AMERICAN GRAND STRATEGY UNDER OBAMA

To my parents Ursula and Werner,
and my wife Lisa

AMERICAN GRAND STRATEGY UNDER OBAMA

Competing Discourses

═══════

Georg Löfflmann

EDINBURGH
University Press

Edinburgh University Press is one of the leading university presses in the UK. We publish academic books and journals in our selected subject areas across the humanities and social sciences, combining cutting-edge scholarship with high editorial and production values to produce academic works of lasting importance. For more information visit our website: edinburghuniversitypress.com

Edinburgh University Press Ltd
The Tun – Holyrood Road
12(2f) Jackson's Entry
Edinburgh EH8 8PJ

Typeset in 11/13 Palatino Light by
Servis Filmsetting Ltd, Stockport, Cheshire

A CIP record for this book is available from the British Library

ISBN 978 1 4744 1976 5 (hardback)
ISBN 978 1 4744 4573 3 (pbk.)
ISBN 978 1 4744 1977 2 (webready PDF)
ISBN 978 1 4744 1978 9 (epub)

CONTENTS

FIGURES AND TABLES

ACKNOWLEDGMENTS

The inspiration to write this book came from a life-long fascination with how different nations, cultures, and peoples experience and interpret the world around them and express these views though their actions and their ideas. This curiosity about the 'big picture' and how it shapes international affairs and national security ultimately led me from a life in Berlin working in the German Parliament to a return to academia, allowing me to write my PhD thesis on Obama and American grand strategy at the University of Warwick in the UK.

Researching and developing the ideas that have informed this book, exchanging thoughts on identity, grand strategy and US foreign policy, the Pentagon and Hollywood with fellow academics, friends, and colleagues in Europe and the United States was an incredibly enriching experience. Finally completing this book has been the most rewarding conclusion to these last five years of inquiry, research, and the intellectual exchange of ideas. Many people have allowed me to undertake this journey and I am forever grateful for their support.

I would like to thank the various people who took time from their busy schedules to see me in the United States in May and June 2013, from Boston to Washington DC and down to Beaufort, South Carolina. Andrew Bacevich, Shawn Brimley, Thomas Donnelly, Christopher Preble, Mark 'Puck' Mykleby, Michael O'Hanlon, and Colonel Greg Schultz all gave me valuable insights and additional background knowledge into the contest of strategic visions under the Obama presidency. At Warwick University and the Department of Politics and International Studies, I have found an intellectual home for my ideas and interests, and I could not have wished for a more encouraging or supportive environment in returning to academia. I also had great support from my publisher Edinburgh University Press with Jenny Daly, Joannah

Duncan and Ersev Ersoy being there every step of the way with valuable assistance.

Most of all, I am deeply indebted to Stuart Croft and Nick Vaughan-Williams, whose friendly advice, constructive criticism, deep knowledge, and great sense of humor have accompanied me through my PhD and the start of my academic career. This book would not have been what it is without them.

Finally, above all I want to thank my parents Ursula and Werner, and my wife Lisa, whose love and encouragement have always given me the confidence to pursue my goals and develop my talents. This book is dedicated to them.

ABBREVIATIONS

―――――

AEI	American Enterprise Institute
ASB	Air-Sea Battle
BCA	Budget Control Act
CAP	Center for American Progress
CFR	Council on Foreign Relations
CIA	Central Intelligence Agency
CJCS	Chairman of the Joint Chiefs of Staff
CNAS	Center for a New American Security
COIN	counter-insurgency
CRS	Congressional Research Service
CSBA	Center for Strategic and Budgetary Assessments
CSIS	Center for Strategic and International Studies
CT	counter-terrorism
DNI	Director of National Intelligence
DoD	US Department of Defense
DSG	*Defense Strategic Guidance*
IR	International Relations
JCS	Joint Chiefs of Staff
NATO	North Atlantic Treaty Organization
NDU	National Defense University
NIC	National Intelligence Council
NSA	National Security Agency
NWC	National War College
ODNI	Office of the Director of National Intelligence
OCS	officer candidate school
ONA	Office of Net Assessment
UAV	Unmanned Aerial Vehicle
PME	professional military education

QDR   *Quadrennial Defense Review Report*
RMA   Revolution in Military Affairs
ROTS   Reserve Officer Training Corps
SEAL   Sea, Air, and Land Teams of the US Navy
UN   United Nations
USMC   United States Marine Corps
WMD   weapons of mass destruction

INTRODUCTION

Under President Obama, the United States was once again debating its decline. Books with alarming sounding titles like *After America: Get Ready for Armageddon, Drift,* or *That Used to Be Us* featured regularly at the top of *The New York Times* best-sellers list.[1] In leading American media and expert publications, from *The Washington Post* to *The National Interest,* the United States under Barack Obama appeared 'shrunken,' its foreign policy one of 'weakness' and 'retreat.'[2] Op-ed columnists, foreign policy experts, and pundits warned of China's territorial ambitions in the South China Sea, Russian incursions into Ukraine, and the multiple crises in the Middle East as dangerous signs that American leadership in the world was waning.[3]

The rest of the world was taking notice as well. The British *Economist* worriedly asked: 'What would America fight for?' and summed up the foreign and security policy of the Obama administration in a damning verdict: 'America is no longer as alarming to its foes, or reassuring to its friends.'[4] In a similar vein, the English-language *Japan Times* stated that the American-led global economic and financial system was broken, while the German international broadcaster *Deutsche Welle* speculated that Barack Obama might be 'the first president forced to deal with the U.S.' downgrading from biggest superpower to co-player on the world stage.'[5]

President Obama, it was argued by critics, did not possess a strategic vision to match Franklin D. Roosevelt or Harry S. Truman, who had successfully led in similar times of geopolitical upheaval and existential threat to the national security of the United States.[6] Obama in turn repeatedly stated that the United States remained the world's 'indispensable nation' today, and for the foreseeable future, declaring in his 2012 State of the Union address that: 'Anyone who tells you that America is in decline or that our influence has waned, doesn't know what they are talking about.'[7] Here, Obama directly referenced an article written by the neoconservative scholar Robert Kagan, titled 'The Myth of American Decline.'[8] In his article, later developed into a best-selling book, *The World America Made*, Kagan argued that the liberal world order that had advanced following World War II, marked by democracy, economic prosperity, and great power peace depended on America's global hegemony and military supremacy.[9]

In political, expert, and media circles, representations of American indispensability and exceptionalism continued to underwrite an overarching elite consensus on America's essential leadership role in world affairs.[10] This geopolitical discourse of perpetual excess firmly established America's material and ideological singularity with both supporters and critics of American hegemony, thus reproducing both its discursive dominance and the militarized practices of Empire.[11]

Yet, at the same time, America's global leadership role was more contested than ever under Obama. While the presidency of George W. Bush had been characterized by frequent debates over American empire, 'hyper-power,' and unilateralism, the discussion had clearly shifted under his successor: the days of American unipolarity seemed numbered, likely to be replaced by a 'post-American world.'[12] In popular media, expert discussions, and official analyses, from *Foreign Policy* magazine to the Center for a New American Security think tank, and the National Intelligence Council (NIC) of the United States, the end of America's ultimate political, military, and economic pre-eminence was characterized as the defining feature of a future geopolitical order.[13] This would result in potentially far-reaching changes to the international system, and a redefinition of the world political role of the United States.[14]

The assessment of tectonic shifts in the geopolitical landscape led to frequent calls that American grand strategy, the 'fundamental tenets guiding the nation's statecraft,' should be reconsidered in order to adapt to a fast-changing international system.[15] According to prominent American grand strategy experts and geopolitical analysts like Zbigniew Brzezinski, Fareed Zakaria, or Charles Kupchan, the United States should no longer seek an elusive and unattainable global primacy, as promoted by Kagan and other neoconservative intellectuals, but pursue a grand strategy of cooperative engagement and joint global responsibilities in a multipolar, less America-centric system.[16]

In contrast to such liberal visions of engagement, calls for America to finally 'come home' likewise gained leverage under the Obama presidency. A much-reported Pew research poll of December 2013 found that among Americans, support for their country's global engagement was at a historic low.[17] Prominent International Relations (IR) scholars, think tank researchers, and American politicians were proposing a grand strategy of restraint that would see the United States and its military less engaged in the world, not more.[18] Decried by their critics as irresponsible 'isolationists,' these voices maintained that the United States was better served, and kept safe at far less cost, by a foreign and security policy of 'non-interventionism,' and 'off-shore balancing.'[19] Here, the failed interventions of the United States in Iraq and Afghanistan served as a cautionary tale against illusions of American omnipotence, the hubris of national exceptionalism, and the blind faith in the efficacy of military force to determine political outcomes according to American preferences.

Grand strategy has been described as the 'highest form of statecraft.'[20] Most of the foreign policy establishment in the United States sees grand strategy as an essential, intellectual prerequisite for the conduct of a successful foreign policy, and the safeguarding of national security.[21] Without a grand strategy in turn, the United States is expected to risk its dominant place in the world, inviting national decline and the unraveling of the liberal world order the United States created and supported.[22] As one author stated, without a grand strategy 'the nation, its leaders, and people will experience a sense of drift and confusion.'[23]

To its critics, grand strategy represents an abstract, purely intellectual exercise for academic theorists and thinks tank analysts, without much practical use for policymaking, since the realities of world politics are deemed too complex as to be subsumed under one coherent narrative.[24] While frequently described as vital prerequisite for America's continued success and necessary world leadership, the idealization of grand strategy, bordering on fetishization in certain academic and media circles, has at times been met with slight ridicule.[25] Other critics, in particular realist IR scholars, have not questioned the premise of grand strategy per se, but saw the United States in pursuit of a dangerous and misguided strategic course of global hegemony and liberal imperialism that overextended the country's resources, and produced global instability rather than national security.[26]

Prominent policymakers and practitioners of US national security and foreign policy have likewise questioned the actual, practical value of grand strategy. President Bill Clinton, for example, rejected the notion that grand strategy was a useful concept altogether. According to Clinton, strategic coherence was 'largely imposed after the fact by scholars, memoirists and "the chattering classes."'[27] President Obama in turn told a reporter of *The New Yorker* that he did not need any new grand strategy: 'I don't really even need George Kennan right now . . .'[28] What he needed rather, the President continued, were 'the right partners' to support his strategic vision of cooperative engagement.[29] Obama's reference to Kennan illustrates how in the United States the Cold War period was predominantly seen as a time when the country last pursued a coherent and consistent national grand strategy – containment – credited for winning the superpower confrontation with the Soviet Union, and securing an unprecedented American unipolarity in the international system. As one author has remarked: 'This period was remarkable for the deep consensus in US society and among our allies on the overall direction of our grand strategy.'[30] Under Obama, however, American grand strategy was perhaps more controversially discussed than ever, revealing a widening rift within the foreign policy establishment, and between elites and the wider public about what America's role in the world should be. The consensus on grand strategy had fractured.

THEORETICAL–METHODOLOGICAL FRAMEWORK

Conventionally understood, an American grand strategy envisions how the United States should best use its various means of power, – military, economic, political – to achieve its desired ends: national security, economic prosperity, and a liberal international order of free trade, great power peace, and the rule of law.[31] Studies following such a conceptualization are mainly interested in measuring grand strategy in terms of input and output, success and failure. In order to function as the 'big picture' of national security, however, a grand strategy discourse has to express deeply-held and widely-shared assumptions and normative convictions about international relations, national security, and the use of force, which orient policy choices.[32] Grand strategy is a worldview. Hegemony, engagement, and restraint in short are not just different and essentially neutral tools for the application of American power in the world, but competing visions of America.[33] Beyond the idea of grand strategy as calculation of material means and ends, lies an ideational dimension of fundamental convictions of truth about the nature of international order, the usefulness of military power, and the character of a nation, its history and purpose. This book therefore moves the realm of identity and discourse into the center of its analysis.

Conceptually, the book has drawn in particular from the critical geopolitics literature in analyzing discourses of grand strategy as intertextual interplay of practical reasoning in political decision-making processes, the formal, intellectual expertise of geopolitical analysts and security experts in the 'strategic community,' and the reflection and co-constitution of these discourses as common-sense understandings in popular media representations.[34] It is this intertextual connectivity between political rhetoric, intellectual expertise, and popular media that establishes constructs of geopolitical identity – such as 'American exceptionalism,' or 'indispensable nation' – as a shared source of national self-identification and guiding principles for political action. The spatialized concept of outside threat, and the external threatening Other were established as key discursive elements by critical works seeking to widen and broaden understandings of IR against conventional definitions, focusing on the writing and rewriting of identity as a key performative function of foreign policy, security practices, and geopolitics.[35] These external threat perceptions continue to play a significant role in discourses of American grand strategy and national security.

However, as explored in the book, the intra-elite conflict over American grand strategy also reveals a significant internal Inside/Outside identity dynamic, where under Obama the constitutive Other against which the hegemonic discourse was employed was domestic rather than foreign. Shifting the analytical focus of grand strategy to competing definitions of America's world political role, then – rather than on the complex of national security designs and external threats – brings into focus an internal dimension of the Self–Other dichotomy, which has been somewhat neglected in critical scholarship.

American grand strategy under Obama, then, did not represent a coherent and consistent framework, linking identity and practice against the external Other, but a contested 'discursive space' within.[36] Here, the established link between the hegemonic identity of American world leadership and a policy course of active military interventionism to support a liberal, international order was challenged on multiple fronts from within the elite network responsible for shaping US foreign and security policy. This resistance to the hegemonic discourse included progressive and libertarian think tanks, realist IR scholars, and even the President himself, who had placed the 'Obama Doctrine' between isolationism and interventionism, declaring that some of the costliest mistakes of the United States had come from a willingness to 'rush into military adventures' without adequate consideration for potential consequences, international support or legitimacy, and the financial and human cost associated with the use of force.[37]

Methodologically, the selection of sources for analysis in this book was concerned with sites that allow for the identification of elite representations and hegemonic knowledges of geopolitical identity construction. Discourses of American grand strategy, linking representations of geopolitical identity to a corresponding performance in US national security and foreign policy, are intertextually linked between popular, formal, and practical sites of knowledge production that include popular culture, intellectual expertise, and political decision-making. In political-practical discourse, official speeches, statements, and strategy documents by President Obama and the White House were examined, as well as strategy and defense policy planning documents produced by the US Department of Defense (DoD). In terms of formal expertise, the focus was on the exchange of competing expert views in the elite opinion outlet *Foreign Affairs* and the wider debate in mainstream IR as well as on policy research outputs on national security by some the most influential think tanks based in Washington DC. Popular reflections of American grand strategy, geopolitical identity, and national security were examined via commercially successful entertainment products in popular culture, such as top-grossing Hollywood movies and best-selling books, as well as leading opinion-forming US media outlets, such as *The Washington Post* and *The New York Times*.

Beyond a strict focus on textual representations, however, the book also engages the social practices that materialize grand strategy as a manifestation of power/knowledge and that are interlinked with ideational paradigms of geopolitical identity. American grand strategy then is not only about textually defining the American Self, but also the actions and processes through which an American worldview operates and becomes actualized, from the production of Hollywood films to the staffing of top positions in the defense bureaucracy and national security establishment in Washington DC.

The materiality of discourses was likewise considered as an analytical category in defining the discursive status of competing American grand strategy visions and their political and societal impact. Domestic box office results of American movies and sales figures of best-selling books have provided measures of popularity used for mapping prevalent grand strategy discourses, and gauging their performance in the public sphere. In the realm of formal expertise, the impact factor and influence rankings of IR journals and Washington think tanks were used to locate the most influential intellectual expertise on American grand strategy. In the discursive realm of US defense planning and political decision-making, the materiality of the Pentagon budget and the practice of American defense policy and military intervention were closely integrated with representations of geopolitical identity. The interlinkage of representation and practice, identity, and policy was thus at the center of the book's intertextual analysis of American grand strategy discourses and their political effects under the Obama presidency presented in the following chapters.

CHAPTER OUTLINE

Chapter 1 will first provide an introduction to the concepts of grand strategy and geopolitics, and their conventional conceptualization in IR literature. This is juxtaposed with the main theoretical and methodological perspectives developed by the literature in critical security studies and critical geopolitics, which have provided the principle framework for the book's underlying research design. The chapter will provide a detailed exploration of the key concepts of power/knowledge, discourse, intertextuality, and identity the book has applied to the study of American grand strategy under Obama. In Chapters 2 and 3, the book will focus on popular culture as a site for the production of constructs of geopolitical identity and practices of national security as common-sense knowledge and conventional wisdom, examining popular Hollywood movies of the 'national security cinema' (Chapter 2), and successful non-fiction books on grand strategy and geopolitics, featured on *The New York Times* best-sellers list (Chapter 3). Here, the analytical focus in particular is on the cultural construction of a geopolitical identity of American leadership, military supremacy, and national exceptionalism, and how key representations have confirmed or contested this construct of the American 'Self' in the popular imagination.

A critical textual analysis and deconstructive reading of popular representations and narratives located with Hollywood films and *The New York Times* best-sellers allows a categorization of basic grand strategy discourses by locating strategic visions in the everyday of security and geopolitics.[38] Rather than using popular culture to intertextually link up to representations of identity already established through the analysis

Intertextual links

⇕

Popular Culture

⇕

Formal Expertise

⇕

Policymaking

Pentagon/

President Obama

Foreign Affairs/

Think Tanks

Hollywood Films/Non-

fiction Best-sellers

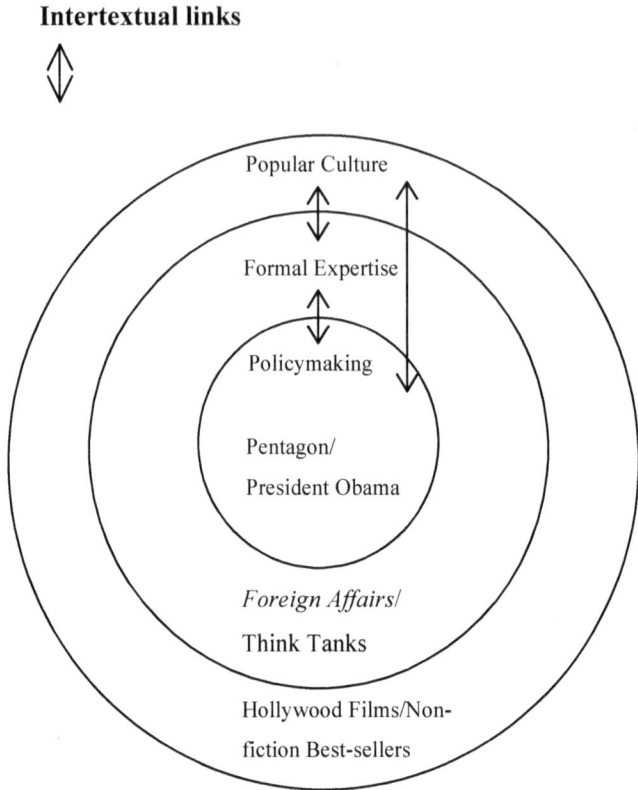

Figure I.1 Model of discourse analysis

of political and media discourses, the everyday of popular culture serves as a discursive location to map out and identify the key themes, basic representations, and core narratives that draw the 'big picture' of grand strategy in the popular imagination.[39]

Having established the basic grand strategy discourses of hegemony, engagement, and restraint through this analysis of the everyday and the cultural production of security, identity, and geopolitics, the analysis then considers the production of grand strategy knowledge as expert opinion and intellectual expertise. In Chapters 4 and 5 the book will analyze the mainstream academic debate in the discipline of IR and policy research outputs by some of the leading think tanks operating in Washington DC. Here, the book focuses on the use of ideational paradigms in the production of the supposedly neutral, scientific knowledge of experts within the American foreign policy establishment, and how

their ideological dispositions have framed their strategic recommendations and policy proposals.

Here, the book first engages in a comprehensive analysis of the
grand strategy debate contained in the pages of *Foreign Affairs* (Chapter
4), which represents a leading elite publication that bridges scholarly
debate and the policy-oriented writing of experts and political practitioners. Chapter 4 also examines in particular how the main theoretical
perspectives of mainstream IR have informed competing grand strategy visions, introducing the concept of hybrid discourses of American
grand strategy: hegemonic engagement and hegemonic restraint. These
expert visions reproduced the dominant representation of American
exceptionalism, and military supremacy, while advocating political
practices that partially reformulated and negated this hegemonic role,
such as the liberal institutionalist concept of deep engagement, or neorealist ideas of offshore balancing.

In Chapter 5, the book will then investigate the grand strategy proposals by some of the leading think tanks operating in Washington
DC, demonstrating how their nominally impartial and independent
research reveals a dominant, bipartisan neoconservative/liberal
internationalist consensus on hegemony that further underlines the
intertextual and practical interconnection between research expertise,
professional knowledge, and policymaking. Finally, the analysis will
examine the center of political-practical discourses of grand strategy
and decision-making on US national security, located with the US
DoD (Chapter 6) and President Obama (Chapter 7). Here, the book
will examine key texts such as the Pentagon's *Quadrennial Defense
Review* reports, the *Defense Strategic Guidance*, or the President's
annual State of the Union addresses. The analytical focus here lies
on how constructs of geopolitical identity, and the basic and hybrid
discourses of grand strategy that have been established through the
previous mapping of popular and formal discourses, have been translated into political practices and the strategic vision of the 'Obama
Doctrine,' and the practical effects this has had on US foreign and
security policy.

The book does not suggest a particular hierarchy in the significance
of grand strategy discourses, in comparison to traditional works, which
would clearly prioritize the elite level of political decision-making in the
White House as the most significant source for the identification and
analysis of American grand strategy, frequently outright equated with
the concept of a presidential doctrine, such as the Obama Doctrine, by

scholars working in the field.[40] However, the book's inversion is deliberate in that it envisions American grand strategy to function as set of
concentric circles of discourse, or communicating vessels, which simultaneously engage in the imagination and re-imagination of US national
security, geopolitics and American identity with frequent intertextual
links between them that document the relatively fluid lines separating
these discursive realms.

As such, the book suggests to travel through these concentric circles
by using popular culture and the 'everyday' as a starting point on the
map in which the key themes, ideas, and narratives of America's role
and position in the world are formulated. The everyday of national
security then represents the basic cultural framework in which more
'traditional' and formal grand strategy discourses operate. The book
then progresses to modes of discourse, which become increasingly
more concerned with traditional practices of national security and their
theoretical contextualization, practical evaluation, strategic planning,
and political execution. While the different discursive sites thus reveal
varying and increasing degrees of involvement with what traditionally is
considered the practice of US national security, the countering of external threats as the ultimate expression of political sovereignty by the state,
they all exist within the same basic cultural-ideational matrix of grand
strategy discourses, documenting their intertextual interdependence
and fundamentally decentralized character. It is precisely this cross-
discursive overlapping in the articulation of the 'big picture' between
popular culture, formal expertise, and political decision-making, which
documents the overall function of American grand strategy. Through its
cultural pervasiveness and boundary-crossing quality, the 'big picture'
of grand strategy is performing the identity of the United States in a
world political context. The role of grand strategy, then, is politically and
culturally much more expansive than an equation of means and ends
and goes beyond a coherent and consistent vision to produce security
externally.

From this critical analysis of grand strategy as set of identity performing discourses, the book will offer the conclusion that American grand
strategy under Obama represented both a contradiction between rhetoric and practice in form of the 'Obama Doctrine,' and an unresolved,
internal identity conflict over America's role in the world. This conflict
occurred between competing elite visions of unipolar primacy, cooperative engagement, and hegemonic restraint. This heterogeneity of elite
knowledges challenged the discursive link between hegemonic identity

and hegemonic practice, fracturing the consensus on American grand strategy from within.

NOTES

1. Rachmann, 'American Nightmare,' Maddow, *Drift*, Steyn, *After America*, Friedman and Mandelbaum, *That Used To Be Us.*
2. Bruni, 'America the Shrunken,' Gerson, 'Obama's Foreign Policy and the Risks of Retreat,' Bremmer, 'The Tragic Decline of American Foreign Policy.'
3. Cohen, 'America Stands Accused of Retreat From its Global Duties. Nonsense,' *New York Times* Editorial Board, 'President Obama and the World.'
4. *Economist*, 'The Decline of Deterrence,' p. 37.
5. Rafferty, 'Where is the Global Leadership?,' Sieren, 'Opinion: The World's Superpower No More.'
6. Bonicelli, 'Five Years is Long Enough to Wait for an Obama Grand Strategy,' Martel, 'America's Grand Strategy Disaster.'
7. White House, 'Remarks by the President in State of the Union Address,' January 24, 2012.
8. Kagan, 'Not Fade Away: Against the Myth of American Decline,' before the State of the Union address Obama apparently mentioned Kagan's article to a group of journalists, referencing individual points in the text, see Rogin, 'Obama Embraces Romney Advisor's Theory on "The Myth of American Decline."'
9. Kagan, *The World America Made.*
10. Luke, 'Hyper-power or Hype Power.'
11. Ibid., p. 21.
12. The term was made famous by the journalist, analyst, and author Fareed Zakaria, see Zakaria, *The Post-American World.*
13. Colby and Lettow, 'Have We Hit Peak America?,' National Intelligence Council, *Global Trends 2030*, Work and Brimley, *20YY. Preparing for War in the Robotic Age.*
14. Whether the result of this geopolitical transition will be a multipolar order, as suggested by Zakaria and others, in which the United States will exist as *primus inter pares*, maintaining a stable, international system in concert with others, or if the end of American hegemony will result in a descent into a volatile non-polarity, where no group of states or international organizations is responsible for global governance, is intensely debated, see for example, Kupchan, *No One's World*, Rachmann, *Zero-Sum World*, Bremmer, *Every Nation For Itself.*
15. Kupchan, 'Grand Strategy: The Four Pillars of the Future.'

16. See, for example, Zakaria, *The Post-American World*, pp. 235–250; Kupchan, *No-One's World*, pp. 202–205, Brzezinski, *Strategic Vision*.

17 Pew Research Center, 'Public Sees U.S. Power Declining as Support for Global Engagement Slips.'

18. Posen, *Restraint*, Preble, *The Power Problem*.

19. Walt, 'Offshore Balancing,' Layne, 'The (Almost) Triumph of Offshore Balancing,' Larison, 'Noninterventionism: A Primer.'

20. Brands, *What Good is Grand Strategy*, p. 1.

21. See, for example, Doherty, 'A New U.S. Grand Strategy,' Mr. Y, 'A National Strategic Narrative,' Brimley and Flournoy (eds.), *Finding Our Way*, Fontaine and Lord (eds.), *America's Path*, Drezner, 'Does Obama Have a Grand Strategy?' O'Hanlon, 'How to Solve Obama's Grand Strategy Dilemma,' Slaughter, 'Does Obama Have a Grand Strategy for his Second Term?'

22. Martel, 'Why America Needs a Grand Strategy.'

23. Martel, 'America's Grand Strategy Disaster.'

24. Zakaria, 'Stop Searching for an Obama Doctrine.'

25. As the IR scholar Dan Drezner wryly remarked, 'every time a US foreign policy expert devised a new grand strategy for the United States, in hopes of becoming the next George F. Kennan, an angel was getting its wings.' Drezner, 'Does Obama Have a Grand Strategy?' p. 61.

26. Mearsheimer, 'Imperial by Design,' Layne, 'The End of Pax Americana,' Posen, *Restraint*, pp. 24–69.

27. Quoted in Talbott, *The Russia Hand*, p. 113.

28. Quoted in Remnick, 'Going the Distance.'

29. Ibid.

30. Martel, 'Why America Needs a Grand Strategy.'

31. For a range of definitions on grand strategy that follow this basic conceptualization, see, for example, Art, *A Grand Strategy for America*, Gaddis, *Strategies of Containment*, Dueck, *Reluctant Crusaders*, Posen, *Restraint*.

32. Art, *A Grand Strategy for America*, p. xv, Neumann and Heikka, 'Grand Strategy, Strategic Culture, Practice.'

33. In staying with the mainstay of US discourses it investigates, the book uses the terms 'America' and 'United States' interchangeably. While this is done for stylistic purposes, and to authentically reproduce the discourse, the author is aware that this reflects a geopolitical imagination that is in itself an expression of hegemony, which equalizes US identity with 'America,' ignoring the other 'Americans' of Central and South America.

34. Ó Tuathail, *Critical Geopolitics*, Ó Tuathail and Dalby, 'Introduction.'

35. Campbell, *Writing Security*, Walker, *Inside/Outside*, Ó Tuathail, *Critical Geopolitics*, Hansen, *Security as Practice*.

36. Stritzel, 'Securitization, Power, Intertextuality.'

37. White House, 'Remarks by the President at the United States Military Academy Commencement Ceremony,' May 28, 2014.
38. Milliken, 'The Study of Discourse in International Relations,' p. 234.
39. Hansen, *Security as Practice*, pp. 59–64.
40. See, for example, Dueck, *The Obama Doctrine*.

Chapter 1

REIMAGINING GRAND STRATEGY

Conventionally understood, a grand strategy envisions how a state can best use its various resources of power – military, economic, political – to achieve security, providing a guideline to the national interest.[1] As the realist scholar Barry Posen has summed up this view, prevailing in the majority of the academic literature on the subject: 'A grand strategy is a nation state's theory about how to produce security for itself.'[2] A large segment of the foreign policy establishment in the United States – consisting of IR scholars, think tank experts, media pundits, diplomats, policymakers, and military professionals – accordingly sees formulating and following a grand strategy as an essential, intellectual prerequisite for conducting a successful foreign policy, and maintaining national security.[3]

As defined by the influential Center for a New American Security (CNAS) think tank, for example, grand strategy is supposed to answer fundamental questions about 'America's core national interest' and 'the purpose of American power.'[4] In the United States, the enduring intellectual legacy of George F. Kennan and containment represent a visionary ideal of American grand strategy as the 'highest form of statecraft'.[5] The key assumption is that a coherent and consistent vision can orient the nation's intellectual energies and material resources to successfully counter external threats and maintain an international system under US leadership. The enduring ends of American grand strategy are thus defined as national security, economic prosperity, and a stable, international order of free trade, great power peace, and the rule of law allowing for the promotion of liberal, democratic values.[6]

Traditionally, the most influential literature in IR on grand strategy has employed variants of (neo)realism with its core theoretical assumptions about structural anarchy and the centrality of the balance of power in the international system as the single most important determinant of state behavior.[7] Following the basic conceptualization of neorealism, laid down by Kenneth Waltz, states are functionally identical actors, only differentiated by the distribution of material power resources among them, sharing the ultimate goal of survival. Operating under the state of anarchy in the international system they try to maximize their security by maintaining a favorable balance of power, which in a zero-sum game brings them in constant competition with each other.[8] John Mearsheimer, in going beyond Waltz's more defensive articulation of structural realism, has stated that states seek to maximize their relative power position at the expense of others.[9] In offensive realism, every great power ultimately pursues a grand strategy of regional hegemony, i.e. to become so powerful that it becomes unassailable by the remaining competitors in the international system.[10] To neorealists then, military power is the ultimate determinant of grand strategy.[11]

Based on different ideal type scenarios of how a state can employ its material resources of power to achieve security in the international system, realists have provided a categorization of grand strategy options, listing the various strategic choices available to the United States.[12] These ideal type scenarios, ranging from unipolar primacy to selective engagement and isolationism reveal the dominant materialist understanding of grand strategy. The end (national security, great power peace, economic prosperity) stays consistent over time, it is how coercively, cooperatively or passively means of power (predominantly military force) are being employed toward this end that defines grand strategy.

The neorealist model however, while highly influential in IR and beyond has been widely criticized as too static and deterministic to allow for variation in grand strategy choices, and to be too inconsistent with developments after the end of the Cold War.[13] Liberal institutionalism, international political economy, and social constructivism have in turn provided alternative perspectives that have emphasized the domestic determinants of grand strategy in politics, economics, society, and culture.[14] Instead of a realist emphasis on state power and an aggregated national interest, the intellectual focus in these investigations has shifted on how domestic actors, institutional processes, political ideologies, and official rhetoric have shaped the 'big picture' of grand strategy and its political effects.[15]

Neoclassical realists have attempted to fuse both perspectives, defining grand strategy as fundamentally concerned with material power, national security, and the survival of the state, and the equation of means and ends, but treating economic and cultural variables as intermitting factors that influence strategic preferences. In his neoclassical realist study of American grand strategy, Colin Dueck, for example, explained how classical liberal assumptions and a historical preference for limited liability in strategic affairs have been two persistent features of American strategic culture that help to explain the various adjustments of the United States and its grand strategy in the twentieth century.[16] The result, according to Dueck, has been a grand strategy of liberal internationalist goals and limited means, resulting in a continuous gap of capabilities and commitments.[17]

Christopher Layne arrived at the contrary result to Dueck, stating that the grand strategy of the United States was marked by an ongoing quest for extra-regional hegemony, not constrained by a cultural inclination toward limited means, but rather following an ideological character and economic logic of expansionism, symbolized in the 'Open Door' policy toward China in the nineteenth and twentieth centuries.[18] According to Layne, the goal of American grand strategy was 'an international system, or "world order", made up of states that are open and subscribe to the United States' liberal values and institutions and that are open to U.S. economic penetration.'[19]

While emphasizing ideational factors, such as a state's individual strategic culture, such works predominantly employed a positivist epistemology, where culture and identity were perceived as relatively stable, given entities, and hence suitable independent variables to explain policy outcomes according to the logic of cause and effect.[20] Overall, the analysis of grand strategy in IR is rooted in epistemological and ontological positivism and an empiricist methodology with social constructivism claiming a 'middle ground,' allowing the latter to avoid having to resort to 'some exotic (presumably Parisian) social theory,' in the words of Peter Katzenstein.[21] In fact, various positivists, like the liberal institutionalist Robert Keohane, the social constructivist Peter Katzenstein, or the neorealist Stephen Walt, all leading scholars closely associated with their respective theoretical school of IR, have questioned the premise of critical constructivism and post-structuralism for the study of national security and IR, due to the latter's skepticism toward the possibility of scientifically and objectively measuring an external reality, and its rejection of a strict dichotic view of social and material reality.[22]

The majority of existing IR literature on grand strategy has thus applied a rationalist and materialist focus of analysis, which largely omitted issues of fluctuating identity constructions, competing narratives, and the role of discourse. Key ideational elements apparently guiding US national security policy then – such as the central concern over American credibility in the world, highlighted prominently by President Obama in April 2016 in *The Atlantic* – and the performativity of identity as dynamic, discursive process of social construction and re-construction were not considered essential in analyzing the 'big picture' of grand strategy.[23] Yet, in order to function as the 'big picture' of national security, any grand strategy has to express deeply held and widely shared assumptions and normative convictions about IR, national security, and the use of force, which orient policy choices.[24] The American strategist William Martel commented that 'fundamentally, grand strategy describes a broad consensus on the state's goals and the means by which to put them into practice.'[25]

A critical discourse analysis explores how through the use of language and social practices this consensus is established, reworked, or contested.[26] This reconceptualizes grand strategy as a knowledge practice, where the hegemonic definition of a world political role and corresponding national security performance constitute a discursive nexus of power/knowledge.[27] Grand strategy attains its relevant political, social, and cultural status through the representational and practical intersection of power networks, responsible for constructing a legitimized social reality through invoking common sense, formal expertise, and political authority. It is this intertextuality that establishes grand strategy as a dominant 'regime of truth.'[28]

DISCOURSE, POWER/KNOWLEDGE AND THE POLITICS OF INTERTEXTUALITY

A critical perspective investigates how a dominant discourse 'produces the social reality that it defines,' questioning the prevailing meaning of such influential ideas and practices as 'security' and 'strategy,' at given times in society.[29] As Peoples and Vaughan-Williams have commented in their analysis of Michel Foucault, 'discourse is understood as a series of practices, representations, and interpretations through which different regimes of truth' are being established and reproduced.[30] To Foucault, discourse was not limited to the textual, or linguistic construction of the social environment, but it included the practices, norms, and rules under which a discursive formation became possible and attained regulative status. The formulation of knowledge then is always embedded in and constituted through relations of power. As Foucault has remarked in *Discipline and Punish*, power produces reality: 'The individual and the knowledge gained of him belong to this production.'[31]

Crucially then, discourse is not limited to the writing and rewriting of identity, but it links identity and policy, representations and practices. The grand strategy vision of liberal hegemony, for example, links a dominant identity construct of American exceptionalism to the material reality of US military supremacy, and security practices such as the forward basing of US troops in Europe, Asia, and the Middle East, the ability for global power projection, and America's 'command of the global commons.'[32] As Lene Hansen has commented on this interlinkage of discourse and practice: foreign policy discourses 'articulate and intertwine material factors and ideas to such an extent that the two cannot be separated from one another.'[33]

The key intellectual concept of power/knowledge as developed by Foucault thus offers an analytical tool to re-evaluate grand strategy from a functional instrument of state power to organize material resources and counter external threats toward a manifestation of hegemonic knowledge produced by elite networks in politics and society. For Foucault, the concept of strategy was predominately 'a question of rationality functioning to arrive at an objective,' and thus not about the performing of identity, but the facilitation of conditions of victory in antagonistic relations, such as war or games.[34] Yet, Foucault clearly identified the societal effect of the reciprocity of power and strategy, described as a 'locking-together of power relations with relations of strategy and the results proceeding from their interaction.'[35] This Foucauldian locking-together of power and strategy manifests as social domination of the 'discursive space' that defines strategic knowledge and establishes a hegemonic discourse against countering visions and discourses of resistance.[36] As Foucault has remarked, 'every strategy of confrontation dreams of becoming a relationship of power and every relationship of power tends, both through its intrinsic course of development and when frontally encountering resistances, to become a winning strategy.'[37]

Thus, from a Foucualdian perspective of power/knowledge, the significance of a particular vision of grand strategy lies not primarily in its functionality of countering external threats in defense of the state's sovereignty, but in its internal identity status and discursive level of dominance. Discourses of American grand strategy attempt to establish a particular definition of the United States in world politics, and to link this identity construct to a set of supporting and reinforcing political practices, from defense spending to military intervention. These security practices in turn reconfirm, adapt, or contest dominant identity constructs. Rejecting the epistemological and ontological conditions of positivism, then, enables a critical analysis to understand how strategic visions and the security policies they sustain are not simply dictated by material conditions or cultural dispositions, but are the product of complex political and societal interactions that authorize and legitimize certain ideational constructs and political outcomes over others.

In his study of classical literature's insights into IR, Charles Hill wrote that literature 'lives in the realm grand strategy requires, beyond rational calculation, in acts of the imagination.'[38] In a similar vein, Lawrence Freedman, who has produced a seminal work on the history of strategy as an intellectual concept, pointed to the central importance of narration in the successful operation of the concept, defining strategy as 'a story about power told in the future tense from the perspective of a leading character.'[39] These interpretations illustrate how a critical reconceptualization of grand strategy as set of geopolitical discourses and manifestation of power/knowledge reflects a wider interest in political science and IR to open up debates about strategy and state behavior beyond the established patterns of analytical rationalism and ontological materialism. A wider, Foucualdian discursive perspective, however, also extends beyond an analysis of textual representations, and considers material indicators and social practices as either confirming or contesting established strategic paradigms. Hence, a critical analysis of grand strategy discourses examines the 'politics of intertextuality' that is embedded in the production of discourse.[40] The politics of discourse production manifests, for example, in the infusion of only certain forms of expertise and think tank policy analysis into the political decision-making process, or the legitimization of political arguments as common-sense knowledge through the referencing of selected pop-cultural artifacts.[41] When in May 2003 George W. Bush, for example, landed in a full military flight suit on board the aircraft carrier USS *Lincoln* to announce 'mission accomplished' – the end of major combat operations in Iraq – he seemed to deliberately invoke the military imagery of the iconic 1980s movie *Top Gun* (1986).[42] Both *The New York Times* and the *New York Daily News* invoked the title of the film to describe Bush's political staging of the event, highlighting the close intertextuality between politics and popular culture in constituting a dominant imagination of US moral and military superiority in world politics.[43]

Hollywood, *Foreign Affairs*, the Pentagon, and President Obama all function as discursive producers centrally involved in the formulation of geopolitical identity, and the definition of national security and the interlinkage of both elements in discourses of American grand strategy. This cross-discursive, intertextual process of reiteration and mutual confirmation is both textual and practical, and builds grand strategy as dominant geopolitical knowledge. As Hansen has declared on this intertextuality of discourse, foreign policymakers are referencing other texts and discourses while 'seeking to establish their own discourse as hegemonic.'[44]

This hegemonic definition, the 'Washington playbook' in the words of Obama, at the same time provokes competing knowledges in resistance to the established paradigm. The central American grand strategy debate during the Obama presidency occurred within the elite circle of the foreign policy establishment, between 'insiders', such as Robert Kagan and the Brookings Institution, advocating a grand strategy of liberal hegemony, and 'outsiders,' such as Stephen Walt, or the Cato Institute, calling for restraint and non-interventionism. These deviant elite voices perceived their knowledge as marginalized by the establishment, for example through its stigmatization as isolationism by producers of the hegemonic discourse, or lacking presence in popular media representations. To defenders of the status quo in turn, these countering voices threatened America's leadership role from within.

CRITICAL GEOPOLITICS: CONSTRUCTING THE 'INSIDE' AND 'OUTSIDE' OF WORLD POLITICS

In shifting the intellectual focus on the intertextuality of practical, formal, and popular discourses, and how this process establishes a particular grand strategy as a dominant worldview and supreme guideline to political action, critical geopolitics offers a highly useful conceptual framework. As Simon Dalby has noted, geopolitics provides the 'discursive context for grand strategy'.[45] Scholarship in critical geopolitics originally sought to question the use of spatialization techniques and geographical discourses for the legitimization of state violence.[46] While still a primary concern of the discipline, critical geopolitics is generally concerned with the 'representations, codes, visions' and 'imaginations' that construct world politics.[47] To analyze the process of imagination which produces the 'big picture' of grand strategy and its political effects then centrally involves the study of geopolitical discourses that construct 'world politics.'[48]

Key to critical geopolitics is the analysis of the world political contextualization of national identity constructs, and their co-constitution in popular culture, intellectual expertise, and policymaking.[49] Such geopolitical representations make up the mental maps of space, power, and order that grand strategists employ to chart a course for the 'ship of state' to follow.[50] Indeed, grand strategy has traditionally been a major concern for those 'intellectuals of statecraft,' who engage in the analysis of geopolitics and seek to guide the nation's policies based on these insights into the 'truth' of geography, politics, and history, from Halford Mackinder to Henry Kissinger.[51] Instead of focusing on the equation of material means and ends, then, a critical analysis of grand strategy centers on key representations of national identity, international order, and global space that are being produced and reproduced as generally accepted knowledge, supposed to guide and legitimize political actions in foreign and security policy.[52] Geraóid Ó Tuathail has distinguished three basic categories of discourse in geopolitics.[53] Formal geopolitics is expressed in geopolitical theories, concepts, and paradigms produced by 'intellectuals of statecraft' in think tanks, universities, and war colleges; the form most closely associated with classical geopolitics, from Mackinder's 'heartland' theory to Alfred Thayer Mahan's emphasis on 'sea power.'[54] Practical geopolitics includes the use of key narratives, practical reasoning, and discursive tropes by political practitioners, policymakers, and bureaucratic officials to conduct foreign and security policy, as, for example, found in official declarations, strategy documents, and public speeches.[55] Popular geopolitics is the representation of world politics in popular culture, created in movies, magazines, novels, comic books, and other creative media.[56] These interconnected, geopolitical discourses, produced by academics, journalists, politicians, foreign policy experts, military officials, and the entertainment industry, serve as a significant self-making resource. They promise strategic insight into coming events and offer orientation to the public over the complexities of world politics, while anchoring the national experience in a spatial-temporal and political framework that links geography, history, politics, and culture.

Here, the study of media and popular culture in particular offers an important discursive site, where the 'everyday' of national security and geopolitics is constructed, and where elite conceptualizations are validated through their recognition as common-sense position.[57] This does not deny the significance of political elites in constructing identity discourses and establishing security practices, but a critical geopolitics perspective stresses how elites are embedded in a nation's framework of reference, and how from this shared resource of identity grand strategy discourses are constructed and linked to political practices in foreign and security policy.

THE GEOPOLITICAL IDENTITY OF AMERICAN EXCEPTIONALISM

The social construction of the Self with the distinct notion of a political and spatial-temporal separation against the external Other, which is a source of threat and danger to national security, shared values, and common identity, provides a central avenue for analysis in critical geopolitics and critical security studies.[58] In order to make the themes of geopolitics and national security understood, binary dichotomies reduce the complexity of reality: the world is established through the use of collective identities: 'Us' and 'Them,' 'friends' and 'enemies,' 'Inside' and 'Outside.'[59]

Constructs of geopolitical identity then provide an interpretation of world politics to be accepted as politically legitimate and authoritative, by tapping into shared resources that constitute the nation as an imagined political community invoking particular historical mythologies and political origins in the process.[60] This shared resource of common understandings, ideas, narratives, and values is then used to legitimize foreign and security policy, projecting domestic identity constructs onto the international realm. These initiatives in turn feed back into the identity discourse. John Ruggie has linked the strategies of engagement American leaders pursued in 1919, 1945, and the early Cold War years to a transformative vision of world order that appealed to the American public because it reflected the 'principles of domestic order at play in America's understanding of its own founding,' reproducing its 'own sense of political community.'[61] In his critical history of US foreign policy, Andrew Bacevich has linked its prevailing theme, a grand strategy of 'openness,' to the economic and political liberalism at the core of the American project.[62]

In case of the United States, a particular and persistent geopolitical imagination constitutes the country as a uniquely moral actor and outstanding force for good with a unique mission to make the world 'safe for democracy.' This spatial and chronological anchoring of geopolitical identity, the uniqueness of America's world political role – from the American Revolution to the War on Terror – establishes the United States as both separate from others and a singular entity in world history. While never uncontested by competing discourses, this dominant identity construct is embedded in the mainstream of political rhetoric, intellectual expertise, and popular culture, and thus acceptable to subsequent generations of Americans as a Self-making resource.[63]

John Agnew has examined how 'exceptionalist arguments offer much the same way of justification today as they did in the early nineteenth century.'[64] In American political debates, media outlets, academic presentations, and pop-cultural artifacts American exceptionalism appears as the ultimate expression of the historic difference of the United States and its political, social, and economic distinctiveness.[65] Frequently, a historic imagination of the United States as a new entity in world politics, and its unique political origin, are brought forward to construct an exceptionalist genealogy of the United States from the first Puritan settlements all the way to the present day, with frequent references to John Winthrop's 'City Upon a Hill' sermon, the Declaration of Independence, quotes by the Founding Fathers, or Alexis de Tocqueville's *Democracy in America* as key founding texts in the exceptionalist myth.[66]

Constructs of geopolitical identity are continuously linked to prevalent national security practices, constituting American exceptionalism as a foundational claim around which a dominant grand strategy discourse of liberal hegemony is constructed. Here, American exceptionalism appears as a widely shared and deeply held belief that America is a special nation with a special role to play in history, with a mission to act on behalf of the worldwide spread of freedom and democracy and in support of a liberal, international order representing core American values.[67] As President Obama declared in 2013: 'The burdens of leadership are often heavy, but the world's a better place because we have borne them (. . .).'[68] Core 'exceptional' American values of freedom, individualism, democracy, the rule of law, and a free-market society, are thus understood by most Americans as a universal formula for peace and prosperity that ideally all mankind should adopt.[69] Under Obama's predecessor George W. Bush this exceptionalist self-perception was translated into a grand strategy vision of unilateral primacy and pre-emptive warfare, with the 2002 *National Security Strategy* (*NSS*) declaring: 'The United States must defend liberty and justice because these principles are right and true for all people everywhere.'[70]

Since the end of the Cold War and the advent of America's 'unipolar moment,' the geopolitical identity of American exceptionalism was frequently linked to a political practice in US foreign and national security policy that legitimized American military interventions abroad and the unrivalled, global supremacy of US power.[71]

Maybe most famously, it was Bill Clinton's Secretary of State Madeline Albright who expressed this strong conviction in the virtue of American exceptionalism in 1998, arguing for US air strikes against Saddam Hussein's Iraq: 'If we have to use force, it is because we are America. We are the indispensable nation.'[72] The belief in American exceptionalism and the universality of American values represents a bipartisan consensus on the desirability, efficacy, and moral righteousness of global US leadership. At the same time, the material and in particular military superiority of American power centrally underwrites the identity construct of American exceptionalism. As the realist IR scholar Stephen Brooks has commented 'one would still be justified in speaking of American exceptionalism on the basis of its military capabilities alone.'[73]

Discourse and power, international order, and national identity become intertwined to such a degree that they are almost indistinguishable from each other, locking together the material and the ideational dimension of American hegemony. No matter how firmly established a link between discourse and practice is, however, geopolitical discourses are always constructed and reconstructed by a multitude of different sources in society, producing multiple identities, visions, and imaginations. This discursive multiplicity includes forms of resistance against established paradigms of identity, security, and geopolitics with countering knowledges envisioning alternative conceptualizations of these phenomena that challenge the hegemonic discourse. In critical geopolitics, this displacement of subjugated knowledges of geopolitics and security is usually examined and critiqued via a focus on marginalized voices, employing, in particular, post-colonial and feminist perspectives.[74] This subjugation, however, can also extend to producers of knowledge, which claim elite status but don't agree with, and are thus excluded from, the hegemonic discourse. In investigating the discursive competition over the Obama Doctrine, then, this book focuses on the heterogeneity of elite knowledges, and the internal dimension of the Self/Other dichotomy in constituting dominant concepts of geopolitical identity and national security practices.

BASIC DISCOURSES OF GRAND STRATEGY: HEGEMONY, ENGAGEMENT, AND RESTRAINT

Under the Obama presidency three basic geopolitical visions about America's preferred role and position in the world competed with each other over dominating the discursive space of grand strategy, forwarding diverging conceptualizations of the identity-security link. These basic discourses of American grand strategy can be identified as hegemony, engagement, and restraint. Before this book provides a detailed analysis in the following chapters, these different grand strategy perspectives will be summarized briefly here to provide an initial overview of their basic construction and political significance. A categorization of basic discourses allows for a structured, analytical perspective on the construction of the discourse-practice link, and how competing American grand strategy visions have articulated the Self/Other dichotomy both externally and internally.[75] These basic discourses differ in their use of key representations of geopolitical identity and their respective linkages to different national security policies. It is important to note, however, that these discourses did not function in strict separation from each other, but indeed showed multiple intertextual connections between each other, constituting various hybrid discourses of hegemonic engagement or hegemonic restraint respectively.

Hegemony is the dominant discourse of American grand strategy. This widely shared and entrenched geopolitical vision is anchored in the idea of the global leadership of the United States as morally preferable and functionally essential. Frequently, such terms as 'hegemony,' 'primacy,' 'indispensable nation,' 'American exceptionalism,' or 'global leadership' are used interchangeably to describe both the dominant position of the United States in world politics – politically, militarily, economically, and culturally – and America's special responsibility to continuously maintain a liberal international order that was established under US stewardship after World War II.[76] Clark, for example, has noted how there has been a persistent conflation of the two concepts of hegemony and primacy in IR literature, in particular concerning the 'many claims to the hegemonic status of the United States.'[77]

A standard trope of the hegemony discourse in the context of US national security is the necessity of the global military supremacy of the United States to deter potential aggressors, preserve regional stability, and guarantee world peace and access to the 'global commons.'[78] In its liberal and neoconservative informed strands, the hegemony discourse also incorporates the special responsibility of the United States to undertake armed intervention on humanitarian grounds, or for the purposes of regime change.[79]

In American politics, academia, and media, geopolitical visions of American 'preponderance' or 'benevolent hegemony' have frequently been associated with the ideological influence of neoconservative pundits and scholars such as William Kristol, Robert Kagan, or Charles Krauthammer.[80] Politically, the neoconservative influence remains associated in particular with the George W. Bush administration and the 'Bush Doctrine' of pre-emptive warfare, as articulated in the 2002 *National Security Strategy*.[81] Conservative proponents of American hegemony or primacy in political and intellectual circles emphasize unilateral action, the pre-emptive use of military power against existential threats to national security, and the perpetuation of the global, unipolar primacy of the United States.[82] It is the geopolitical vision most closely associated with the establishment of the Republican Party and neoconservative intellectuals, who articulate this vision in its most overt form of liberal imperialism.

However, the political and historic singularity and the moral and material superiority of American exceptionalism really serve as a foundational claim constituting a bipartisan Washington consensus on liberal hegemony.[83] The second significant strand of the hegemony discourse is thus predominantly associated with the Democratic Party. Here, the main emphasis lies on how the global leadership role of the United States functions as a central and essential part of a liberal institutionalist framework, with a preference for multilateral action and international cooperation. This discourse is influenced in particular by liberal theories of IR and the Wilsonian tradition in American foreign policy.[84] Nonetheless, the underlying key assumption is that it is the United States which has to provide leadership in these cooperative arrangements, and act unilaterally if necessary. Although often clad in the rhetoric of 'engagement' and partnership, this discourse actually represents a hybrid form of hegemonic engagement, where the United States is a partner but never quite an equal. The hegemony of the United States is imagined as being exercised through a cooperative framework of 'burden sharing' and 'responsible stakeholders,' but with America firmly at the top of a political, economic, and military hierarchy of power and influence.[85]

Basic discourses

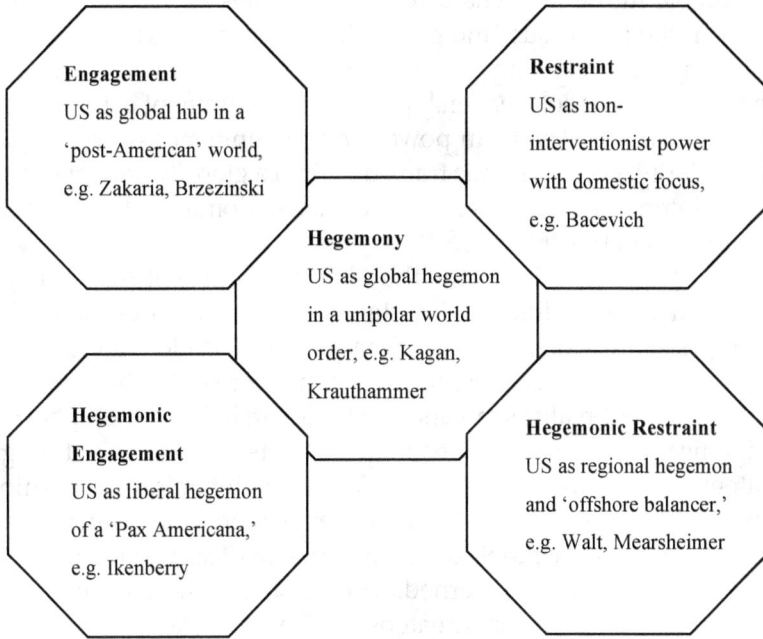

Engagement

US as global hub in a 'post-American' world, e.g. Zakaria, Brzezinski

Restraint

US as non-interventionist power with domestic focus, e.g. Bacevich

Hegemony

US as global hegemon in a unipolar world order, e.g. Kagan, Krauthammer

Hegemonic Engagement

US as liberal hegemon of a 'Pax Americana,' e.g. Ikenberry

Hegemonic Restraint

US as regional hegemon and 'offshore balancer,' e.g. Walt, Mearsheimer

Hybrid discourses

Figure 1.1 Discourses of American grand strategy

Hybrid discourses

Engagement represents the second basic discourse of American grand strategy. This geopolitical vision reflects the key idea that the United States should seek increased international cooperation with partners and allies, and on some issues even with rivals and adversaries, in order to successfully manage international affairs and facilitate global governance in an increasingly multipolar international system marked by a diffusion of power and influence.[86] Rather than the use of America's unmatched military power this discourse emphasizes diplomatic solutions, economic interdependence, 'soft power,' and the importance of international organizations and multilateral institutions.[87] Underlying the engagement discourse is the assessment that the United States is experiencing a relative decline, with its 'unipolar moment' giving way to a 'post-American world.'[88] While the United States is expected to remain the most powerful actor in the international system for the foreseeable future, it is characterized as *primus inter pares* rather than an unchecked 'colossus' and global 'hyper-power.'[89] The United States has to engage with rising powers to maintain a liberal order that can no longer rely on the sole leadership of just one dominant actor. Instead of the singularity of American power and the uniqueness of its position, multipolarity, geo-economic transition, and a globally networked structure of interconnected levels of governance dominate the geopolitical imagination in this discourse.[90]

Restraint is identified as the third basic discourse of American grand strategy. This geopolitical vision stands diametrically opposed to grand strategies of neoconservative primacy, global leadership, and liberal interventionism. Closely associated with the realist school of IR, and such prominent realist scholars as John Mearsheimer or Stephen Walt, a significant strand of the restraint discourse is articulated as grand strategy of 'offshore balancing.'[91] While maintaining its position of regional hegemony in the Western hemisphere, the United States is advised here to only mobilize its military resources when vital national security interests are concerned. Thus, America should only act militarily if an outside actor threatens to likewise establish a position of regional hegemony, as for example attempted by Nazi Germany in Eurasia and Japan in the Asia-Pacific in World War II. Humanitarian intervention, or the individual defense of South Korea or Taiwan on the other hand, should not form part of US national security priorities. To its many critics, restraint and offshore balancing represent a dangerous from of neo-isolationism, a potentially catastrophic disengagement of the United States from the world.[92] Offshore balancing then represents yet another form of discursive hybridity, between regional hegemony in the Western hemisphere and global retrenchment, identified as hegemonic restraint. Politically, the restraint discourse has found support both among conservative libertarians and the Tea Party movement and progressive critics of American imperialism and militarism.[93] A more fully articulated discourse of restraint as proposed, for example, by progressive critics from the left of the political spectrum calls for the United States to substantially cut the defense budget, to further reduce the political clout of the military-industrial and intelligence complexes, and to further prioritize domestic issues such as healthcare, education, and public infrastructure over an expansive and interventionist foreign policy and global military posture.

Considering the underlying geopolitical imagination of the restraint discourse, instead of acting as the 'policeman of the world,' the United States is supposed to emphasize a domestic focus of 'nation-building at home.'[94] The wars in Iraq and Afghanistan are characterized as a waste of financial and military resources and dangerous folly, fueled by geopolitical visions of American omnipotence and exceptionalist hubris.[95] In this view, the overextension of American resources has contributed to the fiscal instability of the United States and has hastened American decline. In need of a strategic course correction, the United States is supposed to decrease its global military footprint, most importantly its global network of military bases and forwardly deployed troops. The restraint discourse calls for Americans to finally 'come home.'[96]

CONCLUSION

Critical security studies and critical geopolitics acknowledge the significance of the nexus of discourse, power, and identity in constructing political and social reality. This critical insight into the production of knowledge about the world and a state's role and position in it provides an intellectual avenue to analyze American grand strategy through a wider lens than previously attempted. So far, research on grand strategy in IR has predominantly focused on a positivist ontology and epistemology in addressing the subject. This has largely reduced the understanding of grand strategy to a neutral-scientific process, concerned with the allocation of material resources, the empiricist assessment of outcomes, and the matching of means and ends, in particular focused on the application of military power and the countering of external threat.

This rationalist-materialist approach, however, has largely omitted issues of discourse and identity, which profoundly influence the national definition of security and the thinking of strategy. Incorporating key insights from critical security studies, and in particular critical geopolitics, then, provides the opportunity to go beyond these limitations, and to examine how American grand strategy comes to be established as a dominant form of knowledge, the political and practical consequences this has, and which external and internal processes of identity formation and Othering this entails. American grand strategy articulates a worldview of particularly American origin and it subjects the international order to Americans' perceptions of their own identity and associated political practices. In looking at who exactly is shaping these visions of 'America,' this book attempts to provide a more nuanced and complex understanding of how the 'big picture' of geopolitics and security comes into being and the political effects the making of grand strategy has, both internally and externally.

NOTES

1. See, for example, Art, *A Grand Strategy for America*, Brands, *What Good is Grand Strategy*, Martel, *Grand Strategy in Theory and Practice*, Posen, *Restraint*. The original idea of grand strategy as a higher level of strategic planning goes back to the writings of British and American military thinkers and scholars of foreign relations, notably J. F. C. Fuller, Edward Mead Earle, and Basil Liddell Hart, and gained prominence in the 1940s and 1950s, see Brands, *What Good is Grand Strategy*, p. 2.
2. Posen, *Restraint*, p. 1.
3. Edelstein and Krebs, 'Delusions of Grand Strategy.'
4. Brimley and Flournoy, 'Introduction,' p. 5. In these conventional conceptualizations of grand strategy, power is usually defined as the ability to effect political outcomes and change the behavior of others through force or coercion, see Nye, Jr., *The Paradox of American Power*, p. 4. The means of grand strategy can include both traditional 'hard power' capabilities (the threat or use of military force and economic reward or pressure), and 'soft power,' the attractiveness of values, ideas, and practices to influence events through persuasion and attraction, for example mediated through cultural diplomacy, international institutions, or popular entertainment, see Nye, Jr., *Soft Power*. Colin S. Gray disputes the value of soft power for grand strategy and advocates the pre-eminence of military power in Gray, *Hard Power and Soft Power*.
5. Brands, *What Good is Grand Strategy*, p. 1, on American grand strategy and containment, see Gaddis, *Strategies of Containment*.
6. Posen, *Restraint*, pp. 5–6.
7. See Garnett, 'Strategic Studies and its Assumptions.' Examples for both neorealist and neoclassical realist perspectives on American grand strategy include Mearsheimer, *The Tragedy of Great Power Politics*, Art, *America's Grand Strategy and World Politics*, Dueck, *Reluctant Crusaders*, Layne, *The Peace of Illusions*.
8. Waltz, *Theory of International Politics*.
9. Mearsheimer, *The Tragedy of Great Power Politics*.
10. Ibid., pp. 21, 40. Waltz himself has stressed that his theory is not there to explain individual foreign policy outcomes, like a particular grand strategy choice, but the structure of the international system, see Waltz, *Theory of International Politics*, p. 58.
11. See Art, *America's Grand Strategy*, Posen, *Restraint*.

12. Bartlett and Holman, for example, have suggested three possible alternatives for American grand strategy: disengagement, global leadership, and balance of power. Bartlett and Holman, 'Grand Strategy and the Structure of U.S. Military Forces,' p. 48. Art identifies seven possible variations for a grand strategy, classified as dominion, global collective security, regional collective security, cooperative security, containment, isolationism, and selective engagement, Art, 'Geopolitics Updated.' Posen and Ross have suggested four main categories of American grand strategy: neo-isolationism, selective engagement, cooperative security, and primacy, see Posen and Ross, 'Competing Visions for US Grand Strategy,' p. 6.
13. Rosecrance and Stein, 'Beyond Realism.'
14. See, for example, Ikenberry, *Liberal Leviathan*, Rosecrance and Stein (eds.), *The Domestic Bases of Grand Strategy*, Johnston, *Cultural Realism*.
15. Goddard and Krebs, 'Rhetoric, Legitimation and Grand Strategy,' Kornprobst, 'Building Agreements Upon Agreements,' Mitzen, 'Illusion or Intention?,' van Apeldoorn and de Graaff, 'Corporate elite networks and US post-Cold War grand strategy from Clinton to Obama.'
16. Ibid., p. 21. Dueck, however, does not question the basic premise of the means-ends equation, defining grand strategy as 'identification of existing and potential resources, and a selection of a plan which uses these resources,' Dueck, 'Realism, Culture and Grand Strategy,' p. 198.
17. Ibid., p. 146.
18. Layne, *The Peace of Illusions*, pp. 28–36. The argument of the Open Door as expansionist and imperialist American strategy has been pioneered and developed by the critical historian William Appelman to which Layne also refers, see Appelman, *The Tragedy of American Diplomacy*.
19. Ibid., p. 30.
20. See, for example, the conventional constructivist interpretation of strategic culture as an independent variable explaining outcomes of state behavior in Johnston, *Cultural Realism*.
21. Jepperson, Wendt, and Katzenstein, 'Norms, Identity, and Culture in National Security,' p. 34. On the ontological middle position of constructivism between structuralism/materialism and critical theory/post-structuralism, see also Adler, 'Seizing the Middle Ground.'
22. Katzenstein, Keohane, and Krasner 'International Organization and the Study of World Politics,' Walt, 'The Renaissance of Security Studies,' Hansen, *Security as Practice*, p. xviii. For a range of essays representing an overview of critical constructivism in the study of security, see Weldes et al. (eds.), *Cultures of Insecurity*.
23. Goldberg, 'Obama Doctrine,' Art, *A Grand Strategy for America*, p. xv.
24. Neumann and Heikka, 'Grand Strategy, Strategic Culture, Practice.'
25. Martel, *Grand Strategy in Theory and Practice*, p. 359.

26. Milliken, 'The Study of Discourse in International Relations,' Müller, 'Doing Discourse Analysis in Critical Geopolitics.'
27. Foucault, *Power/Knowledge*.
28. Foucault, *Discipline and Punish*.
29. Milliken, 'The Study of Discourse in International Relations,' p. 242; see also Mutlu and Mark Salter, 'The Discursive Turn,' p. 113.
30. Peoples and Vaughan-Williams, *Critical Security Studies*, p. 65. See also the treatment of Foucault and his use of discourse in Crowley, *The Politics of Discourse*.
31. Foucault, *Discipline and Punish*, p. 194.
32. See, for example, Brooks and Wohlforth, *World Out of Balance*, Posen, 'Command of the Commons.'
33. Hansen, *Security as Practice*, p. 1.
34. Foucault, *Power*, p. 346.
35. Ibid., p. 348.
36. Stritzel, 'Securitization, Power, Intertextuality.'
37. Foucault, *Power*, p. 348.
38. Hill, *Grand Strategies*, p. 6.
39. Freedman, *Strategy: A History*, p. 609.
40. Stritzel, 'Securitization, Power, Intertextuality,' p. 553.
41. Parmar, 'Foreign Policy Fusion.'
42. Sanger, 'In Full Flight Regalia.'
43. A toy manufacturer would later produce a George W. Bush 'Top Gun' action figure.
44. Hansen, *Security as Practice*, p. 215.
45. Dalby, 'Recontextualising Violence, Power and Nature,' p. 285.
46. Ibid., p. 281.
47. Mamadouh and Dijkink, 'Geopolitics, International Relations and Political Geography,' p. 354.
48. Müller, 'Doing Discourse Analysis in Critical Geopolitics.'
49. Ó Tuathail, *Critical Geopolitics*.
50. Drezner, 'Does Obama Have a Grand Strategy,' p. 61.
51. Ó Tuathail and Agnew, 'Geopolitics and Discourse,' p. 193.
52. Ibid.
53. Ó Tuathail and Dalby, 'Introduction,' p. 5. Ó Tuathail also mentions structural geopolitics, defined as global processes of human experience, such as globalization, the rise of information technology, or the advent of Ulrich Beck's 'risk society,' Ó Tuathail, 'Understanding Critical Geopolitics,' p. 110.
54. On the diverging assessments of Mackinder and classical geopolitics, see, for example, Gray, 'In Defence of the Heartland', and Kearns, 'Naturalising Empire.'
55. Ó Tuathail and Agnew, 'Geopolitics and Discourse.'

56. Dittmer, *Popular Culture, Geopolitics, and Identity*.
57. Weldes (ed.), *To Seek Out New Worlds*, Dittmer, *Popular Culture, Geopolitics and Identity*.
58. Walker, *Inside/Outside*, Campbell, *Writing Security*, Ó Tuathail, *Critical Geopolitics*, Hansen, *Security as Practice*.
59. Campbell, *Writing Security*, p. 9.
60. Dijkink, 'National Identity and Geopolitical Visions.'
61. Ruggie, 'The Past as Prologue?,' p. 89; see also Ruggie, *Winning the Peace.*
62. Bacevich, *American Empire*, pp. 79–116.
63. Ó Tuathail and Dalby, 'Introduction,' p. 3, Kennedy, 'The Manichean Temptation.' Simon Dalby gives an illustrative account of the 'villain of the day' in the techno thrillers of Tom Clancy, set at the end of the Cold War and the early post-Cold War era that reproduce this basic Manichean narrative of a 'good' United States fighting 'evil' enemies, see Dalby, 'Imperialism, Domination, Culture.'
64. Agnew, 'An Excess of "National Exceptionalism"', p. 151.
65. Lipset, *American Exceptionalism*, Madsen, *American Exceptionalism*, McCrisken, *American Exceptionalism*, Brooks, *American Exceptionalism in the Age of Obama*, Restad, *American Exceptionalism*.
66. Hilfrich, *Debating American Exceptionalism*, p.78.
67. McCrisken refers to this interpretation as the 'missionary' strand of American exceptionalism guiding US foreign policy, as opposed to the 'exemplary' strand, where the United States rather serves as an example to be emulated politically, economically, and socially by other nations, see McCrisken, *American Exceptionalism*.
68. White House, 'Remarks by the President in Address to the Nation on Syria.'
69. Kagan, *The World America Made*.
70. White House, *The National Security Strategy of the United States of America, 2002*, p. 1.
71. Krauthammer, 'Unipolar Moment.'
72. NBC, 'Transcript: Albright Interview on NBC-TV.' Available at http://www.fas.org/news/iraq/1998/02/19/98021907_tpo.html (last accessed September 2016).
73. Brooks, *American Exceptionalism in the Age of Obama*, p. 82.
74. Hyndman, 'Mind the Gap,' Sharp, 'Geopolitics at the Margins?'
75. See also Hansen, *Security as Practice*, p. 95.
76. See, for example, Wohlforth, 'The Stability of a Unipolar World,' Layne, *The Peace of Illusions*, pp. 25–28, Posen, *Restraint*, pp. 24–69, Kagan, *The World America Made*, Clark, *Hegemony*, pp. 23–28.
77. Clark, *Hegemony*, p. 24. Clark in turn differentiates between 'primacy' as rooted in the superiority of material resources only, and 'hegemony,' which he defines as also grounded in political legitimacy,' see Clark, ibid.

78. Brooks and Wohlforth, *World Out of Balance*, Posen, 'Command of the Commons.'
79. Ignatieff, 'American Empire.'
80. Kristol and Kagan, 'Toward a Reaganite Foreign Policy,' Krauthammer, 'Unipolar Moment.'
81. Krauthammer, 'The Bush Doctrine,' p. 42.
82. Krauthammer, 'Unipolar Moment,' Project for the New American Century 'Statement of Principles,' Kagan, *Of Paradise and Power*, Romney, *No Apology*.
83. Posen, *Restraint*, Bacevich, *Washington Rules*.
84. Mead, *Special Providence*, pp. 132–173, Ikenberry, *Liberal Leviathan*.
85. Brooks, Ikenberry, and Wohlforth, 'Don't Come Home, America': Brooks, Wohlforth and Ikenberry refer to this grand strategy of liberal hegemony as 'deep engagement,' ibid.
86. National Intelligence Council, *Global Trends 2025.*
87. Brzezinski, *Strategic Vision*, Kupchan, *No One's World*.
88. Zakaria, *The Post-American World*.
89. Brzezinski, *Strategic Vision*, Zakaria, *The Post-American World*, Ferguson, *Colossus*.
90. Slaughter, 'America's Edge.'
91. Kaplan, 'Why John J. Mearsheimer is Right (About Some Things),' Walt, 'Offshore balancing,' Layne, 'The (Almost) Triumph of Offshore Balancing,' Posen, *Restraint*.
92. Bacevich, '70 Years of "New Isolationism."'
93. Blake, 'The Republican Party Likes Rand Paul's Foreign Policy,' Purple, 'Ted Cruz's Fourth-Way Foreign Policy,' Preble, *The Power Problem*, Johnson, *Dismantling the Empire*, Bacevich, *Washington Rules*, Maddow, *Drift.*
94. Preble, *The Power Problem*.
95. Bacevich, *The Limits of Power*.
96. Bacevich, *Washington Rules*, Preble, *The Power Problem*.

Chapter 2

FILMING HEGEMONY: HOLLYWOOD AND THE
MANICHEAN SCRIPT OF GEOPOLITICS

The Pentagon is a church. And the soldiers are the priests.

Oliver Stone[1]

Critically investigating grand strategy as a set of discourses that define America's geopolitical identity and shape its national security policy has no better starting point perhaps than Hollywood. For more than a century the American film industry has perfected the making and remaking of America's image for domestic and foreign audiences. However, this imagination of the United States through film – the 'nation's preeminent form of cultural expression' – extends beyond the seemingly apolitical realm of everyday experience and popular entertainment.[2] Since World War II, Hollywood has been closely linked to the national security state, both reflecting and co-constituting America's global superpower status by portraying the seemingly never-ending struggle against America's sworn enemies – from Nazis to Communists and international terrorists – often working in close cooperation with government institutions like the US DoD in bringing the United States to life on the big screen.[3]

Popular culture provides key discursive sites within the wider cultural and societal context of geopolitics and national security, where deep-seated representations of identity are formulated and reconstituted as common-sense reality in film and TV productions, novels, magazines and comic books, popular music, and other assorted everyday artifacts.[4] When they interrelate with practical discourses of grand strategy, popular representations can help to produce and sustain a generally understood version of political reality, defining the role and place of the United States in world politics and legitimizing its policy choices for national security. Following the 'cultural turn' in IR, the study of popular culture has revealed the numerous connections between the supposedly real world of politics, power, and security, and what is generally considered to lie outside the scope of appropriate IR research, the mundane world of daily experiences, narratives, imagination, media reflections, and the make-believe world of entertainment.[5]

A critical approach which uses popular culture as a key site of analysis rejects this strict dichotomy between grand strategy as the sole realm of military power and high, political calculation, and film as the politically irrelevant world of entertainment and fiction. In the words of Cynthia Weber: 'Culture is political, and politics is cultural.'[6] Popular culture then is neither irrelevant nor dismissible, but one of the sites where power is produced and reproduced. To examine the connection of film and grand strategy is to acknowledge the political significance of storytelling in creating a commonly shared truth. Both film and strategy then focus on the imagination of power as much as they rely on the power of images. The close, institutionalized cooperation of the Pentagon and Hollywood is a striking example, where popular representations and political-military practices intersect in this way. Through the production of film, dominant imaginations of national security, military power, and the role of the Armed Forces are projected and promoted to domestic and global audiences for entertainment and PR purposes, sustaining and reflecting in turn hegemonic, strategic narratives employed by the US defense establishment.

Representations of geopolitical identity and national security, analyzed here in some of the most commercially successful films in the United States released between 2009 and 2015, testify to an enduring popularity of key ideational themes and mythologies, such as American exceptionalism, military heroism, and external threats endangering the existence of the United States, its interests, and values during the Obama presidency. Counter-narratives to this basic Manichean script exist as well, for example when films feature threats to the United States emerging from out-of-control government surveillance efforts, rogue intelligence operations, or secret military programs. However, predominantly these narrative constructs function as outliers and disruptors to the general notion of American innocence and moral superiority, where a defensive United States is called upon on a regular basis to defend freedom and liberty against the disrupting forces of evil and chaos. The serial reproduction of these national security narratives, realized in multi-million dollar film productions, illustrates the cross-discursive leverage of American hegemony over alternative formulations of grand strategy under the Obama presidency. The critical engagement with these pop-cultural artifacts focuses in particular on patterns of cultural production and the way themes of identity and security are established and generalized, rather than a more detailed textual analysis of individual films and their cinematic narratives. It is through the constant repetition of a generic formula of Manichean geopolitics that the Hollywood narrative of national security reproduces a strategic vision of liberal hegemony as common-sense knowledge. The basic tenets of this popular vision were, at the same time, to be found at the center of political-practical discourse and intellectual expertise and policy advice, highlighting the strong intertextual links that exist between entertainment, politics, and research in constructing the geopolitical vision of American grand strategy.[7]

This intertextuality does not suggest that popular entertainment was a monolithic resource exclusively in support of American grand strategy and US national security policy. But, the common-sense status of this discourse, as underwritten by the Pentagon-Hollywood liaison, questions the pervasiveness of existing, alternative grand strategy discourses and their ability to challenge the existing paradigm in the popular imagination. Looking to the popular realm of motion picture entertainment, grand strategy visions present in academic and expert circles – such as cooperative engagement of a less hegemonic United States in a post-American world, or a realist-inspired course of offshore balancing and military restraint – were largely absent from the imagination. In Hollywood, hegemony dies hard.

HEROISM, MILITARIZATION, AND THE GEOPOLITICAL IDENTITY OF THE UNITED STATES ON SCREEN

Identity is maybe the most comprehensively studied issue in the geopolitical analysis of Hollywood films and the popular construction of an American 'security imaginary.'[8] Joanne Sharp and Klaus Dodds, for example, have explored the cinematic construction of gender, masculinity, and patriotism, and how these discursive tropes write 'America's map of world order.'[9] Closely related, yet distinctive from these phenomena, are the ideational themes of heroic individualism and militarism that delineate the American Self from the threatening, un-American Other in US cinema.

In the commercially highly successful *Iron Man* film franchise (2008, 2010, 2013), for example, it is the industrial and entrepreneur Tony

Stark (Robert Downey Jr.), who, due to his technological ingenuity, is able to design and operate a weaponized high-tech armor, taking on the identity of 'Iron Man' in the process. Iron Man/Tony Stark represents a combination of military muscle, self-reliant individualism, technological innovativeness, and entrepreneurial spirit, displaying traits commonly associated with the United States and American society, personified in the character of the superhero. At the same time, *Iron Man* is closely connected to the national security state and US military establishment. While the *Iron Man* films have also offered a tentative critique of the military-industrial complex, the US Air Force featured prominently in these pop-cultural entertainment products. Tony Stark's best friend is Lt. Col. James 'Rhodey' Rhodes (Don Cheadle), who in *Iron Man 2* (2010) takes on the identity of 'War Machine,' supporting Iron Man in fighting the film's main villain, the Russian scientist-turned-terrorist Ivan Vanko (Mickey Rourke), who attacks New York City with an army of drone soldiers. In real life, the *Iron Man* franchise received substantial, official support from the Pentagon and the Air Force, including script research, filming on location at military installations, access to military vehicles, such as fighter jets and helicopters, and the provision of soldiers as extras.[10] The popular imagination of American military power as heroic was underwritten by an intertextuality that was both ideational and practical, linking the military and the superhero both on screen and off.

The American superhero, heroic US soldier, or valiant secret intelligence operative, who defends the United States against existential threats through necessary force, is a theme that has been repeated in numerous popular films and movie franchises released during the Obama presidency. This includes the commercially highly successful *Transformers* science-fiction series (2007, 2009, 2011, 2014), the *Mission Impossible* spy films (1996, 2000, 2006, 2011, 2015), the *G.I. Joe* military science-fiction franchise (2009, 2013), and major superhero blockbusters such as *The Dark Knight Rises* (2012), *Man of Steel* (2013), or Marvel's *Avengers* (2012, 2015), *Iron Man* (2008, 2010, 2013), and *Captain America* films (2011, 2014, 2016). In addition, there were a number of stand-alone military themed films, which were likewise among the annual top-fifty highest grossing films in the United States, such as *Battle: Los Angeles* (2011), *Act of Valor* (2012), *Battleship* (2012), *Lone Survivor* (2013), or *American Sniper* (2014), the top-grossing film in the United States in 2014.[11]

Of course, it cannot be assumed that the popularity of these entertainment products was due to their particular geopolitical imagination, or indeed if a reading of identity was performed by audiences as such. Primarily, audiences seem to focus on aesthetic and artistic qualities in viewing films; however, themes such as military power or American exceptionalism are noticed and engaged with, albeit often in an indirect way.[12] Yet, the continued involvement of the Pentagon in the production of Hollywood films under the Obama administration suggests a conviction on behalf of the US DoD that the predominantly positive image of the American military created in these films was reaching the intended audiences and thus represented a worthwhile investment for public relations, recruitment, and retention of military personnel. In a similar vein, the continued investment into certain geopolitical imaginations of American military power on film can be attributed to the conviction of film producers and movie studios that these films would turn a profit at the box office, justifying in turn further investment in similar entertainment products.

In the cinematic discourse of national security and geopolitics under Obama, then, established representations of identity and security coincided with substantial levels of government support, capital investment, and financial revenues, suggesting their popular appeal and common-sense status. This circular flow of box office success, generic film production, and capital investment represents an often overlooked element in the analysis of popular geopolitics that widens the scope of research beyond a purely representational and textual analysis to include aspects of cultural economy in the evaluation of how the film industry constitutes a Foucauldian nexus of power/knowledge.[13] In this regard, Hollywood as an industry focused on reliable revenue and seemingly winning, creative formulas of economic success represented a powerful voice in defense of the status quo of American hegemony in the popular imagination.[14] In filmic representations of national security, audiences usually encountered a 'virtuous war' in the words of James Der Derian, the simulated use of military power or violent force by the United States and its representatives against America's enemies was morally unambiguous and righteous, surgically executed, successful, and neither produced collateral damage nor post-traumatic stress in the hero.[15] America was fighting a good, clean fight in defense against evil aliens and sinister terrorists.

This glorification of violence and the militarization of American, patriotic identity, however, have not always been a staple feature of American films. During the 1920s and 1930s, for example, Hollywood tended to avoid addressing war as a topic, sensing a public mood that favored pacifism and isolationism.[16] Ever since the entry of the United States in World War II and the emergence of the country as a global military superpower however, the 'good war' narrative and representations of military heroism were dominant in the popular imagination that was presented to American movie audiences, fostering their status as common-sense knowledge.[17] In fact, Hollywood had been enlisted by the US government from the very onset of America's rise to superpower status. Frank Capra's propaganda documentary series *Why We Fight* (1942–1945) and war movies like *Bataan* (1943), *Air Force* (1943), and *Thirty Seconds Over Tokyo* (1944) facilitated popular support for the country's involvement in World War II and ensuing transformation to a globally oriented, interventionist actor defending freedom, democracy, and liberty against the evilness of Japanese imperialism, German Nazism, and Italian fascism.[18] As Tom Engelhardt has remarked, Hollywood was substantial in establishing an American 'victory culture,' which gave purpose to the country's identity within the new geopolitical context of American global hegemony, and which was only interrupted in the late 1960s by the experience of the Vietnam War.[19]

During the Cold War, the Other against which the popular identity of American exceptionalism, innocence, and virtue was constructed appeared as the all-encompassing threat of Communism. This enemy was encountered as both an internal and external threat to the 'American way of life,' and often presented by Hollywood in allegorical form, be it as dangerous monster suddenly appearing in the midst of ordinary Americans in horror movies, or science-fiction films, where the alien invasion theme had become a staple since the 1950s, with the alien invader widely seen as metaphor for a potential invasion by the Soviet Union and a Communist takeover of the American homeland.[20]

Following 9/11, there was a marked resurgence of alien invasion themed films and TV shows in the United States documenting the newly felt sense of the vulnerability and insecurity of the American everyday, and popular anxieties surrounding US national security. As Steffen Hantke has pointed out, the genre can be categorized broadly as either 'inclusionary' or 'exclusionary,' where the alien invasion was revealed to be beneficial for mankind, or an existential threat endangering the survival of the planet and the human race.[21] In either case, the Otherness of the alien and the reaction toward it provided a political commentary on the constructed identity of the Self as either progressing through exchange with the Other, or as existentially threatened and in defense against a villainous enemy.[22]

The Pentagon-supported alien invasion films detailed later in this chapter clearly fall into the latter category. The evil Decepticons in the *Transformers* series, or the invading aliens in *Battleship* and *Battle: Los Angeles*, all function as the ultimate despotic Other, against which the American geopolitical identity of freedom-loving heroism is displayed, reconstituting the quintessential 'good war' narrative and unchallenged 'victory culture' of the 1940s and 1950s, thus attempting to reaffirm the clarity of purpose and certainty of victory that was challenged by the inclusive results of US military campaigns in Iraq and Afghanistan following 9/11, just as Vietnam had challenged earlier Hollywood cinematic incarnations of American exceptionalism and innocence.

The singular exception to a generalized cinematic narrative of American moral superiority and guaranteed victory, which generally also informs the frequent re-imaginations of World War II – from *The Longest Day* (1962), to *Saving Private Ryan* (1998), and *Red Tails* (2012) – then remains the Vietnam War, a conflict whose legitimacy, conduct, and purpose remain highly contested, and that presented a temporary break with the 'good war' tradition. American films about Vietnam took a much more critical stance toward American military power, rewriting the script of the United States as innocent defender of freedom, for example, in *The Deer Hunter* (1978), *Apocalypse Now* (1979), or *Platoon* (1986). Instead, the cinematic focus shifted onto the traumatizing effect of the Vietnam War on American soldiers, and the chaos, nihilism, and madness of war itself.[23]

During the 1980s, however, subsequent films such as *Top Gun* (1986), the *Rambo* series (1982, 1985, 1988) or *Red Dawn* (1984) successfully reemphasized a patriotic, hyper-masculine and militarized imagination of the United States under Ronald Reagan, documenting a renewed ideological determination in the Cold War confrontation against the 'Evil Empire' of the Soviet Union. Following the end of the Cold War and the 9/11 terror attacks, films like *Independence Day* (1996), *Behind Enemy Lines* (2001), or *Black Hawk Down* (2001) similarly reformulated the theme of American geopolitical identity as heroic, morally righteous, and victorious, occasional outliers with more negative depictions of the military ethos and US foreign policy, such as *A Few Good Men* (1992) or *Three Kings* (1999) notwithstanding.[24] The cinema thus served as space where American anxieties over the ambiguity and complexity of geopolitics and international affairs in the 'new world order' were replaced with certainty and simplicity.[25] A function similar to the one American grand strategy was supposed to perform in the political realm.

Common to what Jean-Michel Valantin has dubbed the 'national security cinema' is the perception of threat as an existential danger to survival, security, and order against which American power has to be mobilized. The narratives and visualizations of this theme provide filmic representations of American grand strategy, from failed containment in Vietnam, to the reverberations of American primacy under George W. Bush. As Valantin has noted, the 'history of relationships between the American state and strategy is also that of communication between Washington and Hollywood, which constantly transforms the application of American strategic practices into cinematic accounts.'[26]

This conjunction between entertainment, business, and politics was promoting the public's consent and compliance with the national security establishment and its strategic priorities, making Hollywood a filmic 'chronicler of American empire,' its films celebrating the 'virtue and power' of the United States.[27] To the critical and multiple Academy Award winning filmmaker Oliver Stone, Hollywood was 'selling the idea that America is militarily successful' through patriotic films like *Pearl Harbor* (2001), or *Black Hawk Down* (2001), released just before or shortly after 9/11.[28] The mixed results and costly experiences of the United States in the wars in Afghanistan and Iraq did not fundamentally affect the popularity of this established, cinematic narrative.

G.I. Joe: The Rise of Cobra (2009) and its sequel *G.I. Joe: Retaliation* (2013) are perfect examples that display this enduring pop-cultural construct of a militarized heroism in major Hollywood films under the Obama presidency. Based on an American 1980s cartoon series and toy line, *G.I. Joe* features a fictional, American-led, but formally international, secret organization of Special Forces soldiers, engaged in a global struggle against the evil Cobra terror organization, seeking world domination. The motto of the original cartoon series captures the simplistic, Manichean essence of the film franchise: Every Joe is 'a real American hero.'[29] Under Obama, this popular display of American military power and the heroic soldiers who embody and defend the country's liberal values was mirrored in a militarized, geopolitical imagination in formal and popular discourses. Here, 'American leadership' in the world was rooted in its global military supremacy and the moral purpose behind its power. As President Obama explained at the US Military Academy of West Point in 2014, American leadership and military superiority secured 'peace and prosperity' not just at home but around the globe:

'America must always lead on the world stage. The military . . . is and always will be the backbone of that leadership.'[30]

In the popular realm, this conjunction of heroic identity and military might was displayed most ostentatiously perhaps in the form of American superheroes as defenders of national security. In *Captain America: The First Avenger* (2011), for example, the audience encounters a fictional version of World War II, in which the United States is engaged in the development of a secret program that could turn ordinary soldiers into superpowered individuals. The only soldier who successfully undergoes this treatment is Steve Rogers, who would become the superhero Captain America, tasked to fight the Nazis and the Hydra terror organization. In *Captain America* the United States fights a 'good war,' virtually alone, against the very embodiment of evil, and it is the heroic self-sacrifice of the soldier/hero Steve Rogers that saves New York City from certain destruction by crashing the enemy's WMD-armed bomber in the Arctic.

Captain America quite literally embodies the military heroism of the United States as he is clad in a costume version of the Stars and Stripes. As Jason Dittmer has elaborated in his work on the film's comic book source material, significant to Captain America's role in the process of popularizing geopolitical narratives is his ability to connect the individual experience of the hero to 'political projects of American nationalism, international order, and foreign policy.'[31] The Captain fights for America, but he also is America. The filmic representations of militarized American heroes like Iron Man, the G.I. Joes or Captain America are testament to the enduring myth of American exceptionalism in the geopolitical imagination of the United States, stressing the singularity and material and moral superiority of the United States in world history and international politics.[32]

Superhero movies tap deep into these national myths, featuring such archetypes as the lone Western hero (Batman) and the American immigrant (Superman), and, in particular, the theme of American exceptionalism, and the fight against the barbaric, uncivilized Other on the frontier in the name of truth, justice, and the American way.[33] According to *New York Times* film critics A. O. Scott and Manohla Dargis, for example, cinematic portrayals of American superheroes, which have dominated commercially at the box office since the release of *X-Men* in 2000, were supporting the belief that the United States was 'different from all others because of its mission to make "the world safe for democracy,"' noting that both President Woodrow Wilson and the fictional character

Iron Man had used this key trope of American self-identification as moral crusader for a just cause.[34] As with President Bush's 'Top Gun' moment aboard the USS *Lincoln*, the close intertextuality of politics and popular culture in superhero movies serves to underwrite a geopolitical vision of American liberal hegemony as both functional necessity and moral imperative.

HOLLYWOOD, THE PENTAGON, AND THE CINEMATIC PRODUCTION OF NATIONAL SECURITY

The popular imagination of the United States as defender of national security and global freedom is centrally linked to the cinematic representation of American military power. The US DoD is actively involved in promoting and projecting the geopolitical identity of the United States as the world's only military superpower through its entertainment industry liaison. This long-standing cooperation between the Pentagon and Hollywood has been institutionalized through the Office of Public Relations and the Special Assistant for Entertainment Media, located within the US DoD. Individual liaison offices for the US Navy, the US Army, the US Marine Corps, and the US Air Force exist in Los Angeles. Their frequent involvement in contemporary film productions demonstrates that the Pentagon and the Armed Forces are not just a passive service provider to the film industry, but play an active role in the process of filmmaking.

Officially, the criteria the Armed Forces and the Pentagon apply to determine if they can provide support for a film are accuracy and realism. The portrayal on film is supposed to reflect an authentic image of the US military to domestic and international audiences. The actual support provided to film productions can include technical advice by active-duty or former soldiers, the lending of military hardware like tanks or helicopters for filming, the provision of military personnel as extras, or shooting on location at military installations. This service can save a production substantial costs, but it also allows the Pentagon great leverage in maintaining a positive image of the American military in the films it cooperates with.

Insiders have described the close relationship between filmmakers and the military as 'mutual exploitation.'[35] Hollywood obtains access to military hardware and expertise, acquiring an authenticity it would otherwise have to rent on the free market at substantially higher cost. The Pentagon in return reaps the public relations benefits from starring its technology and soldiers in big blockbusters where America's military heroes save the world. However, the role of the Pentagon goes beyond a mere supplier of technology and free-rider on Hollywood's PR machinery. It actively takes control of the popular image of national security which is being created in the films it cooperates with. As Capt. Russell Coons, director of the Navy Office of Information West declared in an interview in 2014: 'We're not going to support a program that disgraces a uniform or presents us in a compromising way.'[36]

In granting or denying support for a film, and being able to demand script changes, the DoD can apply its own definition of what constitutes a realistic portrayal of national security, and which version of political and historic reality it deems fit to support with expertise, manpower and equipment. This ultimately links the production of film and the popular representation of identity to the political agency and geopolitical imagination of the DoD. Every American soldier, fighter jet, or warship provided by the Pentagon to appear on screen also represents an attempt to legitimize a particular vision of US military power, its use and purpose through the discursive authority of the DoD. The Pentagon-Hollywood liaison then helps to establish a cross-discursive, common-sense position of national security, underwriting a hegemonic, geopolitical vision of America's role and position in the world. James Der Derian has commented how Hollywood is central to a 'military-industrial-media-entertainment network,' which he identified both as a continuation and transformation of the Cold War-era traditional military-industrial complex, and as supporting, legitimizing, and enabling a globe-spanning US hegemony and its militarized security practices through the visual technologies of simulation, surveillance, network-centric warfare, and media dissemination.[37] Hollywood films then represent both an ideational, virtual space in which projections and imaginations of identity and security are constructed and reflected, and a practical resource through which these constructs become the political, social, and economic reality of war and geopolitics.[38]

As the official statements of the various film liaison offices of the American military document, the goal of the Pentagon and the Armed Forces in the production of films is the projection of authentic images. According to the website of the U.S. Army's Office of the Chief of Public Affairs, Western Region (OCPA-West), its mission is to 'educate American and global audiences about the U.S. Army by ensuring realistic/plausible portrayal of Soldiers in the entertainment media.'[39] The Air Force Office of Public Affairs, Entertainment Liaison defines its mission as 'to project and protect the image of the United States Air Force within the global entertainment environment'.[40] The U.S. Navy Information Office West aims to 'ensure an authentic, accurate portrayal of the Navy's assets, policies and people in popular culture.'[41] Finally, the USMC Motion Picture & TV Liaison Office states that a 'production must benefit the Department of Defense, or otherwise be in the national interest' in order to obtain support.[42] As these statements demonstrate, the cooperation of the military with the motion picture industry is not simply for entertainment purposes: 'authentic' images are also meant to 'educate' audiences, further underlining the political significance of these pop-cultural artifacts. As the US Army's liaison office demonstrates, this political education can occur in a highly fictional setting, from alien invasion to gigantic monster attacks, as long as the basic 'good war' narrative is in place:

> Some of the people who will be watching "Godzilla" aren't watching the evening news or keeping up with news about our troops in Afghanistan, but they may learn about the Army from watching this or any other movie or TV show that we supported or provided guidance for.[43]

With an all-volunteer force that represents less than 1 percent of the American population, a majority of Americans obtain their information about the US military through entertainment products such as Hollywood films with concrete political effects. The 1986 film *Top Gun*, for example, which celebrated the daredevil exploits of US Navy pilot Pete 'Maverick' Mitchel, played by Tom Cruise, saw the substantial involvement of the US Navy, and is credited for a subsequent, marked increase in recruitment figures for the US Navy and Air Force.[44] The predominantly male teenage audiences of special effect-driven science-fiction and action movies, with their fast cuts, multiple explosions and fire fights, and visceral audio-visual style, represent a key target group recruiters hope to inspire with a positive image of serving in America's high-tech military. An illusion of realism, film promises the opportunity to experience the excitement of battle, the thrill of violence and destruction, and the spirit of camaraderie that the military embodies. As such, war or military-themed films and video games also feature themes of sexual euphoria and construct fantasies of hyper-masculinity, highlighting a particular gender perspective in the popular imagination of national security.[45]

In the 2012 *Avengers* action blockbuster, however, the representation of the fictional entity of the S.H.I.E.L.D. intelligence agency as a formally international body impeded support by the Pentagon. As Philip Strub, the Pentagon's Special Assistant for Entertainment Media explained: 'We couldn't reconcile the unreality of this international organization and our place in it . . . To whom did S.H.I.E.L.D. answer? Did we work for S.H.I.E.L.D.? We hit that roadblock and decided we couldn't do anything with the film.'[46] This rejection occurred despite the fact that *Avengers* featured a cast of predominantly American superheroes, defending the United States against alien invasion, and were led by Captain America, in the fictional Marvel universe a product of the US Army's 'super soldier' program. While the production team of *G.I. Joe: The Rise of Cobra* (2009) received permission to film at the National Training Center at Fort Irwin in California, according to Vincente C. Ogilvie, Deputy Director for Entertainment Media, the DoD could only provide limited support, in part due to the fact that G.I. Joe was not 'wholly American.'[47]

In the *Transformers* franchise on the other hand, where the military was defending American sovereignty and national security directly 'under U.S. command and control,' the support of the Pentagon even exceeded what was originally asked for.[48] Reportedly, Mr. Strub urged the filmmakers of *Transformers: Revenge of the Fallen* also to include the US Navy and the US Marine Corps in the movie so that the Pentagon would have the opportunity to showcase even more of its weaponry and soldiers.[49] As defined by the DoD, the reality of gigantic, shape-shifting, alien robots could be accepted, provided it conformed to its hegemonic definition of national sovereignty. An international context, however, where the United States was integrated into a supra-national security organization, such as S.H.I.E.L.D. or G.I. Joe, was too unrealistic a projection of national security as it displayed an unwanted dilution of American identity.

The realism of national security which the Pentagon sought to promote, however, was oftentimes far removed from the real-life conflicts involving the US military in the post-9/11 environment. The Academy Award winning *The Hurt Locker* (2009), for example, although hailed by then Secretary of Defense Robert Gates as 'authentic' and 'very compelling' did not enjoy official assistance.[50] The film, centered on a traumatized, renegade bomb disposal specialist in Iraq, who becomes addicted to the adrenalin rush of war and struggles to reintegrate into civilian life, was denied support due its unrealistic portrayal of military life. A movie franchise about alien robots based on a 1980s children's cartoon was, in contrast, deemed sufficiently authentic to be awarded a plethora of military assistance. Unlike *The Hurt Locker*, *Transformers: Revenge of the Fallen* clearly promoted an unequivocally positive military image of the United States saving the world from barbaric enemies.

WHY THE PENTAGON LOVES FIGHTING ALIENS: WINNING AGAINST THE PERFECT ENEMY

According to the Internet Movie Database (IMDB), between 2009 and 2015 a range of American film productions featuring the US military has obtained official support through the Pentagon's entertainment industry liaison, including: *The Messenger* (2009), *Transformers: Revenge of the Fallen* (2009), *Iron Man 2* (2010), *Transformers: Dark of the Moon* (2011), *Battle: Los Angeles* (2011), *Act of Valor* (2012), *Battleship* (2012), *Captain Phillips* (2013), *Man of Steel* (2013), *Lone Survivor* (2013), *G.I. Joe: Retaliation* (2013), *American Sniper* (2014), *Godzilla* (2014), and *Bridge of Spies* (2015). Remarkably, the majority of these films did not depict the military in real-world conflict, but showed American soldiers fighting evil aliens in a series of films that largely subscribed to the science-fiction genre.

During the Obama presidency, a basic, Manichean script of national security and geopolitics was predominantly constructed in a virtual reality where the moral ambiguity, uncertainty of purpose, and questionable outcomes that accompanied US military interventions in the aftermath of 9/11 did not feature prominently. Instead, Hollywood constructed an opponent whose evil Otherness was the perfect enemy to fight and win against in a spectacular fashion: the alien invader. The alien invasion theme, then, reproduced a basic narrative of American innocence that the Pentagon in turn could actively support with the moniker of military authenticity. Just as 9/11 was constructed as an attack out of the blue by 'evildoers' and 'enemies of freedom,' the frequent alien invasion on screen came over America as swift, sudden assault, taking an unprepared nation by surprise.[51]

There was no backstory leading up to events, no 'blowback' of previous American covert or military action, and no insight into the rational for invasion. Just like Nazis, Soviet Communists or Al Qaeda terrorists, the alien invader represented an uncivilized enemy of freedom that America had to defeat in a basic struggle of good versus evil: a cinematic narrative confirming both the material and ideational status of the

United States as the world's pre-eminent power. As then Secretary of Defense Chuck Hagel, for example, declared in 2015 before the Senate Armed Services Committee: 'The United States of America possesses the most lethal, strongest, most powerful military today in the history of the world. We will continue to have that kind of a military. We need that kind of a military to protect our interests.'[52]

Hollywood provides the cinematic narrative and visual spectacle in support of this rationale. A key identity trope in this formula is that the United States is always acting in defense, its supreme military resources only mobilized in response to external threats, establishing the superpower as defender, liberator, and protector. In addition, and unlike historic war films or even contemporary reflections of Iraq and Afghanistan, the entirely fictional scenario of an alien invasion allows the Pentagon to be involved in an even more sanitized version of warfare and military heroism, where post-traumatic stress, civilian causalities, mutilation, or friendly fire incidents are almost completely absent from the popular imagination of war fighting. Finally, unlike the contested political reasons for going to war in Iraq, or the doubtful final outcome of the Afghanistan mission, the moral cause for resorting to the use of force against the invader is unquestionable, and the ultimate outcome a guaranteed, total victory.

In the *Transformers* film franchise, for example, the United States encounters the threat of shape-shifting alien robots, the Decepticons, who seek to exploit earth for its energy resources and technology to rule the universe. America is aided in its fight by another group of robot aliens, the Autobots. The second installment of the series, the 2009 *Transformers: Revenge of the Fallen* is particularly interesting for the unprecedented support that the US DoD provided director Michael Bay in terms of military equipment and personnel. The final confrontation between the American military, the Autobots and the Decepticons occurs in Egypt, shot on location on the US Army's missile range in New Mexico.[53] In *Transformers: Revenge of the Fallen* the American military deploys the entire range of its devastating firepower, representing all branches of the Armed Forces to win a decisive victory in the deserts of the Middle East.

According to the Pentagon 'full-spectrum dominance means the ability of U.S. forces, operating alone or with allies, to defeat any adversary and control any situation across the range of military operations.'[54]*Transformers: Revenge of the Fallen* is full-spectrum dominance in action. At the same time, Bay's *Transformers* films or *Battle: Los Angeles* with their highly visceral, audio-visual effect bombardments and unapologetic relish in destruction appear like the military-entertainment industry's equivalent of 'shock and awe,' or what film critic A O Scott described as 'symphonies of excess and redundancy, taking place in a universe full of fire and metal and purged of nuance'.[55] There is no possibility for diplomacy, compromise, or restraint, but only a violent, decisive confrontation of the forces of good versus the forces of evil.

In contrast to the high-tech desert warfare of *Revenge of the Fallen*, the fighting in *Transformers: Dark of the Moon* and *Battle: Los Angeles*, however, seems much more influenced by an asymmetrical conflict setting, showing the US military engaged in urban combat, essentially employing guerrilla tactics against superior enemy forces. Displaying America's Armed Forces as the underdog appears odd, given the status of the United States as the world's pre-eminent military power. However, these representations partially reflected the costly and frustrating realities of the asymmetrical warfare the US military had to adapt to in the post-9/11 environment. Here, instead of conventional military confrontations with potential peer competitors, counter-insurgency (COIN) and counter-terrorism (CT) emerged as the Pentagon's new focus of war fighting, with US soldiers tasked to police a new frontier between 'uncivilized' space and America's liberal empire. In a remarkable reversal of real-life roles, however, American soldiers were acting as insurgents, and the alien invader represented the occupying force in a series of films deemed explicitly 'apolitical' by the respective liaison offices of the Armed Forces.[56]

The classic narrative of David versus Goliath allows the audience to identify easily with the American citizen-soldier, who defends the homeland with ingenuity and courage against the crushing superiority of the enemy's war machine. At the same time, this cinematic imagination, which the Pentagon promoted through the films it supported, conveniently avoided a critical engagement with the reality of American military power as an occupying force and the role of the US as 'global policeman' and quasi-imperial hegemon. Instead, it is the American homeland that repeatedly comes under attack. In the 2011 *Transformers: Dark of the Moon*, for example, the Decepticons launch an invasion of Chicago in their quest to subjugate Earth. In a costly, final battle the Autobots and a small infantry unit of American Air Force Special Forces soldiers manage to defeat the enemy once again.[57]

Where the US Air Force took the lead in *Transformers: Dark of the Moon*, the United States Marine Corps (USMC) followed with its own invasion movie. *Battle: Los Angeles* is set in modern-day Los Angeles, where a retiring Marine Staff Sergeant (Aaron Eckhardt) must go back into the line of duty to lead American troops during yet another global alien invasion and attack on US soil. Here it is again the Other, rather than the United States, who enjoys the advantage of techno-logical superiority, with the invading aliens operating sophisticated drones that control the skies and rain down death and destruction on American soldiers and civilians. The film's focus lies on a small group of Marines from the 2nd Battalion 5th Marines and the production received substantial cooperation from the USMC, including guidance, equipment, military training of actors, and access to Camp Pendleton in California.[58] The purpose of the alien invasion is ultimately to serve as a backdrop for the display of the heroism and military power of the United States and the Marine Corps in particular. Aaron Eckhardt, the film's leading star, explained at its premier: 'This is a movie about Marines . . . kicking ass. When people see this movie, we want to make sure that they love the Marines.'[59]

In *Battleship*, the defense of national security against invading aliens shifts to the Pacific, where the United States Navy is allowed to take the spotlight. Again the world is threatened by an alien invasion, and again American military power is the planet's last and best hope for survival.[60] The film's naval focus on a military exchange in the Pacific Ocean contrasts with the more ground combat and air power oriented films of the *Transformers* series and *Battle: Los Angeles*. Departing from seemingly Iraq- and Afghanistan-inspired scenarios, *Battleship* is par-ticularly interesting when seen in context with the 'pivot to Asia' the Obama administration announced in 2011, when the Secretary of State declared America's leadership in the Pacific Century in *Foreign Policy*.[61]

Central to the 'pivot' – later relabeled 'rebalancing' – was the deployment of additional military assets to the region, in particular US Navy and Marine forces to check a more assertive China, assessed in Washington as aiming for political, economic, and military hegemony in Asia.[62] Seemingly echoing the pivot's geopolitical reorientation of America's strategic priorities, *Battleship*'s main locations are situated in Asia and the Pacific, while the Japanese Maritime Self Defense Force (JMSDF) aids the US Navy in its fight against the invading aliens. The spirit of the American-Japanese security alliance and the United States' role as Asia's security guarantor are also invoked, when the movie shows the beginning of RIMPAC (Rim of the Pacific Exercise), accord-ing to the US Navy, the 'world's largest international maritime warfare exercise' hosted by the United States. In the words of the US Navy's Chief of Information, Rear Admiral Denny Moynihan:

> We can't take everyone out to our ships, but we can work with Hollywood and bring the Navy to life on the big screen. Consequently, it's in our best interest to engage and make sure that movies like *Battleship* accurately portray who we are and what we do as a Navy.[63]

Although a science-fiction film, *Battleship* both asserts the geopolitical identity of the United States as a 'Pacific power' and underlines the key role of the US Navy and American military power in maintaining security in the region.

In contrast to the multiple Pentagon-supported science-fiction films, major realistic films, depicting the American military under Obama, included *The Messenger* (2009), *Act of Valor* (2012), *Lone Survivor* (2013), *Captain Phillips* (2013), and *American Sniper* (2014). In addition to cooperating with the US DoD, the special aura of authenticity surrounding these particular pop-cultural artifacts resulted from their cinematic depiction of real-life events. *Lone Survivor*, for example, is set during the Afghanistan War, re-telling the events of an unsuccessful US Navy SEALs (Sea, Air, and Land Teams) operation in 2005 to capture a Taliban leader ('Operation Red Wings'), ending with the rescue of Marcus Luttrell (Mark Wahlberg), the sole surviving SEAL team member. *Captain Phillips* is likewise based on a real-life event, featuring the rescue of civilian Captain Richard Phillips (Tom Hanks) by US Navy SEALs from Somali pirates. *American Sniper* is set during the Iraq War, and loosely based on the memoir by Chris Kyle (Bradley Cooper), the most successful sniper in US military history and likewise a Navy SEAL.

A novel development, *Act of Valor* is an entire film dedicated to this elite Special Forces unit of the US Navy that was directly commissioned by the Navy's Special Warfare Command and featured actual SEALs, and not actors, as the protagonists, tracking and eliminating a global terrorist network.[64] *Act of Valor*, *Captain Phillips*, *Lone Survivor*, and *American Sniper*, all prominently featuring the Navy SEALs, serve as a popular reflection of the prominence of Special Forces and covert operations in US national security policy under the Obama administration.[65] This prominence of America's secret soldiers under Obama was highlighted most spectacularly with the assassination of Osama bin Laden by the Special Warfare Development Group (DEVGRU), also known as SEAL Team 6, later fictionalized in the CIA- and Pentagon-supported film *Zero Dark Thirty* (2012).[66]

Only in one instance did the Pentagon lend support to a film that somewhat challenged the narrative of American superior military power as victorious defender of freedom and security. *The Messenger* (2009) features Will Montgomery (Ben Foster), a rebellious US Army Staff Sergeant and war hero who has returned home from Iraq. He is assigned to the Army's Casualty Notification service and partnered with a recovering alcoholic, Captain Tony Stone (Woody Harrelson), to give notice to the families of fallen soldiers. The *Messenger* is a quiet counterpoint to the high-tech firework displays of military muscle in *Transformers* and *Battleship*. The film shows the soldiers fighting America's wars coming back to the home front and the human cost attached to the role of global superpower. Given the backdrop of the Iraq War, *The Messenger* questions both the defensive and victorious representations of military power, and the meaning of military superiority altogether. However, in comparison with the majority of films supported by the Pentagon, and given their respective production cost and box office successes, the cinematic narrative that film producers, the DoD, and the American public apparently embrace most is one where the United States and its military emerge victorious from a basic confrontation of good and evil.

This is even more striking when the Pentagon-supported alien invasion films are compared with a more critical, cinematic reflection of the military in economic terms. According to boxofficemojo.com, in 2011 *Transformers: Dark of the Moon* grossed US$352.4 million domestically and *Battle: Los Angeles* made US$83.5 million, while the Iraq War movie *Green Zone* (2010) grossed US$35 million, the Oscar-winner *The Hurt Locker* (2009) US$17 million, and *In the Valley of Elah* (2007), which featured abuse of prisoners and post-traumatic stress in soldiers, US$6.7 million. Even the critically panned *Battleship* still managed to gross US$65 million in 2012. Between a critical reflection of America's military involvement in the Middle East, and a military fantasy of defending the American homeland against evil aliens, the winner at the box office is clear. While these critical films about America's post-9/11 wars in Central Asia and the Middle East undoubtedly challenge the militarization of US national security and the geopolitical imaginations of the 'good war' narrative – the 'violent cartography' in the words of Michael Shapiro – their modest economic performance at the same time reveals their limited ability to disrupt the common-sense status of a virtual reality in which America saves the world.[67] In the words of one of the US Army's entertainment liaison officers: 'The military enjoys a high level of support among Americans and they don't want to spend their entertainment dollars watching something they don't believe to be true.'[68] Its popularity and commercial success are thus vital elements that establish the government-sponsored national security cinema as a Foucauldian 'regime of truth.'

A particularly interesting entry is the highly-commercially successful and controversial Iraq War movie, *American Sniper*, directed by Clint Eastwood. The film follows its protagonist Chris Kyle, played by Bradley Cooper, from working as an unfulfilled Texas rodeo cowboy to becoming a Navy SEAL sniper, with more than 160 confirmed kills in four tours in Iraq, making him the deadliest sniper in US military history. The film reproduces several key mythological themes of American identity construction, from American exceptionalism to the Western hero, defending civilization out on the ungoverned frontier. In the film, soldiers refer to Iraq as the 'new Wild West of the Middle East,' while the enemy – Iraqi insurgents and Al Qaeda terrorists – are frequently referred to as 'savages' and collectively dehumanized. Iraqis are given no agency on their own, and appear either as helpless victims or terrorists – often disguised as civilians – implying that the Americans ultimately cannot trust the Iraqi population.

The film also avoids any wider political contextualization of why US soldiers are in Iraq in the first place, beyond showing a newsreel of the collapsing Twin Towers on 9/11. In the film, Kyle gives his personal motivation for joining the military and fighting in Iraq as protecting the 'greatest country on earth' and confronting evil in the 'dirt' of Iraq so that it cannot come to New York or San Diego. Yet, like *The Hurt Locker* or *The Messenger*, the film also depicts the struggle of American soldiers to readjust to civilian life. Kyle himself was killed by a fellow veteran suffering from Post-Traumatic Stress Disorder on a shooting range in Texas after returning home from Iraq, a scene the movie does not show directly but mentions in the end credits. As such, the attempt to reconstitute an American heroic identity by portraying the fight against the dehumanized 'savage,' a trope in the cinematic continuity of the classic Western, nonetheless remains ambiguous, as it remains embedded within the wider geopolitical context of the 'War on Terror,' marked by persisting anxieties and uncertainties over the legitimacy, conduct, and effectiveness of US foreign and security policy.[69]

American Sniper shows audiences the mutilation of veterans, the disillusion of some of Kyle's comrades with the Iraq mission, and the strain of multiple overseas deployments on American families, delivering a more nuanced picture, compared to the flag-waving patriotism and military bombast of the alien invasion genre. Yet, *American Sniper* and its protagonist also reproduce a key, mythological narrative in which the military serves as the embodiment of the nation, its warriors united by shared values and a sacred bond, displaying valor and heroism in confronting and defeating America's enemies. This particular imagination of a militarized American identity, while not altogether unchallenged, remains both the most significant and commercially most successful contribution of mainstream Hollywood to the popular discourse of national security and geopolitics.

COUNTER-NARRATIVES IN NATIONAL SECURITY CINEMA

The dominant cinematic narrative in the films surveyed so far establishes the United States as the heroic, powerful, and moral defender of freedom and justice. However, prevailing counter-narratives to this theme also exist in major, popular films outside of independent movies and small-budget productions like *The Messenger*, or the string of Iraq-themed films that all flopped at the box office. In *Avatar* (2009), for example, one of the most successful films of all time, the Resources Development Administration (RDA) that invades the planet of Pandora to mine for natural resources and violently displaces the indigenous population of the Na'vi can be read as an allegory for the United States as imperialist and militarist aggressor in the name of corporate profit.[70] Thus, the film can be viewed as critique of American foreign policy, in particular directed against the grand strategy vision of American primacy followed by the George W. Bush administration in its invasion of Iraq, and conservative circles in the United States accused the film and its director James Cameron of being anti-American.[71]

Another form of counter-narrative concerns the location of threat to the United States not externally but internally. In *Iron Man 2*, for example, the threat to national security arises not only from the mad Russian scientist Vanko but also domestically from corporate greed and the willingness of an American weapons manufacturer, Justin Hammer (Sam Rockwell), to use criminal practices in his pursuit of profit and status. A common element in representing internal threats to national security is through the negative depiction of the Central Intelligence Agency

(CIA), arguably the best known of the seventeen different agencies the United States maintains for intelligence purposes. During the Obama presidency, the theme of rogue agents, for example, who are being hunted down by the CIA because of their knowledge of illegal government activities, has been featured in films such as *RED* (2010) and *The Bourne Legacy* (2012). The perceived threat to national security in these films does not lie in external attack but in the exposure of secrets the US government wants to keep hidden, such as a war crime record of a presidential candidate (*RED*) or the illegal conduct of human experimentation by the Pentagon (*The Bourne Legacy*). In other instances, individual CIA agents act as villains for a film, as criminals seeking illegal profits from selling sensitive information or material (*The A-Team, Knight and Day*), or as sleeper agents who work for a foreign power (*Salt*). In Hollywood, the CIA often represents the dark side of American superpower. It is perhaps the one aspect of American national security most frequently and consistently portrayed in a negative, or at least critical, fashion.[72]

Plots that feature threats emerging from the military-industrial complex, or an out-of-control intelligence establishment have provided the backdrop for a number of highly successful films, notably since the beginning of Obama's second presidential term in 2012. Here, the United States was not represented as heroic defender of national security; on the contrary, institutional secrecy and uncontrolled executive power were themselves shown to be threats to civil liberties and individual freedom. In the commercially highly successful 2014 film *Captain America: The Winter Soldier*, for example, Captain America doubts his role in the national security apparatus and is ultimately forced to fight his own side, the S.H.I.E.L.D. intelligence agency, which has been subverted from within, the result of a widespread Hydra conspiracy, led by a State Department official. The surveillance and intelligence apparatus conceived to counter terrorists appears as a direct danger to the American ideal of freedom embodied by Captain America. As Steve Rogers (Chris Evans) explains, when confronted by S.H.I.E.L.D.'s plans to establish a global, weaponized surveillance satellite network: 'You hold a gun to everyone on Earth and call it protection. This is not freedom. This is fear.'[73]

Captain America: The Winter Soldier offers a critical reflection of the Obama administration's secret intelligence policy and global surveillance activities within the popular framework of a superhero movie. As the film's review in the *Washington Post* stated: 'The Winter Soldier

uncannily taps into anxieties having to do not only with post-9/11 arguments about security and freedom, but also Obama-era drone strikes
and Snowden-era privacy.[74] *Time* magazine noted that the danger in
Captain America: The Winter Soldier did not emanate from a fantasy villain, or an imaginary realm, but was grounded in 'threats from today's
headlines.'[75]

White House Down (2013) is a particularly interesting entry in this
group of more critically-oriented national security movies. On the surface, the film is a standard action thriller that pits a Capitol Hill police
officer John Cale (Channing Tatum) against a group of terrorists who
have taken over the White House and want to take the President of
the United States hostage. In fact, *Olympus Has Fallen*, released in the
same year, featured a virtually identical plot of '*Die Hard* in the White
House,' albeit with North Koreans as the terrorist enemy. The former,
more conventional, film was also the clear winner at the box office,
while *White House Down* was a commercial failure. What makes *White
House Down* noteworthy in comparison, however, is its critical contextualization. As the reviewer for the *New Republic* remarked: 'it manages
to capture the zeitgeist: the movie is more concerned with civil liberties
than foreign threats; the danger is the vaguely Tea Party-esque enemy
within our own borders.[76]

White House Down opens with President John Sawyer, played by
Jamie Foxx, in the midst of negotiating a broad peace agreement with
several countries in the Middle East, including Iran. As part of this
agreement, the United States has announced its willingness to withdraw all its troops from the region. In the film, the President specifically
lays out a foreign policy vision of diplomacy and cooperation against
a perpetual war scenario promoted by the 'military-industrial complex,' which is specifically referred to by this name in the movie. This
focus on cooperative engagement, even with declared 'enemies' of the
United States, seems like a direct, filmic allegory of President Obama's
attempts at engagement with Iran, among others.

In fact, the political similarities between President Sawyer and
President Obama were noted by several critics.[77] In *White House Down*,
the terrorist plot to take over the White House is carried out by right-
wing extremists and former Special Forces soldiers, and is ultimately
orchestrated by the Republican Speaker of the House Richard Jenkins
(Eli Raphelson) and the military-industrial complex in an attempt to
undermine President Sawyer's peace efforts. Conservative critics in
particular criticized Roland Emmerich for directing an anti-Republican,

liberal action-fantasy, where Sawyer/Obama appears as the hero and Jenkins/Boehner as the sinister villain.[78] Within the framework of a standard Hollywood action movie, *White House Down* thus provided a narrative that contrasted a geopolitical vision of diplomacy, compromise, and restraint against the status quo of American hegemony, global power projection, and military engagement overseas. The film appeared like a cinematic endorsement of President Obama's emphasis of military restraint and 'nation-building at home.'[79]

Finally, a major blockbuster that seemed to question the narrative of American exceptionalism and military efficacy is *The Dark Knight Rises* (2012). In the film, Gotham City, a comic book allegory of New York City, is subject to a massive terrorist attack orchestrated by the villain Bane (Tom Hardy). In *The Dark Knight Rises*, the United States does not appear as the triumphant force for good but as a profoundly troubled country, whose national security is easily disrupted and its military power largely ineffectual. The institutions which the American society charges to maintain law and order and keep the country safe cannot be trusted, are corrupt or are rendered useless. Only Batman (Christian Bale), a masked vigilante operating outside the law – and who utilizes methods from illegal wiretapping to interrogation techniques bordering on torture – manages to finally defeat Bane and free Gotham City after months under foreign domination.

The theme of the lone hero is of course a staple of American mythology, and of Hollywood action films and the national security cinema in particular. This theme was made prominent originally by Westerns, where it is down to the courage and determination of the individual – and not the weak, or non-existing institutions of the state – to bring outlaws to justice. And with his superior technological arsenal of weapons and vehicles, martial arts skills, and body armor, Batman arguably represents yet another version of the militarized superhero acting in defense of the nation. *The Dark Knight Rises* then reformulates, but does not replace, the basic Manichean narrative of good versus evil that Hollywood employs to construct the geopolitical identity of the United States on the big screen.

CONCLUSION

Film provides a framework of reference for popular understandings of the world political role of the United States and the national security practices employed to defend and protect this identity. The national security cinema regularly creates a world that appears as a profoundly dangerous place, where America stands largely alone in defending the freedom and safety of its people, and the world at large, against a multitude of existential threats, from international terrorists to monstrous villains and alien invaders. The Pentagon-Hollywood liaison is centered on the constant reproduction of this particular construct of geopolitical knowledge that weaves together themes of American exceptionalism, militarism, and heroic individualism. On screen, this hegemonic vision is offered to audiences as an authentic and real depiction of world politics. Films like *Battleship* reveal a dominant worldview that unites the entertainment industry and the defense establishment. This geopolitical vision is meant to both entertain and educate, establishing global leadership, military supremacy, and the use of force for a just cause as hallmarks of US national security.

As such, films like *Transformers* or *Battle: Los Angeles* are military propaganda vehicles serving the interest of the Armed Forces for positive public relations and recruitment, but they also reveal a prevalent conviction of truth that positions the United States and its military power as the foundation and defender of a liberal world order of peace, democracy, and prosperity, which motivates US policymaking in the White House and the Pentagon. While, occasionally, films also displayed threats to America that emerged domestically – from the military-industrial complex, or the national secret intelligence apparatus – ultimately they did not question the basic Manichean narrative that represented the geopolitical identity of the United States as a morally righteous power on the world stage. Here, aberrations in the pursuit of national security were corrected, when the American secret agent, soldier, or superhero overcame the corruption, subversion, or institutional ineptitude that allowed the United States to be endangered from within.

As such, Hollywood films can both affirm the geopolitical identity of the United States and its heroic, military exceptionalism, and question the excess of secrecy and surveillance that has come to be associated with American grand strategy and national security policy under the Obama presidency. This ambivalence about American power and global hegemony in films like *White House Down* and *Captain America: The Winter Soldier* reflected popular attitudes in the United States at large. Under Obama, ordinary Americans similarly oscillated between expecting American leadership in the world and taking pride in the country's superpower status, and voicing doubt over the use of force, favoring restraint over being engaged abroad. While the heroic past of

Captain America remains a fixture in the country's popular imagination, his future purpose and role seem unclear.

NOTES

1. Oliver Stone, quoted in *Al Jazeera*, 'Empire: Hollywood and the War Machine.'
2. Mintz and Roberts, *Hollywood's America*, p. 27.
3. O'Meara et al., *Movies, Myth and the National Security State*, Robb, *Operation Hollywood*, Suid, *Guts and Glory* (revised and expanded edition), Valantin, *Hollywood, the Pentagon and Washington*.
4. Dittmer, *Popular Culture, Geopolitics and Identity*.
5. Weldes (ed.), *To Seek Out New Worlds*.
6. Weber, *Imagining America at War*, p. 188.
7. Politically, this vision was laid out in key speeches and statements by President Obama, the 2010 and 2015 *National Security Strategy* (*NSS*), or high-level Pentagon documents, like the 2010 and 2014 *Quadrennial Defense Review* (*QDR*) Reports, see Chapters 6 and 7 in this book.
8. O'Meara et al., *Movies, Myth and the National Security State*, p. 19
9. Sharp, 'Reel Geographies of the New World Order,' pp. 152–170, Dodds, 'Gender, Geopolitics, and Contemporary Representations of National Security', pp. 21–33.
10. US Air Force Entertainment Liaison Office, 'Motion Pictures.'
11. All domestic box office results available at boxofficemojo.com (last accessed August 22, 2016).
12. Dittmer and Dodds, 'Popular Geopolitics Past and Future.'
13. Jason Dittmer has recently raised the issue of a greater attention to the role of cultural economy in the analysis of popular geopolitics in Dittmer, 'American Exceptionalism.'
14. See in this context also Giglio, *Here's Looking at You*.
15. Der Derian, *Virtuous War*.
16. Pollard, 'The Hollywood War Machine,' p. 121.
17. William L. O'Neill, 'The "Good War."' This applies in particular to cinematic accounts of World War II as the quintessential 'good war' and its reincarnations in other form as, for example, in *Star Wars* (1977) or *Independence Day* (1996).
18. Der Derian, *Virtuous War*, p. 166, Engelhardt, *The End of Victory Culture*, pp. 10–11, 48. The *Why We Fight* series was originally commissioned to be shown only to US service personnel but was later released to the general public due to its great effect on audiences.
19. Ibid., p. 10.
20. Dixon, *Lost in the Fifties*.

21. Hantke, 'Bush's America and the Return of Cold War Science Fiction,' Engelhardt, *The End of Victory Culture*, pp. 101–107.
22. Hantke, 'Bush's America and the Return of Cold War Science Fiction.'
23. Works such as *Apocalypse Now* and *Platoon* are among the most famous examples of 'anti-war films' hailed for critically exploring the American involvement in Vietnam and its social and political implications, see Anderegg, *Inventing Vietnam*. Others deny an 'anti-war' quality to these films, describing, for example, *Apocalypse Now* as violent spectacle that does not question the legitimacy of the Vietnam War and that is based on the representation of the enemy as the unknown 'Other,' see Hayward, *Cinema Studies*, p. 462.
24. Ó Tuathail, 'The Frustrations of Geopolitics and the Pleasures of War,' Dalby, 'Warrior Geopolitics,' Dodds, 'Hollywood and the Popular Geopolitics of the War on Terror.'
25. Lacy, 'War, Cinema, and Moral Anxiety.'
26. Valantin, *Hollywood, the Pentagon and Washington*, p. xi.
27. Chris Hedges, quoted in *Al Jazeera*, 'Empire: Hollywood and the War Machine.'
28. Oliver Stone, quoted in ibid.
29. Some of G.I. Joe's members, unlike the original all-American cartoon cast, originated from other countries in the film, most likely to increase the global box office appeal of this very American military toy line turned movie franchise; see Sharkey, 'Movie Review G.I. Joe.'
30. White House, 'Remarks by the President at the United States Military Academy Commencement Ceremony,' May 28, 2014.
31. Dittmer, 'Captain America's Empire,' p. 627.
32. See also, McCrisken, *American Exceptionalism*, Dittmer, 'American Exceptionalism,' O'Meara et al., *Movies, Myth and the National Security State*, p. 29.
33. O'Meara et al. identify five key, mutually reinforcing foundational myths that serve as a common, cultural repertoire of American historic memory and national identity: American exceptionalism; the universalism of American liberal values; Manifest Destiny; the frontier experience as conflict between civilization and barbarism; and the American war story; ibid. p. 28.
34. Scott and Dargis, 'Super-Dreams of an Alternate World Order.'
35. Taraby, 'Hollywood and the Pentagon.'
36. Quoted in ibid.
37. Der Derian, *Virtuous War*, p. xx.
38. Ibid.
39. Available at http://www.army.mil/info/institution/publicAffairs/ocpa-west/faq.html (last accessed August 18, 2016).

40. Available at http://www.airforcehollywood.af.mil/ (last accessed August 23, 2016).
41. Available at http://www.navy.mil/local/navinfowest/Welcome.asp (last accessed August 23, 2016).
42. Available at http://www.hqmc.marines.mil/divpa/Units/LosAngeles PublicAffairs/FAQ.aspx (last accessed August 23, 2016).
43. Vergun, 'Soldiers' Take on Godzilla.'
44. Sirota, '25 years later, how "Top Gun" made America love war.'
45. See also Suid, *Guts and Glory*, pp. 6–11.
46 Ackerman, 'Pentagon Quit The Avengers Because of its "Unreality."'
47. Schogol, 'Transformers beat G.I. Joe in battle for DOD support for summer blockbusters.'
48. Ibid.
49. Rose, 'The U.S. Military Storm Hollywood.'
50. Barnes, Parker, and Horn, 'The Hurt Locker sets off conflict.'
51. See in this context, Croft, *Culture, Crisis and America's War on Terror*.
52. Quoted in US Senate Committee on Armed Services, Department of Defense Authorization of Appropriations for Fiscal Year 2015 and the Future Years Defense Program, March 5, 2014, p. 61.
53. Axe, 'Pentagon, Hollywood Pair up for Transformers Sequel.' A B-1 bomber, AWACs surveillance plane and six F-16 Fighting Falcon fighter jets, the US Army's Golden Knights parachute team, armored Humvees, M1 Abrams tanks, M2 Bradley infantry fighting vehicles, and MLRS missile-launchers engage the alien invader from above and on the ground. In addition, the US Navy aircraft carrier USS *John C. Stennis* and a group of real-life United States Marines join the fight on the American side.
54. Shelton, 'Chairmen of the Joint Chiefs of Staff,' p. 61.
55. Scott, 'One Small Step for Man, One Giant Leap for Autobots.'
56. The website *Spy Culture* has obtained a number of documents from the film liaison offices of the US Army, US Air Force and US Marine Corps via a Freedom of Information Request (FOI) detailing this assessment, and the specific cooperation granted to film productions. Available at http://www.spyculture.com (last accessed August 22, 2016).
57. The US Air Force provided 50 airmen from Headquarters Air Force Special Operations Command and the 1st Special Operations Wing for the film as extras, together with a CV-22B Osprey plane and shoots on location at Hulbert Field, Florida and Edwards Air Force Base, California, see US Air Force, 'Transformers: Dark of the Moon filmed at Hurlburt.'
58. Scott, 'Aaron Eckhart Went Through Military Training to Make "Battle: Los Angeles" seem real.'
59. Sauer, 'Retreat, Sell!'
60. In essence, the US Navy features as the protagonist of this film, in particular the Pacific Fleet's real-life Arleigh-Burk class Destroyers USS *John Paul*

Jones and USS *Sampson* and their crews. After the loss of both ships the remaining survivors have to reactivate the film's name-giving battleship, the WW II-era USS *Missouri*, in order to defeat the invading aliens and their main communications outpost on Oahu, Hawaii.

61. Clinton, 'America's Pacific Century.'
62. See, for example, US DoD, *Asia-Pacific Maritime Security Strategy*, pp. 20–21.
63. Quoted in Ewing, 'The Military-Industrial-Entertainment Complex.'
64. Keegan, '"Act of Valor" must balance publicity, secrecy with Navy SEAL.'
65. Hasian Jr., Lawson and McFarlane, The Rhetorical Invention of America's National Security State, pp. 95–130.
66. Ibid., p. 111.
67. Shapiro, *Cinematic Geopolitics*, p. 37.
68. Quoted in Vergun, 'Soldiers' take on Godzilla.'
69. On the role of the Western mythology in constituting American nation-hood, see also Shapiro, *Methods and Nations*, pp. 151–172.
70. Itzkoff, 'You saw what in 'Avatar'? Pass those Glasses!'
71. Shone 'James Cameron Hates America.'
72. On favorable and unfavorable representations of the CIA on film, see also Oliver Boyd-Barrett, Herrera, and Baumann, *Hollywood and the CIA*.
73. Quoted in Foundas, 'Film Review.'
74. Hornaday, 'Captain America.'
75. Collins, 'REVIEW.'
76. Chotiner, 'The Surprisingly Left-Wing Politics of "White House Down."'
77. Barber, 'White House Down.'
78. See, for example, Franke, '"White House Down."'
79. White House, 'Remarks by the President on the Way Forward in Afghanistan,' June 22, 2011.

Chapter 3

COMPETING VISIONS FOR AMERICA – POPULAR DISCOURSES OF GRAND STRATEGY ON *THE NEW YORK TIMES* BEST-SELLERS LIST

═══════

> Anybody around here know how to write a telegram?
> Thomas L. Freidman and Michael Mandelbaum[1]

The New York Times best-sellers list is widely considered to be the pre-eminent account of best-selling books in the United States.[2] As such, it provides an ideal location for a wider mapping of grand strategy discourses in American popular culture. From a post-structural analytical perspective, there exists no distinctive hierarchy between discursive realms in the construction of reality and the legitimization of a generally accepted truth. Geopolitical knowledge is built from political, social, and cultural resources with frequent intertextual links interconnecting these discursive sites and the outputs of individual discursive producers.[3] The stories, images, and ideas that construct American grand strategy must thus be present in the popular imagination if they are to function as a national policy guideline and provide the 'big picture' of a commonly accepted truth of world politics. As David Campbell has noted in his seminal *Writing Security*, the constant '(re)writing of the charter of US society in Foreign Policy texts' suggests that the performance of a particular American identity is the main function of foreign policy practices and occurs through the dichotic distinction of the American Self and the foreign, dangerous Other.

Analyzing *The New York Times* list reveals how, in line with Hollywood's dominant, cinematic accounts at the box office, American hegemony represents the principal theme in these popular foreign policy and national security texts, which constitute a geopolitical identity of American exceptionalism and world leadership vis-à-vis the threatening, volatile Other of global disintegration and chaos. However, among these best-selling books, alternative accounts of the present and future state of American power and international influence were more numerous and varied than in the national security cinema, signifying an internal contest of competing popular geopolitical visions of hegemony, engagement, and restraint in the popular imagination.

The writing and rewriting of security and identity, then, occurs within a fractured national landscape of conflicting elite opinion, and individual texts are articulated primarily against the internal, threatening Other, whose misguided strategic vision is seen as endangering the nation from within. This contest is revealed, for example, in the marked dichotomy of strategic arguments between insiders, such as Robert Kagan, defending a discursive status quo of liberal hegemony against 'misguided' critics, and outsiders like Andrew Bacevich targeting 'Washington' and challenging the prevailing elite consensus through the advocacy of restraint. This reconfirms the centrality of the notion of danger in constituting discourses of American identity and security, yet it neither locates the Other, as explored by Campbell, at the margins of American society, for example, the criminal in the 'War on Drugs,' nor within the realm of the territorialized, foreign enemy, but within the domestic network of foreign policy experts, media pundits, and elite opinion formers, suggesting a greater heterogeneity of elite knowledges than previously explored.[4] The popular manifestation of this heterogeneity of grand strategy visions in the nation's bestsellers in turn reveals a considerable degree of national insecurity and uncertainty over American geopolitical identity at the beginning of the twenty-first century.

Analyzing non-fiction books which have achieved the status of national best-seller, then, illustrates how debates over grand strategy, American identity, and national security are products of both political and popular culture, constructed in the public sphere at the multimedial intersection of entertainment, journalism, academia, and political commentary. As Joanne Sharp has noted in her critical geopolitical analysis of *Readers Digest* and the construction of the Cold War in the popular imagination in the United States, the division between 'international relations and the politics of everyday praxis' should be scrutinized.[5] The 'cultural context of elite discourses' must be understood, since it is through the socialization of common norms and cultural values that meaning is created and geopolitical identities are constituted and stabilized.[6] As Sharp has argued, it is through the consumption of everyday representations of geopolitics that the reader is constituted within a particular discourse of 'Americanness' and understanding of world order.[7]

As such, *The New York Times* best-sellers list, while also an icon of American popular culture, is unlike *Readers Digest*, not one unique and distinct voice, which has shaped a particular popular American imagination, but it is rather a central site where a multitude of voices intersect in competing over the formulation of such an American identity, validated as influential through their presence on this key ranking of popular texts. At the same time, this everyday production of geopolitical knowledge also transcends a clear separation between political practice, formal analysis, intellectual expertise, and popular culture. *The New York Times* non-fiction best-sellers combine popularity, profit-orientation, and mass appeal with the formal authority of expert knowledge, and they frequently engage in practical policy recommendations in their discussion of American grand strategy. This cross-discursive overlapping somewhat blurs the boundaries that the critical geopolitics literature has established between popular, formal, and practical geopolitical discourses.[8]

The popular texts collected on *The New York Times* best-sellers list offer a wide range of liberal and conservative, Democrat and Republican, more internationalist or 'isolationist' inclined views of the United States that have all reached a certain degree of commercial success and mass appeal, and thus can claim some discursive prominence. Furthermore, their respective public status as experts lends these authors a special authority to construct knowledge about geopolitics and national security, with their outputs being recognized as both intellectual expertise and as reflecting popular sentiments.

The authors of these books thus emerge from a wide range of backgrounds and professions, as former government officials, journalists, economists, media pundits, radio talk show hosts, political scientists, and geopolitical analysts. Several of the authors included here also enjoy a considerable media presence and popularity in the United States. Thomas L. Friedman, for example, is a Pulitzer Prize winning journalist and regular op-ed contributor to *The New York Times*. Rachel Maddow hosts the popular *Rachel Maddow Show* on the liberal-leaning MSNBC network, while Bill O'Reilly acts as the figurehead for its conservative counterpart *Fox News*. Robert Kagan is a leading neoconservative scholar, Republican foreign policy advisor, and senior fellow at the prestigious Brookings Institution think tank. Zbigniew Brzezinski, the former National Security Advisor to Jimmy Carter, is a highly respected Democratic grand strategy expert and counselor at the right-of-center Center for Strategic and International Studies (CSIS).

François Debrix has referred to figures like O'Reilly, Brzezinski, and the geopolitical analyst Robert Kaplan, who are all featured as popular book authors in this chapter, as representatives of what he called 'tabloid geopolitics,' a cultural mode of discourse that fuses established concepts of world order and national security with sensationalized media representations of terror, shock, and fear in order to substantiate these intellectuals' ideological predispositions and political agendas for a permanently militarized US security state and American society.[9] Debrix writes in this context of 'mediated discourses' of anxiety, fear, and insecurity through which certain political and cultural realities are produced as 'commonsensical popular truths about the present condition.'[10]

However, rather than understanding 'tabloid geopolitics' as a dominant cultural form of media representations of international affairs and US foreign and security policy in general, this chapter explores how the mobilization of threat and fear within popular culture occurred most strongly within particular grand strategy discourses, especially in the context of neoconservative and nationalist-isolationist conceptualizations of American primacy. Competing discourses of engagement and restraint rather sought de-escalation away from this sensationalized mode of threat inflation that sustains a permanent and institutionalized state of war and militarized global hegemony of the United States. As such, this book does not question the political and cultural significance of 'tabloid geopolitics,' but views it as an instrument employed to varying degrees by competing discursive producers under the Obama presidency.

Overall, the best-selling books analyzed in this chapter feature major works on geopolitics, American grand strategy, and US foreign and security policy published during the Obama presidency. However, it must be noted that even within the relatively narrow confines of *The New York Times* best-sellers list, books on grand strategy and related subjects only represented a minority of the non-fiction works listed during the time period surveyed, the rest consisting of a wide array of books on history, politics, science, sports, and comedy, together with celebrity memoirs, self-help guides, and the multitude of other topics that find interest among the readership of modern American society. While acknowledging this limitation, however, the *NYT* best-sellers which did problematize geopolitical and national security issues provide valuable insights into how competing basic discourses of American grand strategy defined the past, present, and future role and position of the United States in world politics, reflecting a fractured public consensus over the 'big picture.'

HEGEMONY BETWEEN AMERICAN LEADERSHIP AND AMERICAN EMPIRE

Under Obama, a wide variety of best-selling books formulated a grand strategy vision of American hegemony: a global vision of American pre-eminence founded on the country's global military supremacy, economic prosperity, and liberal, democratic ideals.[11] *The World America Made* written by the influential, neoconservative scholar Robert Kagan serves as an intertextual focal point containing many of the basic representations and narratives shared by these works: the unique moral and material superiority of American exceptionalism, the dangerous volatility of any multipolar system, the avoidable character of American decline, and the fundamental desirability of America's enduring military and economic pre-eminence not just to Americans, but to the world at large.

The World America Made opens with a reference to Frank Capra's classic Hollywood movie *It's a Wonderful Life* (1946).[12] Just like George Bailey in the film, the reader is invited to imagine a world without America as the pre-eminent power. It is not, Kagan suggests, a world one should wish for. The book builds its argument for continued global American leadership around one central line of argumentation: the liberal world order that has emerged after World War II, marked by great power peace, economic prosperity, and the spread of democracy relies on American power and the liberal worldview it supports.[13]

Kagan establishes political and economic modernity as a primarily American achievement, rather than the result of world historical processes. According to this narrative, were American power to decline, the liberal vision of an open, peaceful, and democratic world that the United States fostered would lose ground to the strategic visions of other influential states with competing interests and beliefs, such as Russia and China. It was this message of America's enduring global significance that President Obama endorsed by directly referencing Kagan in his 2012 State of the Union address.[14] The intertextual exchange between the scholar Kagan and the politician Obama illustrates how practical, political reasoning and formal, intellectual expertise regularly intersected in constituting and reconstituting a worldview of American leadership, representing US hegemony as both a functional necessity and a moral imperative. Yet, while Obama referenced Kagan in his 2012 address, the Brookings expert, at the same time, served as foreign policy advisor to the presidential campaign of Obama's Republican challenger Mitt Romney, illustrating the bipartisan nature of the Washington consensus on hegemony.

In *No Apology*, Romney would invoke a similar script to Kagan's Manichean narrative of geopolitics, in order to argue for the continuation and renewal of American hegemony. To Romney, the prospect of the United States becoming France, still great but no longer leading on the world stage, was simply 'chilling.'[15] The conservative hegemony discourse constructed a binary opposition between an idealized, international system ruled by American ideals and principles, and a Hobbesian world of disintegration, volatility, and chaos following American decline. This dichotomy, at the same time, reproduced the mythological identity of American exceptionalism, a uniqueness which supposedly exempted the United States from the historic cycle of rise and fall that previous empires and great powers had experienced.[16] Romney directly translated exceptionalist convictions into rejection of a declinist narrative and support for an activist foreign policy in *No Apology*: 'I am convinced that we can act together to strengthen the nation, to preserve our global leadership, and to protect freedom where it exists and promote it where it does not.'[17] Conservative and Republican authors and politicians regularly translated nostalgic reflections of an idealized American past – invoking an exceptionalist mythology with John Winthrop's 'shining city upon a hill' speech and quotes from the Founding Fathers, or using references to Manifest Destiny and the American Century – into rejection of a multipolar, post-hegemonic, 'post-American' future of globalization.

The geopolitical imagination that underwrote the conservative discourse of American hegemony was thus developed from a clear spatial and temporal separation of positive and negative, a moral absolutism that fundamentally did not allow room for variation, alternative, or change in international affairs. A sentimental 1940s Hollywood movie about a man exploring a reality in which he never existed could thus provide a key geopolitical metaphor for the future: only a world with the United States as its leading power was a 'wonderful' world order. This retrograde quality to the hegemony discourse was also reflected in the enduring popularity of nineteenth- and twentieth-century geopolitical thinkers like Halford Mackinder, Alfred Thayer Mahan, and Nicolas Spykman, whose emphasis on the determinism of the Eurasian 'heartland,' the 'rimland,' and 'sea power' centrally informed the writing of modern geopolitical analysts like George Friedman and Robert Kaplan in their American grand strategy best-sellers.[18]

In George Friedman's *The Next 100 Years* and *The Next Decade*, and Kaplan's *The Revenge of Geography*, a determinist analysis of US power and interests, rooted in a supposed scientific neutrality and geographic truth, generally betrayed an imperialist and Manichean worldview, where the United States ranked first among the world's democracies and non-Western powers and regions were perceived through an antagonistic lens and characterized through Orientalist and essentialist attributes.[19] As Agnew and Corbridge have pointed out, geopolitics represents a historical tradition of territorial thinking, boundary drawing, and power politics that is intrinsically tied to the notion of hegemony and hierarchy as a necessary condition of world politics.[20]

Popular books debating American hegemony through the lens of classical geopolitics, however, disagreed on one key issue: how openly imperial the exercise of US power would have to become in order to lastingly secure American interests in a hegemonic order that the United States had established. In *The Next Decade*, Friedman recommended an overtly imperial American grand strategy that would require the American President to freely acknowledge his role as quasi-global emperor and adopt a Machiavellian style in pursuing a 'ruthless' and 'unsentimental' foreign policy.[21] To Friedman, this would also entail ending America's commitments to constraining and outdated alliances and institutions, such as the UN, NATO, and the IMF.[22] Friedman's neo-imperialist vision of American grand strategy voiced doubts over the existing grand strategy consensus on liberal hegemony and US support for free trade and established alliances. This nationalist-exceptionalist discourse, as formulated in *The Next Decade* in 2012, would be echoed in remarkable fashion by the presidential campaign of Donald Trump four years later, attesting to its growing political influence among conservatives in the United States over the course of Obama's second term in office.

An American, imperialist grand strategy of Machiavellian ruthlessness, however, exclusively based on a realist balance of power calculation and a geopolitical analysis of spheres of strategic importance, would directly undermine the institutionalized, liberal world order that Kagan and Romney, for example, identified as a hallmark of American world leadership. The competing hegemonic visions of Kagan and George Friedman thus exposed the deep ideological rift between neoconservatism and realism, liberal conviction and geopolitics existing in the United States, a rift that also opened up between the Republican establishment, represented by Romney in 2012, and the Tea Party and Republican anti-establishment voters, who supported the populist Trump running for president in 2016.

A driving force behind the debate over American hegemony versus American empire was the widespread concern over American decline under the Obama presidency; a concern not limited to conservative and Republican circles, but voiced by a wide spectrum of scholars, pundits, journalists, politicians, and assorted experts since the onset of the global financial crisis and US setbacks in Iraq and Afghanistan.

In *The Revenge of Geography*, for example, Kaplan, a correspondent for the *The Atlantic* and a senior fellow at the CNAS think tank, recommended that the United States should prepare itself for a graceful retreat. Instead of acting as the world's policeman, and engaging in futile attempts at democracy export and regional transformation as in Iraq, the US should establish a Schmittian *Großraum* – a North American empire, encompassing Canada, the United States, and Mexico tied together through close political, social, and economic integration and an emerging 'Polynesian-cum-mestizo civilization.'[23] In most popular best-sellers constructing the hegemony discourse, however, the prospect of decline was acknowledged but rebuked at the same time. In *The World America Made*, for example, decline was presented primarily as a choice, a matter of national willpower.[24] National decline then appeared not as inevitable consequence of global, structural developments and shifting geopolitical and socio-economic parameters that would indicate the diminished international standing of the United States.

In the popular, geopolitical imagination of hegemony, American decline represented the transition from a positive unipolar to a negative multipolar world order. Having discounted external causes, such a transition was ultimately located in a possible transformation of American geopolitical identity at home that would no longer support a vision of global leadership: 'To many Americans, accepting decline may provide a welcome escape from the moral and material burdens that have weighed on them since World War II.'[25] As Kagan would reiterate in an article for the *New Republic* in 2014, attacking President Obama's strategic vision of restraint and retrenchment: 'Superpowers don't get to retire.'

With its triumphalism and pathos, the conservative treatise of *The World America Made* described American grand strategy as an issue that potentially decided the fate of the world. Yet, it was not external threats, such as China or Russia, but the domestic challenges the United States faced in education, healthcare, and the economy that were seen as the greatest risk to its enduring role as global hegemon. Here, Kagan also referred to Thomas Friedman and others to support his argument, those who had debated the issue of America's basic competiveness in the twenty-first century.[26] This reference in *The World America Made* illustrates how the popular discourse of American liberal hegemony represented a remarkable mainstream consensus and nexus of intertextuality among different experts, where neoconservative and neoliberal arguments for America's prescribed role in the world directly interconnected. As Friedman and Mandelbaum, for example, wrote, they too could only fathom a world that was made in America: 'A world shaped by a strong America – strong enough to provide political, economic, and moral leadership – will never be a perfect world, but it will be a better world than any alternative we can envision.'[27]

In *That Used To Be Us*, the issue of American grand strategy was directly entwined with the state of American politics and the American economy, and the need for deep and far-reaching reform of both. Its authors diagnosed severe problems and shortcomings prevailing in the United States, mainly in the areas of high school education, immigration policies, public infrastructure, government debt, and basic innovation and competitiveness in the global economy, perpetuated by a gridlocked, partisan political system that hindered the collective action necessary to overcome these issues.[28] Invoking George F. Kennan's famous 'long telegram' from Moscow which would ultimately lead to the adoption of a new American grand strategy of containment, Friedman and Mandelbaum worriedly ask if anybody still knew how to write such a far-sighted and coherent strategic guideline to the nation.[29]

Containment thus acted as a cipher for yet another reiteration of an idealized past of American benevolent hegemony and visionary strategic thinking. According to the hegemonic consensus uniting neoconservatives and neoliberals, then, American decline was a possibility, mainly due to strategic ignorance and complacency, which resulted in the country lacking an adequate strategic vision for a globalized environment. Indeed, this assessment of globalization as a major disruption driving the necessity for change of established strategic paradigms would unite proponents of hegemony and producers of the competing discourse of cooperative engagement. In the engagement discourse, however, it was the post-American future rather than

America's idealized superpower past that was guiding the formulation of a new strategic vision.

ENGAGEMENT WITH THE POST-AMERICAN WORLD

Two works on *The New York Times* best-sellers list stand out for prominently arguing for a liberal grand strategy vision of cooperative engagement under Obama, employing a narrative of geopolitical and geo-economic transition: *The Post American World: Release 2.0* by Fareed Zakaria and *Strategic Vision* by Zbigniew Brzezinski.[30] In his best-selling *The Post-American World*, originally published in 2008, Zakaria, a popular geopolitical analyst and foreign policy commentator on CNN and former editor of *Time* and *Newsweek*, argued that the dynamic, economic growth of non-Western powers, especially India and China, was redistributing economic power and political influence more evenly across the globe. This would result in a relative decline of the United States. In consequence, the United States would still be a leading power, but would be no longer hegemonic, and should adopt a grand strategy where it maintained excellent relations with everyone, rather than offset and balance against emerging powers.[31]

The updated and revised 2011 *The Post American World: Release 2.0.* characterized these aforementioned, geopolitical trends as having gained momentum since the global financial crisis of 2008, establishing the shift from unipolarity to multipolarity as a central theme of world politics and a structural challenge for Obama and subsequent American presidents: 'I . . . remain convinced that the geopolitical challenge of living in a world without a central, dominant power is one that will be felt everywhere and that too has been amply illustrated over the last few years.'[32]

In *Strategic Vision*, Brzezinski, a highly respected commentator and prolific writer on American grand strategy and geopolitics, who acted as lead political advisor on foreign affairs to Barack Obama's 2008 presidential campaign, shared Zakaria's basic analysis of a multipolar future. According to Brzezinski, in response to this shift of economic and political influence from West to East, the United States should pursue a grand strategy of global cooperative engagement: leading a core partnership around a renewed and 'larger West' encompassing the United States and the European Union, plus Russia and Turkey, and simultaneously engaging China as a relationship of single importance in dealing with the 'new East.'[33] Hence, a central, discursive element that separated the liberal grand strategy vision of engagement from the popular reflections of American hegemony and its conservative leaning authors, was the issue of power transition in the international system.

In their respective books, most proponents of hegemony, usually aligned with the Republican Party, denied that American unipolarity was ending, representing American decline mainly as a domestic and ideological challenge. Zakaria and Brzezinski, however, voices more clearly in support of Obama and the Democratic Party, judged a changing balance of power as an inevitable and structural development of IR and geopolitics.

Where the former discourse sought to defend and preserve the status quo of American primacy and equaled American decline with the end of unipolarity and the dangerous volatility and chaos that would ensue – a dramatic and cataclysmic event described as akin to the fall of the Roman Empire – the latter vision did not necessarily associate geopolitical transition and an emerging multipolarity with the demise of the United States and the liberal world order it supported. As Zakaria, who coined the term 'post-American world' insisted, this story was not about American decline, but about the 'rise of everyone else.'[34] Nonetheless, the shift of economic dynamism and growth away from the United States and Europe toward the rising economies of the 'rest,' most importantly China and Asia, was expected to significantly alter the center of gravity of the international system and dominate the future conduct of American foreign and security policy.[35] Zakaria and Brzezinski thus focused on the transition and dispersion of global power in their arguments for American engagement.

Brzezinski, for example, concluded that given this global transition of power and influence, 'the United States must seek to shape a broader geopolitical foundation for constructive cooperation in the global arena.'[36] Yet, Brzezinski formulated his strategic vision of global, cooperative engagement not only against what he perceived as the futile vision of unipolar hegemony and imperial dominance, advocated by Kagan, Friedman, and others, but also explicitly against the dangers of American isolationism and global retreat.[37] In the words of Brzezinski, 'the ongoing changes in the distribution of global power and mounting global strife make it all the more imperative that America not retreat into an ignorant garrison-state mentality or wallow in self-righteous cultural hedonism.'[38] Zakaria likewise translated these seismic geopolitical and geo-economic changes into a reformulated American grand strategy, a neo-Bismarckian vision of the United States as 'honest broker' of world politics.[39] As Brzezinski would reiterate in 2016 in the *American Interest*, the United States remained the world's most powerful political, economic, and military entity but, it was 'no longer the globally imperial power.'[40]

In the geopolitical imagination of engagement, the United States was no longer able to fulfill the role of global hegemon and sole superpower, as envisioned by Kagan, Romney, George Friedman, or in *That Used To Be Us*, but it also did not retreat into Kaplan's neo-imperial *Großraum*, nor indulge in neo-isolationist fantasies as with Trump's 'America First' slogan. Instead, it served as leading, global partner for international governance and commerce. The hegemony discourse implied that American exceptionalism provided the United Sates with a clear mandate for global leadership and, if deemed necessary, foreign interventionism. In Brzezinski's and Zakaria's geopolitical vision of engagement, the allure of the American Dream was greatest if America successfully demonstrated its unique blend of 'political idealism and economic materialism' at home, making it an attractive model to follow and a coveted partner to the world.

This geopolitical mantra of American leadership through the 'power of our example,' rather than just the example of American power, centrally informed the political grand strategy discourse under Obama. It was represented, for example, in the text of the 2010 *National Security Strategy*, published shortly after Obama entered the White House to signal the departure from his predecessor's strategic vision of unilateral assertiveness and US primacy.[41] As Brzezinski made clear, Obama shared his sensitivity for the complexities of US foreign policy in an increasingly multipolar, globalized, and dynamically changing world: 'What makes Obama attractive to me is that he understands that we live in a very different world where we have to relate to a variety of cultures and people.'[42]

Where the popular articulations of hegemony and engagement coincided, however, was on the issue of domestic reform, as made clear by Brzezinski: 'Americans must understand that our strength abroad will depend increasingly on our ability to confront problems at home.'[43] Comparing the argument for liberal hegemony in *That Used To be Us* with the elaboration of engagement in *Strategic Vision* shows that both deemed overcoming the country's considerable economic and social deficits to be the necessary condition for shaping America's future global role and position.[44] Both discourses also expressed the belief that a prudent American grand strategy had the ability to focus the country's energies and political motivation into a nationally focused response, and to avert the erosion of American influence in the world, just as the United States had successfully met major challenges in the past, from the Great Depression to World War II and the Cold War.

In both the hegemony and the engagement discourse, American decline in absolute terms would mean an end to America's continued capacity to 'play a major world role.'[45] Unlike the hegemony discourse, however, a major domestic reform effort would only guarantee continued American influence in a multipolar world, not perpetuate America's 'unipolar moment.' A grand strategy of cooperative engagement was to secure a safe and secure multipolar world order with the United States firmly at its center. Brzezinski's Eurasian grand strategy, for example, envisioned a 'larger West' that expanded the institutional ties of political, economic, and security cooperation between the United States and Europe to Russia and Turkey. A strategic focus on the 'new East' represented the second-half of this cooperative vision. Here, the United States was supposed to maintain a significant presence through existing and expanding alliances in East and Southeast Asia, and at the same time fashion a substantial political and economic partnership with China. Next to the failed 'reset' with Russia, the 'pivot to Asia' announced by the Obama administration in 2011/2012 represented a geopolitical conceptualization of America as a 'Pacific power' in a 'Pacific Century' that in many ways matched the basic analysis of America's need for expanding political and economic partnerships that Brzezinski outlined in *Strategic Vision*.[46]

Unlike the often triumphalist and exceptionalist language of the hegemony discourse, which treated the issue of grand strategy, world order, and geopolitics almost exclusively as a matter of American agency and willpower, the engagement discourse tacitly acknowledged that world politics in the twenty-first century was at least partially outside American control, and would also depend on the thoughts and actions of other states and foreign populations, and on how their geopolitical identities and historic narratives would shape their respective grand strategies. *Strategic Vision* and the *Post-American World* hence both outlined a geopolitical vision for the United States that sought cooperation and engagement with others, not imperial dominance nor self-adulatory benevolent hegemony.

AMERICA IS COMING HOME: THE CASE FOR RESTRAINT

While the basic discourse of engagement sought to redefine America's leadership role from a hegemonic hierarchy of subject-object relationships to a more level arrangement of cooperative partnerships, it remained fundamentally committed to the idea of a significant global role of the United States in world politics, with a firm belief in the country's positive influence in international affairs. Based on a decidedly more critical assessment of American grand strategy and national security policy, the basic discourse of restraint in contrast sought to further limit the use of American power abroad. Rather than engaging the world through extending global partnerships and multiple commitments, it wanted the United States to focus more on itself and its domestic renewal at home, and to engage less, not more, internationally.

Several books on *The New York Times* best-sellers list did popularize these views in the United Sates: *Washington Rules*, by Andrew Bacevich, presented American grand strategy as a misguided imperial vision of global hegemony, perpetuated by a dangerous American elite consensus in foreign and security policy.[47] In her best-selling book, *Drift*, Rachel Maddow critically assessed the evolution of America's military and national security apparatus that she accused of wasting financial resources and potentially endangering American political and civil liberties.[48] *The Untold History of the United States*, written by film-maker Oliver Stone and historian Peter Kuznick, provided a critical counter-narrative to the dominant historical interpretation of American exceptionalism and the country's benevolent influence in world history and international affairs.[49] That book was complementing a documentary series under the same title, produced and narrated by Stone, which aired in 2012 on the *Showtime* network.

The basic grand strategy discourse of restraint represented the geopolitical identity of the United States fundamentally different from the basic discourses of hegemony and engagement. Rather than American exceptionalism or the American Dream, negative features such as imperialism and militarism were constructed as central characteristics of the United States and its political actions. As Stone and Kuznick pointed out, such critical representations went directly against the mainstream consensus on geopolitical knowledge and established historical narratives that prevailed in the United States; a popular consensus expressed, for example, in the 'good war' narrative perpetuated by Hollywood and the national security cinema. In the words of Stone and Kuznick, this consensus represented a 'popular and somewhat mythic view, carefully filtered through the prism of American altruism, benevolence, magnanimity, exceptionalism, and devotion to liberty and justice.'[50] Its cultural prevalence in American everyday life made it 'part of the air that Americans breathe.'[51]

The central historic narrative of the restraint discourse described the role played by the United States in the past in far less favorable terms. Historic episodes casting the United States in a negative light – such as the CIA's involvement in the overthrow of Iranian Prime Minister Mohammad Mosaddeq in 1953 and Chile's Salvador Allende in 1973, the 2003 Abu Ghraib prisoner scandal involving US Army and CIA personnel, or the civilian casualties in US-bombing campaigns against North Vietnam, Laos, and Cambodia in the late 1960s and early 1970s – were oftentimes ignored altogether, or presented as unfortunate but ultimately negligible aberrations in America's overwhelmingly benign and positive record in international affairs in texts that constructed the hegemony discourse in particular.[52] Stone and Kuznick instead reconstructed these episodes as regular and enduring features of American imperialism and the 'darker side of U.S. history' in their revisionist interpretation.[53]

The basic grand strategy discourse of restraint repudiated a Manichean and reductionist understanding of world history that continuously described the United States as a morally superior force in its enduring, global crusade for freedom. *The Washington Post*'s review of Andrew Bacevich's critical treatise *Washington Rules* summed up this dominant understanding of the geopolitical identity of the United States as follows: 'Power and violence are cleansed by virtue: Because America is "good," her actions are always benign.'[54] Rather than the ideational foundation for a stable, liberal world order of peace, democracy, and free trade, American exceptionalism appeared in the restraint discourse as a dangerous combination of national hubris, ideological self-delusion, unchecked hypocrisy, and missionary zeal. A policy of imperial interventionism born out of this ideology exhausted the country's resources, more often than not produced instability instead of security, and triggered multiple blowback, while engaging the country in activities that betrayed the moral righteousness the American cause of freedom was supposed to represent.[55]

While *The Untold History of the United States* linked the myth of American exceptionalism in particular to the ideological convictions of neoconservatives and their hegemonic designs for 'American empire' and 'military dominance' under President George W. Bush, its influence was not confined to one particular political party or presidential administration.[56] Indeed, in arguing over 'American exceptionalism' during the 2012 presidential campaign and the practical implication of this hegemonic identity construct for the practice of US national security policy, Obama and Romney were not debating two opposing ideological visions of restraint and non-interventionism versus American Empire. Rather, the choice had been between Obama's concept of reformulating US hegemony and American leadership through 'burden sharing' and 'leading from behind,' and Romney's unapologetic assertion of American unilateral primacy, as advocated by Kagan and laid out in *No Apology*.[57]

To proponents of the restraint discourse, Obama had thus placed himself within a continuity of US foreign and security policy, which, in following the Washington consensus over American exceptionalism and liberal hegemony, did not fundamentally reformulate the country's role in the world. In the words of Stone and Kuznick: 'His was a centrist approach to better managing the American Empire rather than advancing a positive role for the United States in a rapidly evolving world.[58] Andrew Bacevich, a West Point graduate, Vietnam veteran, IR scholar, and long-time critic of American foreign and security policy likewise supported the key argument that American hegemony represented a joint vision of the Washington establishment. According to his book *Washington Rules*, American grand strategy continued in its established trajectory under the Obama administration, par some 'cosmetic changes', because hegemony, or 'global leadership,' represented an item of faith for both neoconservatives and liberals.[59] 'The national security consensus to which every president since 1945 has subscribed persists.'[60]

The firm belief in the virtues of America's global pre-eminence was seen as uniting conservatives and liberals, Republicans and Democrats. As Bacevich stated: 'Mainstream Republicans and mainstream Democrats are equally devoted to this catechism of American statecraft.'[61] In the eyes of Bacevich, this basic political Washington consensus about America's global leadership role was constructed around a central paradigm of military power.

Call them the sacred trinity: an abiding conviction that the minimum essentials of international peace and order require the United States to maintain a *global military presence*, to configure its forces for *global power projection*, and to counter existing or anticipated threats by relying on a policy of *global interventionism*.[62]

Not external threats, then, but American militarism, imperialism, and global hegemony represented the dominant, prevailing Other against which the basic discourse of restraint built its own competing grand strategy vision of domestic renewal and self-limitation abroad.

Unlike the basic discourses of hegemony and engagement, which emphasized the political and economic benefits of American leadership – performed either as global hegemon, or leading partner – the restraint discourse also stressed the immense cost Americans had to accept in return for their country's global leadership role. This manifested in the military and financial resources, the 'blood and treasure' America expended, a figure of speech frequently referenced by Obama. The President again reiterated this point, endorsing a more restrained use of American power, during his final State of the Union address in 2016: 'We also can't try to take over and rebuild every country that falls into crisis. That's not leadership; that's a recipe for quagmire, spilling American blood and treasure that ultimately weakens us. It's the lesson of Vietnam, of Iraq—and we should have learned it by now.'[63]

The case for restraint was essentially a call for America to finally come home, as Bacevich made clear in *Washington Rules*: 'With resources currently devoted to rehabilitating Baghdad or Kabul freed up, the cause of rehabilitating Cleveland and Detroit might finally attract a following.'[64] This sentiment was again directly echoed by President Obama on multiple occasions, when he insisted that the United States should engage in 'nation-building at home.'[65] This strong intertextuality between national best-sellers critical of American hegemony and Obama's rhetoric demonstrated the political and practical significance of the restraint discourse. Obama's reproduction of key restraint arguments, then, put his unqualified casting as an American hegemonist in doubt. This was counteracted, however, by the President's use of key ideas and concepts from the basic discourses of hegemony and engagement. Obama's rhetoric exposed the conflicted and incoherent quality of the Obama Doctrine, which simultaneously endorsed elements from such disparate and distinct visions as Kagan's *The World America Made*, Brzezinski's *Strategic Vision*, and Bacevich's *Washington Rules*.

The basic discourse of restraint, however, demanded a clear and unequivocal repudiation of American hegemony, military primacy, and a global ambition to remake the world in America's image. This established, strategic consensus was held responsible not only for causing instability abroad but also for distorting the ideals of the American republic through imperialism and militarism at home. In Maddow's *Drift*, for example, a dangerous historical trajectory in the United States had given rise to militarism, endemic government secrecy, and enormous waste of financial resources: 'With no check on its growth and no rival for its political influence, the superfunded, superempowered national security state has become a leviathan.'[66] The material consequences of a fundamental strategic reorientation in turn would be far-reaching, as the Washington consensus on liberal hegemony and its surrounding political, military, intellectual, and socio-economic structure would be broken up or downsized, with the financial resources supporting the national security state and military-industrial complex diverted to other purposes in education, public infrastructure, and healthcare.[67]

The reorientation of American grand strategy toward restraint, however, targeted first and foremost the ideational definition of national security and the way in which Americans should think about war and the role of the military in defense of the nation. *The Messenger* rather than *Transformers 2* inspired its underlying, geopolitical imagination. In the words of Maddow: 'Our military and weapons prowess is a fantastic and perfectly weighted hammer, but that doesn't make every international problem a nail.'[68] This argument for military restraint would be repeated again using almost exactly those same words by President Obama in his 2014 speech at the Military Academy of the United States in West Point, again documenting the cross-discursive, intertextual links of the basic discourse of restraint between popular culture and policymaking under the Obama presidency and Obama's political reflection of these arguments.[69] This vision of restraint, however, which was partially endorsed by the American President, would be fundamentally challenged by a countering discourse that favored unapologetic nationalism as America's strategic guideline.

NATIONALISM, POPULISM, AND AMERICAN EXCEPTIONALISM

A fourth, decidedly populist discursive strand emerging from an analysis of *The New York Times* best-sellers list constructed a distinct vision of American primacy during the Obama presidency. Beyond best-selling books, this discourse was located at the right end of the spectrum of American conservatism, and most prominently found in nationally syndicated political radio talk shows like the *Savage Nation* and conservative-leaning media outlets such as *Fox News*, or *National Review* magazine.[70] Here, the 'socialist' policies of the Obama administration were endangering America's exceptionalism and its supreme status as dominant, global superpower. This nationalist and chauvinist strand of the hegemony discourse blended an ideological conviction in America's greatness and uniqueness with a peculiar geopolitical vision of isolationist supremacy. As such, it stood apart from the dominant bipartisan consensus over American leadership in a liberal, international order. Yet, it was also distinct from neoconservative ideas about the role of the United States as a global interventionist force, advancing the cause of freedom around the world by military means if necessary.

Published in book form, several of these anti-Obama and America First narratives appeared on prominent places on *The New York Times* best-sellers list, representing a popular and profitable critique of American grand strategy from the right.[71] In August 2016, three of the top five spots on the hardcover non-fiction list were in turn occupied by anti-Clinton books (Gary J. Byrne's *Crisis of Character* at no. 5, Dinesh D'Souza's *Hillary's America* at no. 4, and *Armageddon* by Dick Morris and Eileen McGann at no. 3).[72] Many of these ultra-conservative tractates were written by the same authors who had previously attacked President Obama and his policies, documenting the enduring culture war between conservatives and progressives over defining the meaning of American identity, both at home and abroad.

The language in several of these texts was infused with national, racial, and ethnic stereotypes, essentialist generalizations, distortions, insults, and open prejudice against minorities, foreigners, or social welfare. President Obama in particular was a regular target for attacks. In the words of Michael Savage, for example: 'Like all leftist dictators, Obama is becoming a bloodthirsty monster.'[73] In some cases, the argument presented was bordering on the territory of conspiracy theories, well-illustrated by the title of one of the books by the former *Fox News* commentator and political analyst Dick Morris and his partner Eileen McGann: *Here Come the Black Helicopters!*[74] The book promised to uncover the 'movement afoot to transfer American autonomy to the United Nations.' Here, the case for global governance appeared as a sinister plot of cosmopolitan elites and international organizations to end American, national sovereignty. To these right-wing authors the external and internal decline of the United States represented an existential threat to American exceptionalism, endangering both America's

superpower status abroad and the American ideal of individual freedom and liberty at home.

After America, written by the political commentator and conservative critic Mark Steyn, well-illustrated the general line of argument
in these publications. The decline of the United States was described
as the result of mounting government debt, which was considered to
be unsustainable and undermining American economic and military
strength. In addition, decline was seen as a historic break with an
established continuity, in which an Anglo-Protestant culture had been
the driving force of world history and universal progress. This argumentation showed obvious parallels with the central historic narrative
the hegemony discourse had established, for example in Kagan's *The
World America Made*. The consequences of a geopolitical transition
toward multipolarity were constructed as a global, political, and economic catastrophe, where the victims of American retreat would be the
'many parts of the world that had benefited from an unusually benign
hegemon.'[75]

However, beyond issues of economics, geopolitics, or demographics,
American decline was also seen as a symptom of a deeper American
identity crisis, originating from a misguided, liberal internationalist ideology, progressive change, permissive-relativist social climate,
and cultural decadence. Promiscuity, drug abuse, uncontrolled immigration, environmentalism, multiculturalism, the dictate of political
correctness, and the elimination of individual responsibility by
government entitlement programs and socialist ideology were identified as undermining the ideational exceptionality of the United States.[76]

While abhorring a future without America as the world's dominant
power, this right-wing discourse of American supremacy and exceptionalism also partially negated the neoliberal-neoconservative consensus on grand strategy and national security. In the words of Steyn: 'To
its worshippers, globalization is some kind of mysterious metaphysical
force that's out there remaking our assumptions about the planet.'[77] In
After America, elite establishment voices, such as the liberal journalist
Thomas L. Friedman and *The New York Times*, as well as the (former)
neoconservative scholar Francis Fukuyama and his seminal work *The
End of History*, were singled out for promoting such a misguided liberal
ideology of globalization.[78]

To these conservative critics, the existing bipartisan consensus had
committed the United States to maintaining a system that served the
interests of a detached, cosmopolitan political and business elite, instead

of the American people. Globalization was thus represented as an elitist project, an ideology of 'globalism' designed for the interests of the global financial industry, international organizations, and government bureaucracies.[79] This populist, anti-globalist discourse of American exceptionalism and isolationist supremacy, sought to exploit prevalent fears over American decline to establish a grand strategy vision of 'America First.' This vision would centrally inform the Republican presidential campaign of the New York real estate mogul and TV celebrity Donald Trump with his promise to 'make America great again.' Trump's grand strategy vision, which connected in particular with male, white and non-college-educated voters, was accordingly laid out in 2015, in the best-selling *Crippled America*, which called for hard-line anti-immigration measures, an anti-interventionist foreign policy, and greater protectionism in American trade and economic policies.[80]

The key message in the primacists' America First discourse was clear: the United States should focus its energies domestically and strengthen its economic and political system at home. Yet, this nostalgic, retrograde vision to reclaim an imagined, idealized past of American greatness was also a political response of American conservatives to fast-changing demographics that had accelerated during the Obama presidency, and that would significantly alter the racial and ethnic composition of American society before the middle of the twenty-first century. During the George W. Bush administration, a notable, conservative scholar like Samuel Huntington had already characterized growing multiculturalism and mass immigration from Latin America as incompatible with US-American identity.[81] This dramatic demographic change threatened the cultural hegemony of Anglo-Saxon Protestantism that had shaped the ideals and values of the United States since its founding, and that was seen by conservatives as the indispensable foundation of American exceptionalism.[82]

Finally, in its support for small government, its embracing of libertarian-conservative ideas of economics, and its concern with conserving national resources, the exceptionalist-isolationist discourse advanced its own version of the restraint argument, not as a progressive critique of American militarism and imperialism, but as a conservative charge against 'big government' and 'un-American' multilateralism. There was a general consensus that a liberal grand strategy vision of cooperative engagement and multipolarity would only serve to strengthen America's enemies and leave the United States weaker and more endangered.[83] Significant elements of cooperative engagement in Obama's foreign policy – from attempting to 'reset' relations with Russia and seeking a 'new beginning' with the Muslim world, to the Iran nuclear deal and visiting Cuba – and his apparent endorsement of Zakaria's vision thus appeared as a dangerous and potentially fatal weakening of the United States, as Steyn made clear: 'In a post-American world, the kind of world Barack Obama is committed to building, America will be surrounded on all sides by hostile forces . . .'[84]

Against the Otherness of globalization, socialism, and multiculturalism, an exclusive, national-conservative interpretation of American exceptionalism was presented as the true and original identity of the American Self, an enduring source of strength and national greatness, and thus the ideational foundation that should animate the country's grand strategy and foreign policy. In the best-selling *Exceptional*, former Vice-President Dick Cheney and his daughter Margaret Cheney, a former State Department official, laid out just such an exceptionalist vision of US foreign and security policy.[85] Invoking once again the unique material and moral superiority of the United States – 'the most powerful, good, and honorable nation in the history of mankind, the exceptional nation' – the Cheneys argued for the restoration of US military power and the reconfirmation of its mission to spread freedom and democracy across the globe, against Obama's anti-exceptionalist vision of 'ending wars,' 'appeasing' America's enemies, and 'disarming America.'[86]

One of the main charges brought forward against Obama by his conservative and right-wing critics was, thus, that he did not believe in American exceptionalism and did not employ it as a foundation of American grand strategy. As Bill O'Reilly, multiple best-selling author and host of the *Fox News Channel*'s top-rated *The O'Reilly Factor*, explained: 'Barack Obama is an internationalist, which means he believes America does not have an "exceptional" place in the world.'[87] *The Obama Diaries*, which topped *The New York Times* best-sellers list for non-fiction hard cover books on August 1, 2010 devoted its entire opening chapter to the issue of American exceptionalism and its endangered status under the Obama administration.[88] Written as a satirical 'insider's account' of the administration by the conservative political commentator and radio talk show host Laura Ingraham, the book stated: 'As described by the president, the United States seems like just another defective member of the League of Nations.'[89]

Beyond Obama, Hollywood liberals such as James Cameron, Oliver Stone, and Tom Hanks were singled out here for undermining the belief in American exceptionalism and its historical foundations in movies such as *Avatar* or the *Green Zone* which cast the United States in a villainous role.[90] Ingraham thus acknowledged the popular significance of motion pictures in shaping perceptions of identity and producing everyday knowledge, while simultaneously repeating a long-established conservative charge against the liberal bias of the mainstream media in general and Hollywood in particular. However, far from undermining American exceptionalism, the majority of popular Hollywood movies released under Obama in fact supported the image of military heroism and a 'good war' narrative with America saving the world time and again on the big screen.[91]

To Obama's conservative critics, his approach to IR and foreign policy was deeply flawed, because it was supposedly not rooted in the belief in American exceptionalism but motivated by a negative view of the international role the United States had played in the past. Obama, who had frequently stressed international cooperation and multilateral approaches to global governance, and who distanced himself from the unilateralism associated with the previous Bush administration, was criticized for constantly 'apologizing' for America.[92] The idea of cooperative engagement with countries that were weaker than the United States, or acknowledging historic wrongs perpetrated by America, thus appeared as a violation of the unique values and moral superiority American exceptionalism was supposed to represent.

The argument that American grand strategy under President Obama was repudiating American hegemony, and essentially negating American exceptionalism, was further developed and pursued in its most extreme fashion by *Obama's America*, which was followed by a successful political documentary, both created by the conservative political commentator and author Dinesh D'Souza.[93] Here, President Obama was accused of purposefully aiming to weaken the United States and hasten American decline due to an ideology rooted in radical anti-colonialism, inherited from his Kenyan father.[94] Fears that President Obama, due to his multicultural background and ideological disposition, was somehow 'un-American' were frequently raised on the American right.[95] Beyond a mere dispute about politics, the foreign and security policy of President Obama and his vision of American grand strategy were thus attacked by conservative and right-wing critics on grounds of national identity, revealing a deep cultural divide over the appropriate role of government at home and America's role in the world.

CONCLUSION

Employing *The New York Times* non-fiction best-sellers list as a discursive site for examining popular constructs of geopolitical imagination has revealed three basic American grand strategy discourses of hegemony, engagement, and restraint that competed over defining America's role in world politics under Obama in the public sphere. Hegemony, engagement, and restraint, while not representing completely independent entities that operated in isolation from each other, formulated distinct geopolitical visions that sufficiently set them apart from each other to be identifiable as separate discourses. They prioritized different historic narratives, they differed in their basic perception of the trajectory of power transition in the international system and its implications, and they recommended fundamentally different designs in foreign and national security policy, defense matters, and the projection of military power.

While separated as basic discourses, there also existed considerable overlap and congruence between these popular visions with strong cross-discursive links and intertextual connections demonstrating the centrality of particular ideational constructs in the public debate on American grand strategy. Both Brzezinski and Bacevich, for example, deemphasized the usefulness of military power in world politics and denounced an American grand strategy of unipolar primacy favored by neoconservatives. As expressed in *The World America Made* and *The Post-American World*, discourses of hegemony and engagement both shared a fundamental assumption that American leadership, either as 'benevolent hegemon' or 'honest broker,' was a necessary, beneficial, and stabilizing influence in international affairs. The critique of the national security apparatus by Maddow or Bacevich and the right-wing polemics of *After America* in turn all shared a concern with America's fiscal situation and the waste of economic resources by acting as the world's policeman.

In *Washington Rules* Bacevich attributes the production and reproduction of the dominant grand strategy discourse of hegemony and exceptionalism to 'Washington' – an interlocking set of institutions, combining the government, the military, mainstream media, defense corporations, big banks, leading universities, national security think tanks, and select interest groups, which together form an elite consensus on national security and geopolitics. Although Bacevich does not make it explicit, from a critical perspective 'Washington' represents a concentration of power/knowledge that defines grand strategy through dominant discourses of geopolitics and national security in elite power networks, from Hollywood to *The New York Times*, and the Pentagon to the Council of Foreign Relations, ranging from the popular to the formal and practical realm. Hence, it is in the realm of discourse where a critical analysis can deconstruct and contextualize Bacevich's charge of an ongoing continuity of hegemony, or the conservative counter-argument that described the foreign and security policy of President Obama not as continuation of American Empire but as a globalist antithesis to the idea of American exceptionalism and supremacy.

The analysis of grand strategy discourses via these national best-sellers further demonstrates how American leadership represented a dominant identity construct in the popular geopolitical imagination. Under Obama, neoconservative scholars, liberal political commentators, and anti-establishment populists alike employed a historic narrative of hegemonic stability and American exceptionalism. Any alternative formulation of American grand strategy had to contend primarily with this vision of hegemony that was firmly embedded in American culture. In its populist interpretation, elements of American nationalism and the racial and cultural superiority of Anglo-Saxon Protestantism were seen as defining features of the exceptional role of the United States. This nationalist-exceptionalist vision in turn provided the foundation for a sustained campaign against President Obama's un-exceptional policies on the American right, revealing the significance of divisive identity politics in painting the 'big picture' of American grand strategy at home.

NOTES

1. Friedman and Mandelbaum, *That Used To Be Us*, p. 15.
2. The list is published weekly in *The New York Times Book Review* magazine, with the Sunday edition of *The New York Times*, and as a stand-alone publication. For analysis, the online account of the weekly 'New York Times Best Sellers' list was used, in the category of non-fiction hardcover, with rankings from no. 1 to no. 35 (from August 2014, only rankings from no. 1 to no. 20 were available) starting on January 4, 2009, available at http://www.nytimes.com/best-sellers-books/2009-01-04/hardcover-non-fiction/list.html (last accessed August 24, 2016). The list was analyzed in monthly intervals until September 4, 2016, available at http://www.nytimes.com/best-sellers-books/2016-09-04/hardcover-nonfiction/list.

html (last accessed August 23, 2016). Rankings reflect sales reported by vendors offering a wide range of general interest titles. The sales venues for print books include independent book retailers; national, regional, and local chains; online and multimedia entertainment retailers; supermarkets, university, gift, and discount department stores; and newsstands. Sales of both print books and e-books are reported confidentially to *The New York Times*. The best-sellers lists are prepared by the News Surveys and Election Analysis Department of *The New York Times*. Information taken from *The New York Times*, 'About the Best Sellers.'

3. Ó Tuathail and Dalby, *Rethinking Geopolitics*.
4. Campbell, *Writing Security*.
5. Sharp, *Condensing the Cold War*, p. 557.
6. Ibid., p. xiii.
7. Ibid., p. xiv.
8. As, for example, laid out in Ó Tuathail, *Critical Geopolitics*.
9. Debrix, *Tabloid Terror*, pp. 37–39, 146–149.
10. Ibid., p. 5.
11. Kagan, *The World America Made* [*NYT* best-seller, no. 29, March 4, 2012], Friedman and Mandelbaum, *That Used To Be US* [*NYT* best-seller, no. 2, October 2, 2011], Friedman, *The Next 100 Years* [*NYT* best-seller, no. 5, February 15, 2009], Friedman, *The Next Decade* [*NYT* best-seller, no. 3, February 13, 2011], Kaplan, *The Revenge of Geography* [*NYT* best-seller, no. 10, September 30, 2012], Romney, *No Apology* [*NYT* best-seller, no. 1, March 21, 2010].
12. Kagan, *The Word America Made*, p. 3.
13. Ibid., p. 8.
14. White House, 'Remarks by the President in State of the Union Address,' January 24, 2012, Rogin, 'Obama Embraces Romney Advisor's Theory on "The Myth of American Decline."'
15. Romney, *No Apology*, p. 10.
16. The idea of American exceptionalism draws from multiple historic genealogies; among these are: the colonial period and the cultural and religious heritage of Puritanism and Protestantism, the republican and democratic foundation of the United States and its inauguration in a deliberate political act through the Declaration of Independence, its relative geographic isolation, and the liberal tradition of entrepreneurism and capitalism, see also Lipset, *American Exceptionalism*.
17. Ibid., p. 30.
18. Slaughter, 'Power Shifts,' Kaplan, *The Revenge of Geography*.
19. See, for example, Richardson, '"Blue National Soil" and the Unwelcome Return of "Classical" Geopolitics.'
20. Agnew and Corbridge, *Mastering Space*.
21. Friedman, *The Next Decade*, p. 28.

22. Ibid., pp. 28–29.
23. Kaplan, *The Revenge of Geography*, p. 339.
24. Kagan, *World America Made*, p. 105.
25. Ibid., p. 133.
26. Kagan, *The World America Made*, pp. 130–131.
27. Friedman and Mandelbaum, *That Used To Be Us*, p. 351.
28. Ibid., pp. 17–23.
29. Ibid., p. 15.
30. Zakaria, *The Post-American World: Release 2.0* [*NYT* best-seller, no. 27, July 3, 2011], Brzezinski, *Strategic Vision* [*NYT* best-seller, no. 10, February 12, 2012].
31. Zakaria, *The Post-American World*.
32. Zakaria, *The Post-American World: Release 2.0*, p. xiii.
33. Brzezinski, *Strategic Vision*.
34. Zakaria, *The Post-American World*, p. 1.
35. Of special significance here was the assessment of future economic growth by developing economies, in particular the so-called BRIC countries (Brazil, India, Russia, China), a term originally coined by Jim O'Neill, an analyst of Goldmann Sachs, see O'Neill, 'Building Better Global Economic BRICs,' see also Khanna, *The Second World*.
36. Brzezinski, *Strategic Vision*, p. 1.
37. Ibid., p. 2.
38. Ibid.
39. Zakaria, *The Post-American World: Release 2.0*, p. 233.
40. Brzezinski, 'Toward a Global Realignment.'
41. White House, *National Security Strategy (2010)*, p. 10.
42. Barron, 'Zbigniew Brzezinski.'
43. Brzezinski, *Strategic Vision*, p. 46.
44. Ibid., pp. 46–54. Both discourses of hegemony and engagement counted the residual strengths of America's innovative economy, its demographic dynamics, and liberal democracy as hopeful indicators against the possibility of American decline, Brzezinski, *Strategic Vision*, p. 55, Friedman and Mandelbaum, *That Used To Be Us*, pp. 13–32, Kagan, *The World America Made*, pp. 127–129.
45. Brzezinski, *Strategic Vision*, p. 74.
46. Löfflmann, 'The Pivot between Containment, Engagement and Restraint.'
47. Bacevich, *Washington Rules* [*NYT* best-seller, no. 29, September 6, 2010].
48. Maddow, *Drift* [*NYT* best-seller, no. 1, May 6, 2012].
49. Stone and Kuznick, *The Untold History of the United States of America* [*NYT* best-seller, no. 15, December 2, 2012].
50. Ibid., foreword.
51. Ibid.
52. As, for example, in Kagan, *The World America Made*.

53. Stone and Kuznick, *The Untold History of the United States*, p. xi.
54. De Groot, 'Andrew Bacevich's "Washington Rules" and John Dower's "Cultures of War."' Bacevich sees this historic narrative for example in the 'Disneyfication' of World War II and the Cold War, a term coined by Paul Fussell, see Bacevich, *The Short American Century*, p. 236.
55. See in this context also, Johnson, *Dismantling the Empire*.
56. Ibid., p. xv.
57. See Löfflmann, 'Leading from Behind,' see also Chapter 7 in this book.
58. Stone and Kuznick, *The Untold History of the United States*, p. 566.
59. Bacevich, *Washington Rules*, p. 21.
60. Ibid., p. 20.
61. Ibid., p. 21.
62. Ibid., p. 14, original emphasis.
63. White House, 'President Obama's 2016 State of the Union Address.'
64. Bacevich, *Washington Rules*, p. 240.
65. White House, 'Remarks by the President in Address to the Nation on the Way Forward in Afghanistan and Pakistan,' December 1, 2009, White House, 'Remarks by the President on the Way Forward in Afghanistan,' June 22, 2011, White House, 'Remarks by the President in State of the Union Address,' January 24, 2012.
66. Maddow, *Drift*, p. 248.
67. Ibid., p. 240. A similar argument was made in Preble, *The Power Problem*.
68. Ibid., pp. 250–251.
69. *New York Times*, 'Transcript of President Obama's Commencement Address at West Point,' May 28, 2014.
70. These are, for example, The Rush Limbaugh Show (radio), The Glenn Beck Program (radio), Glenn Beck (2009–2011, Fox News), The Sean Hannity Show (radio), Hannity (Fox News), The Laura Ingham Show (radio), The Savage Nation (radio), and The O'Reilly Factor (Fox News).
71. These include, for example, Steyn, *After America* [*NYT* best-seller, no. 4, August 28, 2011], Buchanan, *Suicide of a Superpower* [*NYT* best-seller, no. 4, November 6, 2011], Coulter, *Adios, America* [*NYT* best-seller, no. 2, June 21, 2015], Savage, *Trickle Down Tyranny* [*NYT* best-seller, no. 3, April 22, 2012], Morris and McGann, *Screwed!* [*NYT* best-seller, no. 3, May 27, 2012], Ingraham, *The Obama Diaries* [*NYT* best-seller, no. 1, August 1, 2010], O'Reilly, *Pinheads and Patriots* [*NYT* best-seller, no. 2, October 3, 2010], D'Souza, *Obama's America* [*NYT* best-seller, no. 5, September 2, 2012].
72. Szalai, 'Inside the List.'
73. Savage, *Trickle Down Tyranny*, p. 281. Michael Savage, who is banned from entering the United Kingdom for 'seeking to provoke others to serious criminal acts and fostering hatred,' is host of one of the most successful radio talk shows in the United States. *The Savage Nation* is ranked as the

third most listened to radio talk show in the country, reaching an average audience of more than 8 million listeners according to *Talkers Magazine,* 'The Top Talk Radio Audiences.'

74. Morris and McGann, *Here Come The Black Helicopters!* [*NYT* best-seller, no. 12, October 28, 2012]. The title refers to a popular myth in certain right-wing, anti-government circles in the United States, according to which unmarked black helicopters are a sign for an impending takeover of the United States federal government, or the UN.

75. Steyn, *After America*, p. 325.

76. See Buchanan, *Suicide of a Superpower*, D'Souza, *Obama's America*, Ingraham, *The Obama Diaries*, Savage, *Trickle Down Tyranny*, and Steyn, *After America*.

77. Ibid.

78. Steyn, *After America*, p. 17.

79. Morris and McGann, *Screwed!*, p. 1, Savage, *Trickle Down Tyranny*, p. 302.

80. Trump, *Crippled America* [*NYT* best-seller, no. 5, November 22, 2015].

81. Huntington, *Who Are We?*

82. Jones, 'The Eclipse of White Christian America.'

83. See Steyn, *After America*, p. 347.

84. Ibid., p. 279, see also Savage, *Trickle Down Tyranny*, pp. 302–350, Morris and McGann, *Screwed!*.

85. Cheney and Cheney, *Exceptional* [*NYT* best-seller, no. 19, October 11, 2015].

86. Ibid.

87. O'Reilly, *Pinheads and Patriots*, p. 87.

88. Ingraham, *The Obama Diaries*, pp. 24–30.

89. Ibid., p. 13.

90. Ibid., p. 20.

91. In this context see also the exploration of American exceptionalism in Hollywood film in O'Meara et al., *Movies, Myth and the National Security State*.

92. Ibid., p. 12, O'Reilly, *Pinheads and Patriots*, p. 31, Cheney and Cheney, *Exceptional*, pp. 123–130.

93. The documentary *2016 Obama's America* grossed over US$33.45 million in the United States, and was distributed in over 2,000 movie theaters. It is the second-highest-grossing political documentary since 1982, topped only by *Fahrenheit 9/11*. Available at http://boxofficemojo.com/mov ies/?id=2016obamasamerica.htm (last accessed August 23, 2016).

94. D'Souza, *Obama's America*, p. 10.

95. D'Souza, *Obama's America*, Savage, *Trickle Down Tyranny*, Steyn, *After America*.

Chapter 4

THE AMERICAN GRAND STRATEGY DEBATE IN INTERNATIONAL RELATIONS

The most powerful voices tend to dominate the discussion, regardless of the merits of their ideas.

David M. Edelstein and Ronald R. Krebs[1]

Grand strategy as an intellectual concept originated from the scholarly attempt to analyze the most appropriate use of state power toward the goal of national security. This basic idea continues to exert a powerful influence in the academic discipline of IR and relevant sub-fields like strategic studies, security studies, or foreign policy analysis.[2] At Yale University for example, the Brady-Johnson Program, which secured a US$17.5 million, fifteen-year endowment in 2006, lets students examine the theory and practice of grand strategy, defined as a 'comprehensive approach to achieve large ends with limited means' in order to 'promote effective leadership in a complex and globalized world.'[3] As demonstrated earlier, visions of geopolitics and national security are regularly being popularized for the consumption of mass audiences, constituting them as a dominant form of knowledge in the realm of common-sense experience. From this critical analysis of two significant sites of American popular culture, hegemony, engagement, and restraint were identified as three basic discourses that frame the context in which American grand strategy is debated and contested. Building upon these findings, this chapter continues the critical analysis of American grand strategy discourses under Obama, and looks at how geopolitical visions of national security were constructed around the concept of expert knowledge that claims authority through its status as formal expertise. In particular, the focus is on the experts' use of basic constructs of geopolitical identity which link intellectual outputs to the wider political context and the cultural dimension of grand strategy as a set of identity performing discourses.

Predominantly, the intellectual outlook and production of knowledge on American grand strategy remained conventional, reductionist, and retrospective, focused on geopolitical antagonisms that perpetuated a militarized imagination of US foreign and security policy. As Meaney and Wertheim have observed, referring to the Brady-Johnson Program, 'Yale's grand strategists openly long for the intellectual certainties they associate with the Cold War, when the Soviet threat made strategy seem indispensable.[4] John Lewis Gaddis, a leading conservative historian of the Cold War, and together with Charles Hill and Paul Kennedy one of the teachers of the Yale program, explained that grand strategy was 'endangered' due to the absence of sufficiently grave threats to concentrate strategic thinking.[5]

The particular set of formal grand strategy discourses produced by IR scholars, security experts, and foreign policy intellectuals can be defined as technical, scientific knowledge considered to be 'true, objective and incontestable.'[6] Within academia, understood here as the mainstream of IR research in the United States, it was, then, mainly a contest between realism and liberalism on the one hand, and within the realist school of IR on the other hand, that informed the theoretical debate on American grand strategy under Obama.[7]

As Biersteker has pointed out, the reciprocal interrelationship of theory and practice in IR and the sub-field of international security is manifold, from the use of theoretically informed framework concepts of world politics, consciously or unconsciously, by political practitioners to the interpretation of international practices by IR scholars.[8] As such, formal expertise can serve as an information base for political decision-making and the education of the general public, but may only be challenged and called into question by other experts, the knowledge itself considered a-political and non-ideological, due to its supposed scientific impartiality. Beyond merely offering a neutral, scientific observation, however, grand strategy experts actively seek to influence political decision-making and guide the pursuit of national security, with their knowledge both politically motivated and ideologically biased.

This intellectual closeness between national security expertise and practice in the United States locates the formal discourse of American grand strategy at the nexus of political science and policymaking with *Foreign Affairs* as a key outlet of choice, where practitioners, policy experts, and IR scholars regularly intersect in articulating the leading debate on the subject. Reviewing the American grand strategy debate in *Foreign Affairs* under Obama, then, and examining the interlinkage of IR theory and political practice reveals a frequent discursive crosso-ver between an established identity paradigm of American leadership and hegemony and countering visions of engagement and restraint. Neorealists and liberal institutionalist scholars offered 'offshore bal-ancing' or 'deep engagement' as best possible, theoretically informed alternatives of American grand strategy. From a discursive perspective, however, these geopolitical visions were ultimately unable to reconcile fully strategic policy recommendations for cooperative partnerships or careful self-limitation with an ideational foundation in national excep-tionalism and hegemonic thinking, rooted in the pre-eminence of mili-tary power and economic supremacy.

This conflict between identity and practice in the mainstream IR debate confuted the reductionist logic of grand strategy as a unitary, coherent, and consistent equation of means and ends. This hybridity in turn reflected the complexity and multidimensionality of grand strategy thinking in a globalized international system lacking an overriding exis-tential threat to US national security, and the synchronicity of several basic discourses that operated in constant competition with each other under Obama.

FOREIGN AFFAIRS AND ELITE OPINION ON US FOREIGN POLICY

Foreign Affairs regularly advertises its status as an elite outlet for expert opinion on foreign policy matters with a quote from President Harry Truman: 'Not all readers are leaders, but all leaders are readers.' The *Encyclopaedia Britannica* describes the journal as 'one of the most pres-tigious periodicals of its kind in the world.' From a Foucauldian per-spective of power/knowledge, this prime expert publication on US foreign policy, IR, and world politics holds significant value for the analysis of American grand strategy discourses and their construction as intellectual expertise.[9] Most significantly, the journal does not only feature examples from academic research in IR, usually realist and lib-eral institutionalist theory-based expertise, but frequently represents the views and opinions of prominent political practitioners and policy experts. Active and former secretaries of state and defense, ambassa-dors, US senators, and generals are among those who regularly publish in this prestigious format of knowledge production and exchange. In 2007, for example, at an relatively early stage of his presidential campaign, Barack Obama, then a US Senator from Illinois, published a widely-read article in *Foreign Affairs* sketching out a foreign policy vision to renew American leadership after the damage the Bush administration had done to America's international legitimacy and political clout.[10]

Importantly, articles in *Foreign Affairs* are not subject to the double-blind peer-review process that usually applies to academic publications and that guarantees anonymity of evaluation. The prominence of certain authors' names plays a significant role in the selection of outputs, and in underwriting the journal's elite status, beyond merely the intellectual quality of the contributions featured. Within the particular genealogy of American grand strategy, this expert publication also holds special significance to strategists and foreign policy analysts due to its historic legacy. It was the pages of *Foreign Affairs*, where the famous Mr. X article was first published in 1947, in which would be spelled out a grand strategy of containment against the Soviet Union.[11] George F. Kennan, later revealed as Mr. X, had developed the article from his 'long telegram,' written as deputy chief of the US mission in Moscow. Kennan is considered the quintessential grand strategist and his work the ideal example of what any successful American grand strategy should aspire to be. As Michael Hirsh has remarked, 'the diplomatic world keeps pining away for the next George Kennan, someone who might sum up the country's overall mission in a strategic concept as simple as containment.'[12] In the words of Kennan's biographer, John Lewis Gaddis, the idea of containment 'removed the danger of great-power war, revived democracy and capitalism, and thereby enhanced the prospects for liberty beyond what they ever before had been.'[13]

Kennan himself later denounced the militarization of American Cold War policies under containment, and the over-simplification of US foreign and security policy into one central paradigm. At a meeting in the White House in 1994, America's ultimate grand strategist urged President Clinton to convey policy in a 'thoughtful paragraph or more, rather than trying to come up with a bumper sticker.'[14] The almost mythical quality of the Mr. X. article and containment in representing the ideal of American grand strategy were remarkably reiterated, however, when in 2009 a Mr. Y article was published, titled 'A new strategic narrative.' The article invoked the image of Kennan to advocate a complete overhaul of strategic thinking in Washington away from a narrow fixation on national security, military power, and threat.[15] The recantation of Kennan and the plea of Mr. Y, however, have done little to undermine the enthusiasm for a reductionist, military-centric grand strategy discourse in political and intellectual circles in the United States. Under Obama, the adoration for Kennan and containment regularly ushered in demands for a new 'bumper sticker' grand strategy as succinct and coherent as its Cold War predecessor, while critics simultaneously attacked Obama's lack of strategic vision in comparison.

Methodologically, for the analysis of formal discourse *Foreign Affairs* is considered in particular due to the measure of influence and impact that is being assigned to the academic research and expert knowledge presented in this medium. As with the material indicators of popularity in best-selling books or highest-grossing movies in popular discourse, then, the impact rankings of academic research and intellectual expertise produced by IR journals and leading think tanks act as confirmation for their respective discursive status as relevant sites of power/ knowledge. Here, *Foreign Affairs* stands out as a publication which is consistently being regarded as both world-leading in its field, as a dominant voice in the intellectual debate on American grand strategy, and as a site were the opinions of experts and practitioners on the subject regularly intersect.

This influence is also expressed in statistical measures, such as the impact factor index of publisher Thompson Reuters. Impact factors are statistical measures by which the significance of academic journals is evaluated based on the number of citations of published articles.[16] In 2013, for example, *Foreign Affairs* achieved an impact factor of 3.347, ranking it as the most influential journal in the field of IR. Between 2009 and 2015 the journal was consistently ranked among the top ten IR journals.[17] The impact factor, then, appears as one of the 'instruments that form and accumulate knowledge,' in the words of Foucault, with the production of knowledge embedded in established mechanisms of power and social regulation.[18]

HEGEMONY AND THE IDEOLOGICAL BIAS OF EXPERT KNOWLEDGE

The American grand strategy debate in *Foreign Affairs* reveals a strong ideological bias of most American political scientists, policy experts, and practitioners toward perpetuating a geopolitical vision of liberal hegemony, based on the country's superior economic and military power. Arthur Krepinevich Jr., for example, a former US Army officer, leading defense analyst, and president of the Center for Strategic and Budgetary Assessments (CSBA) think tank, related the necessary 'global dominance' of the United States to the country's 'overwhelming advantage in technology and resources,' giving the American military an unrivalled capacity for global power projection.[19]

The blow to US-style laissez-faire capitalism through the 2008 global financial crisis, which overshadowed the onset of the Obama presidency, was therefore primarily understood by experts supporting primacy as weakening America's global power position, most notably vis-à-vis China which was predicted to gain in global importance.[20] In this neorealist zero-sum perspective of world politics, the diminished ability of the United States to provide global leadership, due to domestic concerns from public indebtedness to growing inequality and mounting healthcare costs, was directly correlated with a rise in external threat levels, from a possible 'reversal of globalization' to the 'disintegration of Pakistan.'[21] The German political commentator Josef Joffe, while doubting American decline, encapsulated this expert opinion on hegemony in 2009, characterizing the United States as the essential 'liberal empire' necessary to underwrite global stability.[22]

While hegemony, understood as a neoconservative vision of military supremacy and unilateral primacy, came under scrutiny with many foreign policy and security experts, the idea of global leadership of the United States remained pivotal to the majority of geopolitical thinking in these expert circles. As a consequence, the focus of their expertise shifted from the 'unipolar moment' and the singularity of US power to 'burden sharing' and cooperation, incorporating elements of multilateral engagement within the hegemony leitmotif. In a similar way, proponents of retrenchment sought to lower the costs and risks of the United States' global posture, and especially to reduce its military footprint, while maintaining a vision of American leadership in the world, a form of hegemonic restraint, or 'leading from behind.'[23]

Some neoclassical realists, like Stephen Brooks and Will Wohlforth, promoted the global leadership role of the United States as a necessary condition for the functioning of a liberal world order.[24] They did not perceive America to be in decline nor expected an end of the structural unipolarity dominating the international system. As a consequence of the overextension in Iraq and Afghanistan, they proposed a grand strategy of hegemonic engagement, or what they referred to as 'deep engagement,' continuing the established trajectory of American hegemony.[25] This intellectual expertise on US hegemony most clearly reflected the mainstream in American grand strategy discourse and was a close intertextual match with more popular geopolitical reflections, such as Michael Bay's *Transformers* or Friedman's and Mandelbaum's *That Used To Be Us*.

The majority of intellectual expertise, then, served to strengthen further the political consensus on American grand strategy, which the critical neorealist Posen defined as fundamental agreement over the 'big picture,' that 'the United States should dominate the world militarily, economically, and politically.'[26] The *Foreign Affairs* articles by Secretary of Defense Robert Gates, Secretary of State Hillary Clinton, and other political and military officials, appearing in a major outlet of academic research and intellectual exchange, revealed the close intertextual link between formal analysis and the realm of policymaking in constituting this worldview. In the words of Gates, for example: 'The United States is the strongest and greatest nation on earth . . . The power and global reach of its military have been an indispensable contributor to world peace and must remain so.'[27]

This advocacy of hegemonic engagement also reveals a discursive point of connection between neorealism and liberal institutionalism, as the co-authorship of Brooks and Wohlforth with John Ikenberry documents. Leading representatives of neoclassical realism and liberal institutionalism together argued against retrenchment, urging America not to 'come home.'[28] At the same time, this outspoken belief in the virtue of America's global leadership also formed a cornerstone in the political rhetoric of major officials in the Obama administration, as laid out in the pages of *Foreign Affairs*.

However, the attention given to the limits of American power, to 'burden sharing' and 'responsible stakeholders' also demonstrated that the grand strategy discourse in the Obama White House was not a simple reproduction of the 'unipolar moment' and the 'indispensable nation,' which had featured so prominently under the Clinton and Bush administrations. In his 2010 *Foreign Affairs* article Gates, for example, referring to the new Pentagon's *Quadrennial Defense Review*, in effect announced an end of large-scale ground operations and forced regime change as military tool of US foreign policy.

The Iraq War scenario, the invasion and occupation of foreign territory with large American ground forces was supposed to have become a thing of the past, never to be repeated again. Instead, the United States would focus on 'building partner capacity,' to enable other countries to provide for their own security, in order to save American treasury expenditure and the necessity for 'boots on the ground.'[29] Providing this military assistance effectively and as part of a comprehensive approach was described as a crucial tool to guarantee America's 'global leadership' and 'U.S. security', reformulating American grand strategy to be both less ambitious and less costly.[30]

Yet these cooperative security partnerships and alliances were clearly executed under American hegemony, rather than in equal standing with the United States. Published in the very same journal in which the US Secretary of Defense laid out a vision for cooperative security management, George Packard described how Gates demanded implementation of a US-Japanese agreement about the Futemna US Air Base on Okinawa, rather than agreeing to renegotiate it, when a new Japanese government under Prime Minister Hatoyama came into office.[31] In political practice, engagement functioned within the context of hegemony rather than as an alternative to it.

Echoing Gates, Hillary Clinton centered her 2010 *Foreign Affairs* article on the problem of American leadership, and how to sustain it among a 'crucible of challenges.' [32] Here, Clinton argued for developing and strengthening the civilian power of the United States. Similar to the Pentagon's *Quadrennial Defense Review*, Clinton launched a Quadrennial Diplomacy and Development Review (QDDR) for the State Department and US AID, designed to 'align its resources, policies, and strategies.' Mainly referring to this key strategy document of political-practical discourse, Clinton's article was the civilian counterpart to Gates' military-centric perspective of national security and grand strategy. For both, 'American leadership' represented the crucial geopolitical characteristic of the United States that needed to anchor any strategic vision and policy initiative. As Clinton explained in 2010: 'My big-picture commitment is to restore American leadership . . .'[33] As the IR scholars Stephen Brooks and William Wohlforth have argued, the 'unipolar moment' as strategic guideline for the George W. Bush administration fueled 'illusions of omnipotence' about the global supremacy of the United States and its ability to dictate political outcomes militarily.[34]

The neoconservative agenda, however, merely represented a particularly military power-centric, unilateral, and expansive definition of the mainstream consensus on American hegemony, which, under Obama, continued to dominate in most of the political class and expert circles of US foreign policy in Washington DC. Only nuances separated the neoclassical realists Brooks and Wohlforth and the liberal institutionalist John Ikenberry from the neoconservative Kagan, when they located the greatest threat to American primacy as emerging from within,[35] and described any alternative to American leadership as potentially catastrophic: 'Were American leaders to choose retrenchment, they would in essence be running a massive experiment to test how the world would work without an engaged and liberal leading power. The results could well be disastrous.'[36]

From this joint expert perspective, a reformulated grand strategy of 'deep engagement' acted as an instrument for the better management of American hegemony that ended the neoconservative squander of national resources and unnecessary wars of choice. It did not mean the advent of a post-American world, or a true multipolar international system. In the words of Melvy Leffler: 'The United States' quest for primacy, its desire to lead the world, its preference for an open door and free markets, its concern with military supremacy . . . its sense of indispensability all these remained, and remain, unchanged.'[37]

As such, neither the policy statements by Gates and Clinton, nor the formal expertise by Brooks, Ikenberry, and Wohlforth represented cooperative engagement as a true alternative to existing American thinking on grand strategy. Global leadership could not be executed jointly, in an equal, balanced partnership with others, but only through the political, military, and economic pre-eminence of the United States. The renewal of institutional relationships that Brooks and Wohlforth, for example, advocated in *Foreign Affairs* was intended to support a clear continuity of hegemony, perpetuating an international hierarchy of power and influence that benefitted the United States over all others. This was also revealed in the way in which the United States was supposed to convince others of the benefits of the leadership it provided, as Brooks and Wohlforth declared: 'What constitutes a public good is not always straightforward, so the United States needs to persuade others that what it is supplying is important.[38]

The provision of 'global goods' and guaranteed free access to the 'global commons' represented a cornerstone in the geopolitical imagination of the hegemony discourse. It was seen as one of the hallmarks of American world leadership, and one of the key services the liberal hegemon supposedly offered to the states of the world, whose need for these service and compliance with US actions in providing them in turn legitimized America's hegemonic role. However, if these services were objective truths it seems unclear why the United States would have to persuade others of their value. The 'global goods' argument was above all else a necessary trope within the domestic discursive context of hegemony to internally justify a military apparatus designed for global power projection and a forwardly deployed presence with US troops stationed in nearly 150 countries.

The idea that the global commons could be managed jointly, as, for example, the international response to the piracy problem off the coast of Somalia since 2009 suggested, therefore did not enter the hegemony discourse. This absence of multipolarity and a non-America-centric multilateralism in the hegemonists' expertise in *Foreign Affairs* mirrored its ideational construction as the dangerous, volatile Other in Kagan's popular argument for world order in *The Word America Made*, the neo-imperial fantasies of Kaplan and Friedman, or the liberal treatise of Friedman and Mandelbaum in *That Used To Be Us*. In both the popular and expert discourse of hegemony, whether in its neoconservative, neoclassical realist, neoliberal, or institutionalist version, the absence of American leadership equated geopolitical volatility and increased risks, not a possibility for greater international cooperation and the common management of security. The only world imaginable was a world led by America.

In addition, the Washington elite circle of foreign and security experts constructed an ever-increasing list of existential threats to the United States, from failed states to cyber warfare, global terrorism, rising powers, the spread of WMD, hybrid warfare, and regional instability.[39] A number of data sets and research outputs, like the study undertaken by Harvard psychology professor Steven Pinker, have suggested that events like 9/11, the annexation of Crimea, or the rise of Islamic State (ISIS or ISIL) notwithstanding, overall levels of inter-state and intra-state violence have decreased considerably, in particular since the end of World War II and the end of the Cold War.[40] Since 2001, far more US citizens were killed by fellow Americans with guns than by terrorist acts.[41] President Obama himself apparently did remark on a number of occasions to his White House staff that in the United States the fear of terrorism was overblown, with the likelihood of drowning in the bathtub far higher than falling victim to terrorists.[42] The perception of US national security under Obama, however, was predominantly one of deterioration, not improvement.[43]

The continued representation of national security threats as both growing and ever more dangerous guaranteed the existence of the massive infrastructure of the military-industrial complex and the mushrooming intelligence industry that had grown enormously since 9/11, representing substantial political, bureaucratic, and economic interests embedded in the hegemony discourse.[44] This also included the plethora of think tanks and security experts of the 'military-intellectual complex' which provided the specialized expertise in support of the status quo.[45] The military-entertainment industrial complex and the national security cinema likewise functioned within this nexus of existential threat projections and Manichean 'good war' narratives that the discourse of hegemony employed, and that constituted both a political ideology and lucrative business model.

The significance of military power to counter these external and existential threats and the guaranteed material superiority of the United States in this category were central to the experts' hegemony discourse and the geopolitical imagination invoked by leading political figures. In 2016, for example, *Foreign Affairs* dedicated its September/October issue to the significance of military power for US national security and the future necessary adjustments to American defense strategy under Obama's successor. Here again, a clear majority of authors recommended the perpetuation of America's global military supremacy. Guaranteed access to the 'global commons' of sea, air, outer and cyber space, the forward basing of US troops, and prevention of the rise of a competing hegemonic power were all seen as essential parameters for US defense that should guide the allocation of resources and the statement of American intentions.[46] Michael O'Hanlon, Senior Fellow at the Brookings Institution, and David Petraeus, former Director of the CIA and Commander of US Central Command, described the ability to fight multiple large-scale conflicts simultaneously as enduring bipartisan political consensus that should remain the standard measure to size US forces, while also calling for a reversal of sequestration induced defense budget cuts and increased efforts to contain Russia, China, and the Islamic State.[47]

In the expert discourse on hegemony increased US military involvement was accordingly seen as improving global security, despite potentially further destabilizing conflicts in Eastern Europe or the South China Sea, where US military build-ups, either directly or indirectly, could be perceived in turn as threatening China or Russia. Remarkably, O'Hanlon and Petraeus suggested that despite negative experiences with COIN operations in Iraq and Afghanistan, the US would find itself again invading and occupying foreign lands, due to 'the pull of events and the logic of turbulent situations on the ground.'

The regional instability and hundreds of thousands of civilian casualties that US military interventions caused directly or indirectly since 2001 remained an intellectual blind spot in these expert assessments.

This attitude of undaunted liberal imperialism was prevalent among most US foreign policy and defense experts, where America's 'awesome military' underwrote 'peace, security, and international stability.'[48] Countering this entrenched doctrine of 'military activism,' Andrew Bacevich in turn argued in *Foreign Affairs* for a radical departure of conventional wisdom and established paradigms that made American world leadership and global military presence the country's highest strategic priorities, suggesting instead that the presence of US troops could no longer be needed in some – and even be detrimental in other – regions.[49] An alternative grand strategy would see US troops withdraw from Asia and Europe, and terminate America's NATO membership by 2025. The central intellectual debate on American grand strategy thus occurred between those experts who wanted to 'lean forward' and those who wanted to 'pull back.'[50]

REALISM AND HEGEMONIC RESTRAINT

Leading neorealists, such as John Mearsheimer or Stephen Walt, directly opposed a grand strategy of American primacy as advocated by key establishment figures in *Foreign Affairs*, proposing an alternative grand strategy of restraint and offshore balancing.[51] Based on a neorealist focus on military power, they proposed to reorient US national security from an expansive liberal agenda of global leadership and frequent interventionism to a more limited set of goals, built around maintaining a favorable balance of power for the United States. The prevailing political and expert consensus on liberal hegemony was seen by these deviant producers of elite discourse as a dangerous overextension of American resources, while the United States could be kept safe at far less cost to the American taxpayer and the US military.[52]

'Global hegemony' or 'global dominance' thus appeared as a misguided grand strategy, in place since the end of the Cold War, and that continued under Obama, albeit with more liberal institutionalist auspices.[53] As Mearsheimer argued in *The Atlantic*:

> The United States needs a new grand strategy. Global dominance is a prescription for endless trouble – especially in its neoconservative variant. Unfortunately, the Obama administration is populated from top to bottom with liberal imperialists who remain committed to trying to govern the world, albeit with less emphasis

on big-stick diplomacy and more emphasis on working with allies and international institutions.[54]

Applied to the discourse analytical framework of American grand strategy, Mearsheimer's assessment of 'neoconservatives' versus 'liberal imperialists' attested to the two strands of the hegemony discourse, between unilateral primacy and the more cooperative vision of hegemonic engagement. Their advocacy of an alternative 'offshore balancing' strategy in turn placed neorealists firmly within the restraint discourse that opposed both Republican and Democrat proponents of hegemony and shunned America's role as the 'indispensable nation' to 'promote a world order based on international institutions, representative governments, open markets, and respect for human rights.'[55]

However, unlike other prominent and more outspoken critics of American primacy, imperialism, and militarism on the left – such as Tom Engelhardt, Chalmers Johnson, or Oliver Stone – these realist scholars did not envision a grand strategy of demilitarization or a post-hegemonic international system. Instead, they recommended a managed 'retrenchment' of the United States from Europe, Asia, and the Middle East, while maintaining capable military forces 'over the horizon.'[56] Restraint, as a realist concept, was primarily concerned with the preservation of US power. In the words of MacDonald and Parent:

> We define 'retrenchment' as a policy of retracting grand strategic commitments in response to a decline in relative power. Abstractly, this means decreasing the overall costs of foreign policy by redistributing resources away from peripheral commitments and toward core commitments.[57]

In the realist view of retrenchment, military force existed to act as deterrent to other great powers, and in last consequence as an intervening force should another actor try to establish a position of regional hegemony that could strategically challenge the United States, in particular in Asia, Europe, or the Middle East.[58] Realism's focus on economic and in particular military power as a key determinant of state behavior and security in IR dominated the geopolitical imagination of this expert vision.

Crucially, these neorealist critics of the Washington consensus on hegemony emphasized that strategic reorientation and retrenchment was not meant as American disengagement from the world in order to avoid the stigma of isolationism, used to discredit alternative, more limited formulations of American grand strategy.[59] Walt, for example, explained that: 'Offshore balancing is *not* isolationism, however, because the United States would still be diplomatically engaged in many places and committed to intervening in key areas if and when the balance of power broke down.'[60] The power-centric analysis and geopolitical imagination which assigned regions of primary strategic concern to the United Sates documented how offshore balancing actually represented a hybrid discourse of hegemonic restraint. The global military posture of the United States was reduced, but it remained a regional hegemon dominant in the Western hemisphere, maintaining the ability to exert ultimate control over Spykman's pivotal 'rimland' zones in Europe, Northeast Asia, and the Persian Gulf.

While trying to avoid the 'isolationist' label, a realist offshore balancing strategy contested the neoconservative vision of quasi-imperial global primacy as well as liberal internationalist goals of humanitarian intervention. The expert visions of neoconservative primacy, or neoclassical realist/liberal internationalist 'deep engagement,' both drew heavily on the notion of American exceptionalism and the country's liberal identity and political culture to argue for its unique responsibility to lead the world and promote its universal values. The utter lack of idealism in the realist vision of offshore balancing in turn had previously limited its political traction among Washington decisionmakers and media pundits. Walt, for example, criticized the lack of realist ideas among policymaking circles and mainstream media in the United States.[61] Indeed, these neorealist experts formulated a decidedly anti-exceptional American grand strategy, where the United States was expected to essentially behave like other successful great powers and empires of the past in defending its position, while avoiding the historical mistakes of 'imperial overstretch.'[62]

However, over the course of the Obama presidency, realist ideas of restraint increasingly crossed over from a primarily academic discourse and point of debate among intellectuals and IR scholars into a wider sphere of popular and practical discussion. Ideas of offshore balancing, for example, informed a 2011 op-ed article by Thomas Friedman in *The New York Times*, supporting US withdrawal from both Iraq and Afghanistan.[63] Prominent members of the Tea Party, like Texas Senator Ted Cruz, or the libertarian Senator from Kentucky Rand Paul, indicated support for a non-interventionist US foreign policy in 2015.[64] While using an aggressive, derogatory, anti-immigration, and anti-Muslim rhetoric, key ideas on foreign policy voiced by Republican presidential nominee Donald Trump were also reflecting realist ideas for offshore balancing. Trump, for example, had suggested that the United States could withdraw its troops from South Korea and Japan, resulting in these countries providing for their own defense independently, including with their own nuclear weapons arsenals.[65] Indeed, both Obama and Trump challenged elite opinion and conventional wisdom by suggesting greater salience for realist ideas of grand strategy.

In the White House, at the highest level of strategy making, the lessons of the failed military interventions in Iraq and Afghanistan had been translated by President Obama into a political maxim that the United States should avoid making 'stupid' mistakes, resulting from moral absolutism, exceptionalist hubris, and a misguided faith in military solutions to complex political problems.[66] In this assessment, some of the costliest mistakes of the United States had not come from undue military restraint, but from a willingness to 'rush into military adventures' without adequate consideration for potential consequences, international support or legitimacy, and the financial and human cost associated with the use of force.[67]

The hegemony discourse was fundamentally based on the premise of the US as sole superpower facing multiple dangers and growing threats to its national security. The expert discourse of restraint relied in turn on a geopolitical imagination, where a more limited role of the United States, and especially a less engaged American military, did not result in rising threat levels. In the words of Zenko and Cohen: 'In an era of relative peace and security, the U.S. military should not be the primary prism through which the country sees the world.'[68] In fact, the restraint discourse argued that a more limited international role and downsized military profile would likely make the United States safer. These realists argued that a grand strategy of 'prudent retrenchment,' could bring a range of benefits to the United States by limiting the country's exposure to 'potential flashpoints,' encouraging US allies to provide more for common defense, and reducing enmity toward America.[69] However, the neorealist experts conceded that following such a grand strategy would run directly counter to the prevailing political consensus, where a maximum of global military power was equated with a maximum of security for the United States.[70] Hence, presidential leadership was seen as a necessary course corrective to drive lasting strategic change in the United States.[71]

The expert debate in *Foreign Affairs* between the two camps, then, produced completely contrary demands on presidential leadership. Undersecretary of Defense for Policy Michèle Flournoy, co-founder of CNAS, and former Deputy Assistant Secretary of Defense for Plans Janine Davidson, for example, called on Obama to maintain the status quo, declaring that 'the president must resist calls for retrenchment and continue to champion the United States' unique leadership role in the world.'[72] Against a 'misguided' notion of restraint these security and defense experts advocated a policy of 'forward deployment' in *Foreign Affairs*.

The simultaneous but contradictory influence of competing ideas of hegemony and restraint, as articulated in the competing expert visions of 'deep engagement' and 'offshore balancing,' would be reflected in the Obama White House in a hybrid discourse of hegemonic restraint, or what would become known in the in the context of the 2011 Libya intervention as 'leading from behind.'[73] This hybridity and multidimensionality of the Obama Doctrine, which linked the more limited use of American military power and America's enduring status as the world's 'indispensable nation,' at the same time produced a sustained criticism among both realist and liberal foreign policy experts that attacked Obama's strategic incoherence. Obama, then, lacked an adequate and consistent grand strategy to either maintain American world leadership or finally depart from the misguided path of primacy; he neither leaned forward nor did he finally pull back.

LIBERALISM AND HEGEMONIC ENGAGEMENT

Where the realist vision of offshore balancing was anchored in material power calculations and traditional geopolitics, the intellectual expertise on cooperative engagement was clearly rooted in the IR theory of liberal institutionalism and the foreign policy tradition of Wilsonian idealism. Here, the analytical focus was on the cooperative potential of the international system, due to commonly shared norms and values and mutually beneficial institutional and economic arrangements.[74] Arguing from a liberal institutionalist perspective, John Ikenberry, for example, predicted that the liberal world order would endure even with a weakened United States.[75] In this expert vision, the benefits of free trade, open sea-lanes, and a rule-based system of international norms, institutions, and organizations applied to all major and rising powers in the international system, and there was no competing ideology or alternative institutional design that could rival the prominence and advantages of the liberal order installed by Washington after the end of World War II.[76]

Ikenberry and the liberal institutionalists thus argued against primacy and the exclusive focus on unipolar stability theory underlying the unilateral strand of the hegemony discourse, doubting the pessimist predictions from analysts such as Kagan or Kaplan for the negative effects of shifting power balances. In line with Zakaria, the rise of other states was emphasized over the decline of the United States.[77] Thus, America should pursue a grand strategy of engagement, or 'liberal order building' that acknowledged shifting economic and political parameters in world politics, and sought to maintain a cooperative management of the global institutional framework, while simultaneously restoring America's standing as a global leader.[78] The United States' 'unipolar moment' and an associated grand strategy of global primacy had come under scrutiny with both realist and liberal authors in *Foreign Affairs*, due to the costly experiences in Iraq and Afghanistan, and the economic difficulties of the United States persisting at home.

In response to these developments and the failure of neoconservative designs for regime change and regional transformation in the Middle East, alternative geopolitical visions were explored that sought to redefine America's leadership role toward a more cooperative position in managing IR and sustaining a liberal world order. Here, the US would 'renegotiate the bargains and institutions of the past decades but retain its position as hegemonic leader.'[79] This grand strategy vision of hegemonic engagement Ikenberry saw as a guiding principle behind Obama administration's foreign policy. Within the engagement discourse, the grand strategy of President Obama regularly appeared as a direct contradiction of the unipolar vision of his predecessor.

To Walter Russell Mead, a multilateral and liberal 'Wilsonian' vision informed the actions of the Obama administration, which he described as a deliberate and calculated break with the unilateral and confrontational 'Jacksonianism' of President Bush.[80] Brzezinski and Kupchan both characterized the foreign policy of President Obama as a reversal of that of Bush, as the former was supposedly guided by a grand strategy of engagement. To liberals, the 'reset' of relations with Russia, the administration's efforts for nuclear disarmament, the President's Cairo speech announcing a 'new beginning' with the Muslim world, sustained efforts to negotiate agreements on Iran's nuclear program and global CO2 emissions, or the President's push for far-reaching free-trade agreements with Asia and Europe, all demonstrated Obama's strong emphasis on multilateral cooperation, liberal institutionalism, and global engagement.[81]

Obama's focus on engagement and the ideational connection to liberal institutionalism was the clearest intertextual link of IR theory-building and practical American grand strategy discourse. The emphasis on cooperative multilateralism and the mutual benefits of a liberal world order had traditionally been at the center when Washington elites described America's world political role to domestic and foreign audiences.[82] These themes were reemphasized under the Obama administration.[83] However, ideationally this vision of engagement and cooperation was formulated from the clear assumption that the United States remained the indispensable leader in world affairs, rather than becoming just one of many nodes in a networked, multipolar system. The discourse of hegemonic engagement thus reemphasized America's leading position at the center of a liberal international order of its own making.

A more fundamental shift to a grand strategy vision of cooperative engagement that deemphasized the leadership role of the United States would alternatively lead to a 'post-hegemonic,' 'post-American liberal order,' where 'the United States exercised less command and control over rules and institutions.'[84] Instead, global leadership would be exercised through international institutions and global collective action, between bodies such as the UN, and more informal groups like the G-20 that combined established and rising powers, such as the United States, the EU, China, and India.[85] In *Foreign Affairs*, such a geopolitical vision of a 'post-hegemonic' cooperative partnership was recommended by a number of leading grand strategy experts such as Brzezinski, Henry Kissinger, or Charles Kupchan.[86]

Here, engagement represented a geostrategic alternative rather than an auxiliary element that functioned to continue American primacy. On the pivotal US relationship with China, for example, Kissinger, like Brzezinski considered a doyen of American grand strategy thinking and geopolitics, envisioned a relationship based on cooperative partnership and mutual respect rather than turning the People's Republic into a 'responsible stakeholder' in the eyes of Washington.[87] Anne-Marie Slaughter, head of the US State Department's policy planning operation between 2009 and 2011, likewise envisioned the United States as a globalized networking power, concluding that: 'In the twenty-first century, the United States' exceptional capacity for connection, rather than splendid isolation or hegemonic domination, will renew its power and restore its global purpose.'[88] A more fundamental reformulation of American grand strategy toward a vision of cooperative engagement as implied by Brzezinski or Slaughter therefore reimagined the geopolitical identity of the United States, stressing equality and interdependence rather than exceptional and indispensable singularity.

An expert discourse of engagement that stressed cooperation both ideationally and practically offered a distinct alternative in defining America's role in the world. In a similar vein, Joseph Nye Jr., who had coined the term 'soft power,' demanded a new narrative to replace the 'American Century' and 'American primacy,' arguing that the United States had to develop a 'smart power' strategy, a term later adopted by Clinton as Secretary of State for her civilian power concept, defined as exercising 'power with others as much as power over others.'[89] Leslie Gelb, president emeritus of the Council on Foreign Relations (CFR), concluded that a US foreign policy based in 'common sense' had to acknowledge that 'mutual indispensability is the fundamental operating principle for power in the twenty-first century meaning that the United States is the indispensable leader but needs equally indispensable partners to succeed.'[90]

However, as Gelb demonstrated, there remained an irresolvable contradictory tension in the majority of the liberal expert discourse on engagement, where the singularity of American leadership precluded a notion of equivalence toward other powers. While Gelb, for example, seemingly endorsed a vision of engagement as cooperative partnership, he remained convinced that only the United States 'alone among nations can provide the leadership to solve the problems that will otherwise engulf the world.'[91] Nye likewise was unwilling to accept a multipolar international system, or a post-American future where the United States was reduced to the status of *primus inter pares*.[92] American decline, 'becoming just another great power' in the words of Gelb, would mean that the exceptionalist identity of the United States as a global superpower would be challenged. America would become 'a nation barely worth fearing or following.'[93] This representation of the United States as a country, which could only have a meaningful existence in world affairs as long as its superior power could elevate it above its allies and enemies alike, revealed the hegemonic imagination underwriting most liberal experts' arguments for engagement.

Many liberals had denounced the 'unilateralism,' or 'hubris' of the Bush administration, and the neoconservative 'Vulcans,' and their imperial delusions of American primacy.[94] Yet the strategic vision of liberal engagement predominantly served to realize the established hegemony of the United States in a more cost-effective and cooperative fashion, not to fundamentally redefine America's role in world politics.[95] The sacrosanct mantra of American world leadership and indispensability remained in place and continued to dominate the geopolitical imagination. Under Obama, a geopolitical vision of hegemony, then, represented an overarching expert consensus on identity shared by neoconservatives, unilateral primacists, neoclassical realists, and liberal institutionalists.

The result of this conflation of hegemonic identity and cooperative practice was a hybrid grand strategy discourse of hegemonic engagement, where the United States remained the world's dominant power tasked with exercising global leadership, but where the unilateralism of Bush and the neoconservative vision of primacy were replaced with a more conciliatory approach of multilateral cooperation and consultation. Under Obama, then, expert visions of hegemony, engagement, and restraint simultaneously sought to reformulate American grand strategy, and were all reproduced to some degree in political-practical discourse, resulting in many experts finding it difficult to actually identify the Obama Doctrine.[96]

Here, Obama appeared either as 'softheaded idealist, cold blooded realist, or a naïve incompetent.'[97] This confusion and exasperation in expert circles with Obama and his seemingly inconsistent articulation and execution of grand strategy was due to the multiplicity of discourses, IR theories, and foreign policy traditions that informed the Obama Doctrine.[98] Obama invoked the rhetoric of American exceptionalism and indispensability in defending a liberal world order and he frequently resorted to the use of force, while also doggedly pursuing cooperative engagement with former sworn enemies of the United States, such as Iran and Cuba, and demonstratively practicing military restraint in places like Syria and Ukraine.[99] According to Gideon Rose, Obama was prepared to save, maintain, and expand the 'core' of the liberal order by pivoting to Asia and remaining engaged in Europe, while sacrificing the 'periphery,' downsizing and withdrawing from the Middle East.[100]

There was not one single dominant geopolitical vision either of hegemony, engagement or restraint, neoconservatism, neorealism or liberal institutionalism: 'The tone has been neither that of American triumphalism and exceptionalism nor one of American decline.'[101] As Dan Drezner pointed out, the result of this was that grand strategy under

Obama seemed 'poorly articulated.'[102] Obama, then, did not meet the experts' expectations for delivering a coherent narrative and convincing rationale for the administration's behavior. In the eyes of the left-of-center Brookings Institution, for example, Obama in his first term had not yet 'developed a clear strategy' for the readjustment of America's role in a changing global order.[103] However, such assessments were based on a rationalist-positivist interpretation of grand strategy dominant in IR and academic and expert circles in the United States, which demanded that a reductionist logic was imposed over the complexity of world politics through stringent narratives and coherent equations of means and ends. The many acolytes of Kennan in American academe were mostly unable to allow for complexity, nuance, and multidimensionality in the analysis and formulation of American grand strategy, demanding instead a new 'bumper sticker.'

CONCLUSION

The expert debate on American grand strategy remained dominated by a geopolitical imagination of hegemony, framing the discussion of America's global leadership role, and the necessary conditions to sustain it among shifting geopolitical and domestic parameters. This corresponded with the dominant position of hegemony in the common-sense realm of cinematic imagination, where America's military heroes had to save the world on a regular basis, as well as with the majority of national security and geopolitics best-sellers that envisioned the United States as the indispensable center of world politics. However, no single expert vision was altogether dominant in shaping strategic thinking under the Obama administration, frustrating academic preferences for clear rationalist explanatory models and coherent, reductionist arguments. The academic discourse also largely failed to deliver a more holistic and comprehensive reformulation of American grand strategy that not only suggested political-practical course correction, but a more fundamental and deep-reaching reorientation of America's world political role by addressing core underlying assumptions and key tropes of identity construction.

Here, neorealists went furthest in departing from the Washington consensus on hegemony, reformulating the world political role of the United States from a liberal empire to a defensive balancer of last resort. Ideationally, however, the identity of the United States as a hegemon, albeit one limited to the Western hemisphere, and its ambition to exert ultimate control over the globe in terms of the balance of power remained in place. Predominantly, liberal experts stayed even closer to the common foundation of geopolitical identity, envisioning engagement as more a multilateral exercise of hegemony, but not fundamentally questioning the indispensable and exceptional role of the United States in leading and supporting a world order designed in Washington's image.

The contradictory impulses in American grand strategy discourses, however, did not signal the absence of strategic thinking under the Obama administration. Instead, they revealed the existence of a fixed matrix of ideas in the elite establishment of US foreign policy and national security. These ideas operated in constant competition with each other in trying to shape the geopolitical imagination and to establish their respective expert vision as hegemonic. Obama's multiplicity responded to the discursive logic of power/knowledge. As Foucault remarked 'there can exist different and contradictory discourses within the same strategy.'[104] It was this synchronicity and tension that defined American grand strategy under the Obama presidency.

NOTES

1. Edelstein and Krebs, 'Delusions of Grand Strategy.'
2. Study programs in Grand Strategy are currently run by several universities in the United States, notably Yale University, Duke University, the University of Texas, Columbia University, and Temple University.
3. Yale University's 'The Brady-Johnson Program in Grand Strategy' seeks to promote effective leadership in a complex and globalized world. In the program, the study of historical and contemporary cases of grand strategy focuses on past and present great powers, from the Roman Empire to the United States, and the established pantheon of strategic thinkers from Thucydides to Machiavelli, Clausewitz, and Kissinger. The course concludes with a crisis simulation exercise where students take on the role of leading US national security officials.
4. Meaney and Wertheim, 'Grand Flattery.'
5. Quoted in ibid.
6. Edkins, 'Ethics and Practices of Engagement,' p. 66.
7. See also Green, 'Two Concepts of Liberty,' on IR theory as a site of academic knowledge production, see, for example, Milliken, 'The Study of Discourse in International Relations,' p. 238.
8. Biersteker, 'Theory and Practice in International Security Studies.'
9. *Encyclopaedia Britannica*, 'Foreign Affairs.' Available at http://www.bri

tannica.com/EBchecked/topic/213341/Foreign-Affairs   (last   accessed August 29, 2016).

10. Obama, 'Renewing American Leadership.'
11. Kennan, 'The Sources of Soviet Conduct,' see also Nicholas Thompson, 'Review Essay. Ideas Man.'
12. Hirsh, 'The Clinton Legacy,' p. 89.
13. Quoted in ibid., p. 151.
14. Quoted in Meaney and Wertheim, 'Grand Flattery.'
15. Mr. Y, 'A National Strategic Narrative.'
16. Thompson Reuters, 'Thomson Reuters Research Analytics Unveils 2013 Release of its Journal Citation Reports.' Available at http://thomson-reuters.com/press-releases/062013/2013-journal-citation-reports   (last accessed August 29, 2016). In a given year, the impact factor of a journal is the average number of citations received per paper published in that journal during the two preceding years. The impact factor is then used to compare different journals within an academic field, such as IR. According to Thomson Reuters, its Journal Citation Reports (JCR), which calculate the annual journal impact factors, are the world's most influential resource for evaluating peer-reviewed publications.
17. See appendix.
18. Foucault, *Society Must Be Defended*, p. 32.
19. Krepinevich Jr., 'The Pentagon's Wasting Assets.'
20. Altman, 'A Geopolitical Setback for the West,' Birdsall and Fukuyama, 'The Post-Washington Consensus,' Subramanian, 'The Inevitable Superpower.'
21. Subramanian, 'Globalization in Retreat.'
22. Joffe, 'The Default Power.'
23. Gelb, 'In Defense of Leading from Behind.'
24. Brooks and Wohlforth, *World Out of Balance.*
25. Brooks, Ikenberry, and Wohlforth, 'Don't Come Home, America.'
26. Posen, 'Pull Back,' p. 116.
27. Gates, 'A Balanced Strategy,' p. 39.
28. Brooks, Ikenberry, and Wohlforth, 'Lean Forward: In Defense of American Engagement,' pp. 130-142.
29. Gates, 'Helping Others to Defend Themselves.'
30. Ibid., p. 6.
31. Packard, 'The United States-Japan Security Treaty at 50.'
32. Clinton, 'Leading Through Civilian Power.'
33. Quoted in Hirsh, 'The Clinton Legacy,' p. 83.
34. Brooks and Wohlforth, 'Reshaping the World Order.'
35. Brooks and Wohlforth, 'The Once and Future Superpower.'
36. Brooks, Ikenberry, and Wohlforth, 'Lean Forward,' p. 142.
37. Leffler, '9/11 in Retrospect.'

38. Brooks and Wohlforth, 'Reshaping the World Order.'
39. Zenko and Cohen, 'Clear and Present Safety.'
40. Pinker, *The Better Angels of our Nature*.
41. Jones and Bower, 'American Deaths in Terrorism vs. Gun Violence in one Graph,' using numbers from the Centers for Disease Control and Prevention and the US State Department, CNN found that between 2001 and 2013 the number of people killed by firearms in the United States was 406,496 (this data included all manners of death, including homicide, accident, and suicide). The number of US citizens killed overseas as a result of terrorist incidents between 2001 and 2013 was 350.
42. Kristof, 'Overreacting to Terrorism?'; according to *The New York Times*, 464 people drowned in in the United States in bathtubs in 2013, while in 2014 only seventeen were killed by terrorists.
43. Zenko and Cohen, 'Clear and Present Safety,' p. 81.
44. Priest and Arkin, 'A Hidden World, Growing Beyond Control.' *The Washington Post* has launched a special website dedicated to the investigation of 'top secret America.' Available at http://projects.wash ingtonpost.com/top-secret-america/ (last accessed September 14, 2016).
45. Morrissey,' Architects of Empire,' Walt, 'Military-Intellectual Complex?'
46. Thornberry and Krepinevich Jr., 'Preserving Primacy.'
47. O'Hanlon and Petraeus, 'America's Awesome Military.'
48. Ibid., p. 17.
49. Bacevich, 'Ending Endless War.'
50. Brooks, Wohlforth, and Ikenberry, 'Lean Forward,' Posen, 'Pull Back.'
51. Mearsheimer and Walt, 'The Case for Offshore Balancing.' See also, Mearsheimer, 'Imperial by Design,' Layne, 'The End of Pax Americana,' Walt, 'Offshore Balancing.'
52. Drezner, 'Military Primacy Doesn't Pay,' p. 79.
53. Kaplan, 'Why John J. Mearsheimer Is Right (About Some Things).'
54. Quoted in ibid.
55. Mearsheimer and Walt, 'The Case for Offshore Balancing,' p. 71.
56. Ibid.
57. MacDonald and Parent, 'Graceful Decline?' p. 11.
58. Mearsheimer and Walt, 'The Case for Offshore Balancing.'
59. Mearsheimer and Walt, 'The Case for Offshore alancing,' Kaplan, 'Why John J. Mearsheimer Is Right (About Some Things),' Walt, 'Offshore Balancing.'
60. Walt, 'Offshore Balancing.'
61. Walt, 'A Bandwagon for Offshore Balancing?' On the ideological significance of liberalism and idealism for the foundation and development of American grand strategy, see for example Layne, *The Peace of Illusions*, pp. 118–132, Dueck, *Reluctant Crusaders*, pp. 21–26.

62. The concept has been developed by the historian Paul Kennedy and refers to the process of great power decline as a result of foreign engagements and military commitments outstripping diminishing domestic capacities and economic resources, see Kennedy, *The Rise and Fall of the Great Powers*. Kennedy predicted American decline as early as the 1980s, see ibid., pp. 514–532.
63. Walt, 'Offshore Balancing.'
64. Blake, 'The Republican Party Likes Rand Paul's Foreign Policy,' Purple, 'Ted Cruz's Fourth-Way Foreign Policy.'
65. *New York Times*, 'Transcript: Donald Trump on NATO, Turkey's Coup Attempt and the World.'
66. Goldberg, 'The Obama Doctrine,' p. 73.
67. *New York Times*, 'Transcript of President Obama's Commencement Address at West Point,' May 28, 2014.
68. Zenko and Cohen, 'Clear and Present Safety,' p. 93.
69. Parent and MacDonald, 'The Wisdom of Retrenchment,' Mearsheimer and Walt, 'The Case for Offshore Balancing.'
70. Ibid., p. 33.
71. Ibid., p. 39.
72. Flournoy and Davidson, 'Obama's New Global Posture,' p. 63.
73. Ibid. The phrase was coined by an unnamed official in the Obama administration to characterize the Obama administration's approach toward using military force against Gaddafi, following a UN Security Council resolution to protect the civilian population in Libya from the dictator's reprisals in the wake of the Arab Spring. After the United States had undertaken the initial round of attacks, it soon transferred responsibility for the mission to NATO, in particular to France and the United Kingdom.
74. As an exemplary overview, see Keohane, *After Hegemony*, Ikenberry, *After Victory*.
75. Ikenberry, *Liberal Leviathan*.
76. Ikenberry, 'The Future of the Liberal World Order.'
77. Ibid.
78. Ikenberry, *Liberal Leviathan*, pp. 333–360.
79. Ibid., p. 306.
80. Mead, 'The Tea Party in American Foreign Policy.'
81. Brzezinski, 'From Hope to Audacity,' Kupchan, 'Enemies Into Friends,' Indyk, Lieberthal and O'Hanlon, 'Scoring Obama's Foreign Policy,' Rose, 'What Obama Gets Right.'
82. Ruggie, 'Past as Prologue', pp. 108-109; Bacevich, *Washington Rules*.
83. Sanger, 'Pursuing Ambitious Global Goals, but Strategy is More.'
84. Ibid., p. 302.
85. Ibid., p. 303.

86. Brzezinski, *Strategic Vision*, Kissinger, 'The Future of U.S.-China Relations.'
87. Kissinger, 'The Future of U.S.-China Relations.' Arguing from a decidedly realpolitik balance of power perspective, and as a prominent former practitioner who facilitated the original rapprochement between the United States and the People's Republic, Kissinger warned against a confrontational grand strategy toward China that would try to replicate containment, based on an American tendency to overemphasize ideological differences with non-democratic actors. As such, he also criticized a hegemonic rhetoric in American politics, which defined China as a 'rising power' with the need to 'mature' and behave 'responsibly.'
88. Slaughter, 'America's Edge,' p. 113.
89. Nye Jr., 'The Future of American Power.'
90. Gelb, 'Necessity, Choice, and Common Sense,' p. 71.
91. Ibid., p. 72.
92. Nye, 'The Future of American Power.'
93. Gelb, 'Necessity, Choice, and Common Sense,' p. 71.
94. Mann and Mann, *Rise of the Vulcans*.
95. On the continuity of grand strategy thinking from Bush to Obama, see Leffler, '9/11 in Retrospect.'
96. Drezner, 'Does Obama Have a Grand Strategy?'
97. Rose, 'What Obama gets Right,' p. 2.
98. Kaufman, *Dangerous Doctrine*, pp. 27–61.
99. Ibid.
100. Ibid., p. 7.
101. Indyk, Lieberthal, and O'Hanlon, 'Scoring Obama's Foreign Policy,' p. 31.
102. Drezner, 'Does Obama Have a Grand Strategy?' p. 58.
103. Indyk, Lieberthal, and O'Hanlon, 'Scoring Obama's Foreign Policy,' p. 42.
104. Quoted in Edkins, *Post-structuralism and International Relations*, p. 54.

Chapter 5

THINK TANKS AND THE WASHINGTON CONSENSUS ON HEGEMONY

One striking feature of foreign policy discussions in the United States is the widespread assumption that this country is the 'indispensable nation' in the international system.

Ted Galen Carpenter[1]

The think tank scene is a fixture of political life in Washington DC. Think tanks form a 'specialized community of security intellectuals' that analyze, comment, evaluate, and recommend US national security and foreign policy.[2] As 'epistemic communities' they share a 'common worldview,' seeking to translate their political beliefs into public policy.[3] The aim of these think tanks is to formulate a course that 'over several decades and multiple administrations' can align means and ends, domestic and foreign issues, and bring about a world 'that is most conducive to American interests.'[4] Unlike IR scholars with a usually predominantly academic interest in debate and intellectual exchange, their formal research and advice is decidedly policy oriented, motivated by the ambition to 'capture the political imagination' of political decision-makers and the public, and effect practical outcomes.[5]

This intellectual community of security and strategy experts has traditionally played a key role in the public debate on grand strategy in the United States. As discursive producers, they occupy an intermediary, intertextual position, providing both policy expertise and acting as informers of the public on matters of national security. The individual think tanks, set up as independent, non-profit organizations for political research, analysis, and advice, offer professional expertise in a wide range of formats. They publish books, research papers, policy briefs, media articles, and press releases; they organize workshops, talks, and conferences, provide policy experts for media inquiries or

Congressional hearings, and engage in professional networking with government, businesses, and political parties. Some think tanks are decidedly bipartisan organizations; others pursue a clear ideological agenda. Their common goal, however, is to have an impact on the political agenda setting in Washington. As James McGann has explained in his study on think tanks and policy advice in the US, their primary function is to 'help government understand and make informed choices about issues of domestic and international concern.'[6] In this role they identify, articulate, and promote policy issues, build networks, provide personnel, and function as forums of intellectual exchange.

The think tanks examined here have been selected to assess those independent research outputs on US national security and foreign policy considered to have had the greatest policy impact, while also reflecting the widest possible range of political views on American grand strategy.[7] Under Obama, the majority of leading US think tanks adhered to the central ideational paradigm of American hegemony and the indispensability of the United States in their research outputs, reproducing, not challenging 'conventional' wisdom.[8] This production of 'self-defined knowledge' of policy research and analysis further illustrates how the geopolitical imagination of hegemony and global military supremacy represented a Washington consensus that was deeply embedded and widely shared, lying at the center of political discourse, popular imagination, and formal expertise.[9] This limited bandwidth of expert opinion had considerable implications for American grand strategy in that continuity was overwhelmingly emphasized over change and alternative thinking in envisioning America's world political role and recommending policy options to fulfill that role.[10]

The analysis has concentrated on two policy issues in particular which were prominent in the policy debate on national security under Obama: budget sequestration and the 'pivot to Asia.' Both issues were of special discursive significance, because they were consistently framed as fundamental long-term challenges to the global role of the United States and the definition of its overarching grand strategy for the twenty-first century.[11]

BUDGET HAWKS VERSUS DEFENSE HAWKS: GRAND STRATEGY UNDER SEQUESTRATION AND THE DEBATE ON THE RIGHT

Before the background of the 2003 Iraq War, Edward Said explained in an updated preface to his book *Orientalism* that a specific American contribution to the discourse of empire and imperialism was the 'specialized jargon of policy experts,' in particular singling out the influence of neoconservative intellectuals under the George W. Bush administration.[12] Here, the American Enterprise Institute (AEI), founded in 1943, stands out as a leading neoconservative think tank with close links to the Republican Party that enjoyed special prominence under President Bush, with several of AEI's members occupying important positions for foreign policy, defense, and national security.[13] According to Republican vice-presidential candidate of 2012 Paul Ryan, the think tank was 'one of the beachheads of the modern conservative movement.'[14] During the Obama presidency, AEI continued to serve as an intellectual home for prominent neoconservatives, such as Paul Wolfowitz, John Bolton, or Richard Perle, who all had been signatories of the Project for a New American Century (PNAC), a group closely associated with AEI that had promoted a grand strategy of American primacy and pre-emptive warfare since the late 1990s.[15]

Central to PNAC's geopolitical vision of 'benevolent global hegemony' and 'strategic and ideological predominance' was the emphasis of a unipolar world order, with the United States as its undisputed leader and outspoken support for large defense budgets to perpetuate America's technological and military supremacy. This was combined with a stark distrust of international organizations and multilateral institutions for infringing on American sovereignty, and a strong ideological conviction in the moral righteousness and superiority of American exceptionalism and American values of freedom, liberty, and democracy.[16] This neoconservative vision of American primacy, and in particular the strategic emphasis to act unilaterally and pre-emptively when national security seemed threatened, provided a key intellectual foundation of the 'Bush Doctrine' and the 2003 invasion of Iraq.[17]

Under Obama, AEI continued to promote American primacy, including a militarized, interventionist foreign policy. This was despite the heavy criticism the financially and militarily costly Iraq and Afghanistan Wars had produced on the political stage, in academic circles, and in the American media against this neo-imperial vision of American power. Politically, however, the contestation of American primacy was not confined to the liberal end of the spectrum. Under Obama, a growing split manifested on the American right concerning the preferred role and position of the United States in world politics, resulting in diverging grand strategy discourses between neoconservatives, nationalist-conservative populists, and libertarians.[18]

Here, the conservative Tea Party movement which gained prominence after 2009 with a strong ideological platform of limited government, general tax cuts, and fiscal austerity, came into direct conflict with the political demands of establishment conservatives for continued large-scale defense budgets of the kind that were introduced after 9/11.[19] In the decade following the 2001 terror attacks, US military spending had been increased by 50 percent, adjusted for inflation.[20] The budget hawks of the Tea Party and the libertarian Cato Institute thus moved in opposition to GOP defense hawks and neoconservative think tanks such as AEI. This political confrontation resulted in competing expert visions of primacy and restraint, where conservative think tanks formulated fundamentally contrary policy recommendations for national security and American leadership in global affairs in order to square financial resources, political ambitions, and their underlying identity constructions.

In 2012, for example, AEI published a policy brief arguing against mandatory defense budget cuts, to be implemented as a result of the 2011 Budget Control Act (BCA).[21] Known as 'sequestration,' these across-the-board cuts in projected federal discretionary spending would amount to US$1.2 trillion over ten years, in the period of 2013–2021, distributed evenly between defense and non-defense related expenditures.[22] This would mean a reduction of US$487 billion from the US defense budget for the envisioned period.[23] In addition to cuts already implemented through the 2011 BCA, sequestration would ultimately result in fiscal reductions for national defense of almost US$1 trillion compared to original estimates. These automatic cuts were ultimately put into effect in late 2012 after the failure of the Congressional Joint Select Committee on Deficit Reduction to find a political compromise between Democrats and Republicans on fiscal spending reduction. Sequestration would thus occupy center stage in the political debate on grand strategy, national security, and defense policy matters in Washington.[24]

To neoconservatives, the political practice of federal defense spending was directly related to sustaining a grand strategy vision of American primacy and the ability to 'maintain a military capable of keeping the great powers of the world at peace.' The discourse of primacy thus linked the identity construct of American indispensability to a material reality of defense expenditures exceeding US$700 billion annually.[25] Here, AEI identified a continuity of American hegemony 'from the Cold War to the post-9/11 world' and a rationale of maintaining a liberal world order that directly matched the identical correlation of US military supremacy and world peace constructed in popular and formal grand strategy discourses of hegemony, from the 'national security cinema' to *Foreign Affairs*. Primacy, however, also constituted a mainstream conservative consensus on national security and geopolitics, as a joint paper by AEI, the Heritage Foundation, and the Foreign Policy Initiative (FPI) documented, titled: *Defending Defense: Defense Spending, the Super Committee and the Price of Greatness*.[26] The report, which strictly opposed defense budget cuts, concluded with a quote from Winston Churchill: 'The people of the United States cannot escape world responsibility.'[27] Here again, national willpower, resolve, and determination were singled out as the most important and supposedly endangered resource of American grand strategy.

Any deviation from a grand strategy of American hegemony, even a modest reduction in America's global military posture, such as sequestration implied in practice, was thus to be discredited ideationally through the stigma of isolationism, and cast as the dangerous and irresponsible disengagement of the United States from world affairs. The ideologically motivated continued re-imagination and invocation of World War II and the Cold War also applied to the threat perception of China's rise as destabilizing the Asia-Pacific.[28] Here, China was cast as potential successor to Nazi Germany, Imperial Japan, and the Soviet Union; a revisionist, authoritarian power that could seek to establish regional hegemony and upset the established international order promoted by Western democracies. In fact, in the eyes of AEI this struggle between the United States and China for mastery of the Asia-Pacific region was already underway.[29] In Asia, AEI had the United States subsequently increase and strengthen its military presence on all levels.[30]

Checking and deterring a rising China provided a main rationale for AEI's fiscal policy recommendations for continued substantial investments in US defense capabilities, including increased research and development (R&D) expenditures for future weapons systems.[31] Overall, containment of China as America's prime strategic rival had become integral to the neoconservatives' primacy discourse.[32] An alternative grand strategy of offshore balancing, as advocated by the rival libertarian Cato Institute and supported by neorealist IR scholars like Walt, Mearsheimer, or Posen, was accordingly discarded by AEI, because it would 'undercut deterrence' of potential adversaries and undermine the confidence of America's alliance partners in the reliability of the United States to come to their defense.[33]

Under Obama, however, calls for a grand strategy of restraint and offshore balancing were no longer limited to an academic debate among IR scholars, but found support among prominent Republican politicians, such as Kentucky Senator Rand Paul.[34] In February 2013, for example, Paul gave a foreign policy speech at the Heritage Foundation in which he declared that 'a more restrained foreign policy is the true conservative foreign policy, as it includes two basic tenets of true conservatism: respect for the Constitution, and fiscal discipline.'[35]

The political scientist Walter Russell Mead has described foreign policy views in the Tea Party as dominated by two strands of populist sentiment.[36] The first was a unilateral Jacksonianism that combined a firm belief in the singularity of American exceptionalism with skepticism toward the continued role of the United States as sole guarantor of a liberal world order. As demonstrated in Chapter 3, this popular view found expression in multiple conservative bestsellers such as *After America*, *Trickle Down Tyranny*, or *Screwed!* that laid out this populist vision of nationalist-isolationist exceptionalism. The second strand, Mead defined as Jeffersonian neo-isolationism, which sought to minimize the use of American military power abroad and focus on domestic issues, economic growth, and fiscal prudence, the strand most closely associated with libertarian conservatives.

This deviant, conservative elite discourse of 'non-interventionism' was promoted in particular by libertarians like Paul and prominent Tea Party members, such as Texas Senator Ted Cruz.[37] Both strands of conservative populism, then, Jacksonian nationalism and Jeffersonian neo-isolationism, were highly critical of 'liberal internationalism' and challenged the Washington consensus supported by neoconservatives and liberals.[38] Against this challenge, the Washington establishment repeatedly invoked the stigma of isolationism to discredit ideas of restraint and ideologically reconfirm the bipartisan consensus on hegemony, based on the supposed 'lessons of history.'[39]

In an op-ed article for *The Washington Post* in April 2013, for example, former Senators Joe Lieberman, a Democrat, and John Kyl, a Republican, stated: 'We must not wait for another catastrophe to persuade us of the continuing importance of American internationalism.[40] When a Pew research poll in 2013 found that 52 percent of Americans agreed that 'the U.S. should mind its own business internationally and let other countries get along the best they can on their own,' the historian Bill Keller explained in *The New York Times* that this 50-year high of 'isolationism' indicated not just an aversion to war, but 'a broader reluctance to engage, to assert responsibility, to commit.'[41] The Washington consensus on hegemony thus also represented a deeply embedded, widespread, and powerful emotive linking of restraint with isolationism. This stigmatization of restraint as negative, timid, or amoral isolationism by think tanks like AEI, or leading media outlets like *The Washington Post* or *The New York Times*, attempted to narrow the spectrum of acceptable expert and public opinion on grand strategy, resulting in a political debate that largely revolved around the better management of American primacy.

Cato in turn attempted to de-couple this discursive linkage, devoting an entire website to the issue of differentiating 'non-interventionism' from 'isolationism,' explaining that 'interventionists brand their opponents as isolationists to delegitimize them and to stifle debate.'[42] While 'leadership' and its assorted discursive tropes represented an intertextual and ideological fixture in the establishment's view, elevating it to the status of a faithful mantra, 'isolationism' was the nemesis of this idea, the ultimate, unthinkable taboo of US foreign policy to be avoided at all cost. In contrast to this elite insider's view, then, Cato acted in resistance to the hegemonic discourse, declaring that a foreign policy of restraint was 'particularly appropriate in the modern era as threats to the United States have waned, and as the high costs and dubious benefits of a hyperactive, interventionist foreign policy are glaringly apparent.'[43]

The attempt to sideline or discredit the 'isolationist' ideas of the libertarian Cato Institute and realists like Walt or Mearsheimer, at the same time, reveals how proponents of primacy within the US foreign policy establishment viewed domestic critics, and not foreign enemies or geostrategic rivals, as the more serious threat to US national security. According to Kagan, American world leadership and global hegemony were a question of national willpower; unless Americans could be convinced domestically of the virtues of US leadership, the international order was likely to disintegrate further.[44] Political proponents of hegemony frequently invoked a US-centric narrative of world history and IR, emphasizing American victories in World War II and the Cold War, which had not only made the world 'safe for democracy,' but also supposedly created a global system of peace and prosperity that could not operate without US military protection.[45]

The libertarians at Cato, on the other hand, drew historical lessons from more recent events: US failure in Iraq and Afghanistan. Here, the immense drain on financial and military resources these interventions had produced for the United States, and the failure to establish lasting democratic transformation and regional stability, were seen as a cautionary tale about the dangers of 'imperial overstretch' and the folly of over-committing America abroad. Considering individual policy issues, Cato accordingly translated a vision of restraint into concrete plans for changing rather than perpetuating the established national security design of the United States. On the 'pivot to Asia,' for example, directly contrasting policy recommendations made by AEI, Cato explained that 'America ought to pivot home,' and 'lessen and ultimately remove the forward-deployed U.S. military presence in the region, helping establish more powerful national militaries in like-minded states.'[46] The President should therefore encourage 'Asian nations to work together on security issues without the United States leading the way.'[47]

Considering sequestration, Cato likewise recommended a policy course that contradicted primacy, outlining cuts of more than US$1.2 trillion over ten years.[48] These were presented not only as unproblematic, but indeed favorable to the United States. However, far from merely trimming the defense budget for fiscal reasons, Cato proposed a fundamental change in grand strategy thinking that would maintain US national security at far less cost to the American taxpayer. 'The United States confuses what it wants from its military, which is global primacy or hegemony, with what it needs, which is safety. We can defend ourselves with far more restrained military objectives, at far less cost . . . .'[49] A re-imagination of America's world political role and geopolitical identity was thus directly translated into a radically different political-military and fiscal practice. A change to a grand strategy of restraint and offshore balancing would, for example, entail a substantial downsizing of US military capabilities on all levels and termination of US overseas deployments and basing arrangements. While such measures were viewed as an unacceptable and irresponsible risk to national security in a context of hegemony, for Cato, sequestration presented the opportunity to finally reorient and refocus the role and position of the United States while 'avoiding needless military conflict and protecting our prosperity.'

REBALANCING HEGEMONY – THE ASIAN PIVOT, THE OBAMA ADMINISTRATION, AND THE BIPARTISAN CONSENSUS ON AMERICAN LEADERSHIP

Both AEI and Cato criticized the grand strategy of the Democratic Obama administration, yet for diametrically opposed reasons. To the neoconservative primacists at AEI, the grand strategy of Obama was one of retrenchment and withdrawal, both in the Middle East and Asia, where the pivot was seen as mere rhetoric, not substance.[50] To Cato, Obama pursued a grand strategy of hegemony on the cheap. Here, Obama appeared neither fully committed to American primacy, nor was he changing to an altogether alternative course of restraint and off-shore balancing. In Asia, this grand strategy in-between had resulted in an attempt to simultaneously contain and engage China; a policy Cato succinctly referred to as 'congagement.'[51]

While AEI and Cato stood politically and ideologically close to the oppositional Republican Party, the think tanks belonging to the centrist spectrum in turn either carefully stressed bipartisan neutrality, or were openly sympathetic to the Obama administration. Similar to the close relationship between AEI and the George W. Bush Administration, the left-of-center-leaning Brookings Institution, for example, enjoyed close links to both the Clinton and Obama administrations. Brookings is con-sidered to be one of the most prestigious and influential think tanks in Washington DC.[52] The president of Brookings, Strobe Talbott, served as Deputy Secretary of State under President Bill Clinton. Susan Rice, who served as Permanent Representative to the UN, and from July 2013 on as Obama's National Security Advisor, worked at Brookings as a senior fellow in foreign policy from 2002 to 2009. However, Brookings also counted the leading neoconservative Robert Kagan among its senior fellows, underlining its bipartisan credentials.

Brookings' centrist position did not demonstrate the clear ideo-logical neoconservative or libertarian preferences for all-out primacy or restraint, but rather projected a bipartisan mainstream vision of American grand strategy, anchored in the well-established imagination of America's essential global leadership, its responsibility for maintain-ing a liberal international order, and the central importance of engaging US allies and partners politically, economically, and militarily.[53] Within this discourse of hegemonic engagement, policy recommendations on rebalancing to Asia, or cutting the defense budget, were formulated that were not intended to fundamentally alter the national security design of the United States.

On sequestration, for example, Brookings occupied a middle ground. In early 2013, the think tank published a paper, where instead of accept-ing or opposing sequestration outright, it argued for modest defense cuts of US$200 billion over ten years.[54] An essential role of the US military for global deterrence and intervention was centrally linked by

Brookings to the ability to carry out two major wars simultaneously.[55] Full sequestration, however, Brookings assessed as 'unwise,' 'excessive and ill-advised,' curtailing the capability of the United States for global power projection and armed intervention, limiting its armed forces to conduct only one major ground combat operation.[56] This would result in 'dramatic changes in America's basic strategic approach to the world.'[57]

On the Asian pivot, Brookings concluded that Obama had struck a careful balance between 'diplomatic engagement' and 'military off-shore balancing,' one however that did not negate America's leadership role or alliance responsibility, as neorealists or the libertarians at Cato demanded. Interestingly, Brookings thus alluded to the competing impulses of the Obama Doctrine, between liberal ideology and exceptionalist identity on the one side and practical restraint and realist considerations on the other side: 'What is novel about Obama's version of offshore balancing is its moral dimension, which centers on America's exceptionalism—including its respect for human rights—rather than just its hegemony.'[58] The Asian pivot, then, represented yet another expression of the hybridity of grand strategy discourse under Obama that simultaneously incorporated elements of hegemony, engagement, and restraint.[59]

This discursive multiplicity had frequently led to charges that Obama was missing a grand strategy altogether.[60] Indeed, as Richard Betts from CFR argued, the Obama administration did not really have a 'grand strategy in the usual sense of the term. . . .'[61] This expert assessment that Obama was largely doing the 'right thing,' but did not offer a clearly defined or articulated strategic vision, represented yet another commonplace among centrist think tanks. Indeed, the overall variation in ideational representations and policy recommendations among these mainstream adherents to the hegemony consensus was fairly low. CSIS, for example, ultimately constructed a grand strategy discourse that put somewhat greater emphasis on military means than the Brookings Institution, while reconfirming a geopolitical vision of hegemonic engagement. In response to the perceived challenge by China, in particular its development of military technologies that could potentially hinder American access to and movement within the Asia-Pacific region, labeled 'A2/AD,' the United States should strengthen its position through a combination of diplomatic engagement, military rebalancing, and increased alliance cooperation: 'The overall trend should be toward more jointness, integration, collaboration, and presence across the region.'[62] An alternative grand strategy of offshore balancing for the region was in contrast characterized as 'ahistorical and counterproductive.'[63]

In 2012, CSIS was asked by the DoD to 'commission an independent assessment of U.S. force posture in Asia' in compliance with Section 346 of the 2012 National Defense Authorization Act.[64] This extensive report, directly addressed to then Secretary of Defense Leon Panetta, not only demonstrated the prominent role of external policy advice and research for the formulation of US national security policy, but it also represented an important document in American grand strategy discourse, again reconfirming the significance of an established bipartisan Washington consensus on the global leadership role of the United States between intellectual expertise and policymaking. In the report, CSIS concluded that:

> America sustained a remarkably consistent defense policy for fifty years of the Cold War because our national leaders at the outset established a durable consensus on national challenges and strategic objectives. We now need a comparable framework for the next thirty years in Asia.[65]

Against this continuity of conventional wisdom, the discursive nuances between the left-of-center Brookings and the right-of-center CSIS were largely cosmetic in nature.

How blurred the lines between the formally independent expertise of think tank research and the practical discourse of policymaking could be, was shown when an article in *The Boston Globe* reported in 2013 how a speech by Secretary of Defense Chuck Hagel at an Asian security summit in Singapore had actually been drafted by security experts of CSIS, rather than by Hagel's own Pentagon staff.[66] Ernest Z. Bower, one of the CSIS experts identified as involved in preparing Hagel's Singapore speech, later published an article on the CSIS website, titled 'Engagement in the Indo-Pacific: The Pentagon Leads by Example.' Here, Bower applauded the Secretary and the Pentagon for taking the lead in the administration's Asia strategy, highlighting the very same speech he had apparently helped to write: 'Hagel took engagement with ASEAN to a new level during his June speech at the Shangri La Dialogue in Singapore . . . .'[67] The episode demonstrates how the dominant consensus on grand strategy was reinforced through the intertextual and intellectual exchange between policy circles and research experts, and how it operated through an elite network of active and former government officials, military officers, defense contractors, security experts, and geopolitical analysts, all concentrated in Washington DC with frequent intersections that were both ideological and professional in nature.

This prevalent mainstream consensus was somewhat modified however by another integral member of the foreign policy establishment, the centrist CFR.[68] CFR is a highly influential and prestigious institution in American public policy discourse, publishing the prominent *Foreign Affairs* journal and counting senior politicians, former presidents, CIA directors, Secretaries of State and Defense, as well as high-profile bankers, lawyers, professors, and senior media figures among its members.[69] Unlike other think tanks, CFR officially takes no institutional positions on matters of policy, but aims to serve as an independent source for information and intellectual exchange. CFR, like CSIS and Brookings, essentially promoted a bipartisan grand strategy vision of liberal hegemony, where the United States exercised its global leadership role through a broad cooperative network of political, economic, and military engagement in a rule-based international order.[70] This cooperative vision of American grand strategy nonetheless clearly represented the United States at the center and on top of the international system. As Richard Haass, the president of CFR explained, 'the United States stands first among unequals.'[71] At the same time, Haass connected primacy and an increased diplomatic, economic, and military engagement in Asia, with a new focus on restraint, ending 'wars of choice' and 'wholesale efforts to remake societies like the invasion of Iraq in 2003 and the surge in Afghanistan in 2009.'[72] Instead, the United States was supposed to focus on its domestic renewal, investing more in public education, improving its infrastructure, and further reforming healthcare, following a doctrine of 'restoration.'[73] Haass essentially spelled out a geopolitical vision of simultaneous hegemonic engagement and restraint that President Obama and the country should pursue.

Yet in apparently following such a multidimensional course of action, Obama at the same time provoked charges of missing a clear-cut geopolitical vision in foreign policy and national security from conservative and libertarian think tanks, as well as from prominent academics, and even scholars associated with such centrist organizations as Brookings or CFR itself.[74] Ultimately, the expert argument of restraint and domestic renewal ill fitted with an established mainstream notion of global leadership and historic continuity that underwrote the Washington consensus on grand strategy.[75]

A NEW WAY FORWARD? A PROGRESSIVE GRAND STRATEGY OF SUSTAINABLE SECURITY

The idea of renewing America's international standing by restoring the domestic base of its economic prosperity unified libertarian, neoconservative, centrist, and progressive policy experts. In fact, the very idea of Congressional sequestration had been born out of concern over the future fiscal sustainability of the United States, given the vast increase in federal debt due to Obama's economic stimulus packages and healthcare reform program. Arguments for fiscal sustainability and economic restoration, however, did not necessarily result in political demands for geopolitical retrenchment and greater restraint. On the progressive end of the political spectrum, the Center for American Progress (CAP) was one of the most prominent proponents for holistically reorienting US national security policy, yet it also called for an expansion of American engagement.

CAP was founded in 2003 by John Podesta, former chief of staff to President Clinton, with a liberal policy agenda to improve 'the lives of Americans through progressive ideas and action.' Politically, the think tank was clearly aligned with the Democratic Party.[76] Departing from the usual national security-centric perspective of defense, existential threats, and national interests, CAP contributed a genuinely innovative element to the policy discourse of grand strategy by stressing 'sustainability' as an essential component of any overarching American security design.[77] The 'project for sustainable security' at CAP thus aimed to rethink national security by linking it to 'human security' and 'collective security,' interconnecting diplomacy, defense, and development in a global grand strategy vision that stressed the interdependence of American security with the security of foreign states and individuals.[78]

Instead of focusing almost exclusively on American leadership and military power, CAP's grand strategy vision of sustainability stressed multilateral responsibility and international cooperation to jointly manage 'global transnational threats.[79] This included policy recommendations for increased development aid, an institutionalized government capacity for the promotion of global poverty reduction and economic growth, a strengthening of US alliances, and the 'reform and creation of strong international institutions.'[80] Similar to the restraint argument made by Cato or CFR, the narrative of ill-fated US attempts in nation-building in Iraq and Afghanistan served as a central argument for changing the established national security paradigm. Rather than a reorientation and limitation toward restraint and offshore balancing, however, CAP envisioned a strengthening and expanding of the US engagement in world politics, as part of a global network for crisis prevention, human development, and conflict resolution.

Within the sustainability discourse, the geopolitical identity of the United States continued to be represented through the ideational paradigm of global leadership; the exclusivity, singularity, and superiority of the United States and its material power however were stressed far less prominently than with the conservative or centrist think tanks. Instead, this progressive vision of grand strategy highlighted global interconnectedness as a central feature of geopolitics in the twenty-first century. Next to Cato's libertarian ideas for offshore balancing, the progressive vision of sustainable security promoted by CAP envisioned the most holistic policy change to American grand strategy. In US national security policy, CAP translated this reformulated grand strategy into policy recommendations for further cuts to the defense budget and military equipment.[81] Where sequestration envisioned cuts of US$487 billion from originally projected federal spending, a 2012 report by CAP pointed out that, despite sequestration, in 2017 'the Pentagon's base budget will be larger than it is today and larger, in real terms, than it was on average during the Cold War.'[82]

This was characterized as unfounded overinvestment in military resources and imbalance toward other political priorities: 'We face no existential threats abroad at a time when we are long overdue for investment at home.'[83] Similarly, on the Asian pivot, CAP countered conservative assessments of China as challenging US hegemony, and emphasized diplomatic engagement and economic cooperation over the military dimension of the American rebalancing to Asia. As John Podesta remarked in 2012, in a speech at the Sasakawa Peace Foundation in Japan: 'The rise of one country need not come at the expense of another, and ... power does not need to be a zero-sum game.'[84]

Sustainable security thus represented a direct repudiation of neo-realist and neoconservative assessments of IR and geopolitics. As such, it negated neoconservative primacy as well as realist calls for offshore balancing. Intertextually, this progressive expert discourse primarily connected with popular notions of engagement, as forwarded by Brzezinski and Zakaria, which had likewise stressed the cooperative vision of American grand strategy in a global, multipolar network system. The most obvious link between this policy expertise and IR research was in the emphasis of cooperative and human security and the theoretical assumptions of liberal institutionalism.[85] A 2008 report by CAP stated, for example:

> Offered up by academia and Washington's think tanks, the concepts of 'soft power,' 'integrated power,' and 'smart power' bear in common the counsel that America must recalibrate its foreign policy to rely less on military power and more on other tools that can foster change and enhance our security.[86]

A second, more surprising discursive connection linked this liberal-progressive agenda for policy change to the very center of American military power and global hegemony. Written in the Pentagon, but published by the liberal Woodrow Wilson Center, the 2011 'Mr. Y' article, titled 'A National Strategic Narrative,' provided an articulation of the sustainability argument that was directly encouraged by then Chairman of the Joint Chiefs, Admiral Michael Mullen.[87]

The article, later revealed as the work of US Navy Captain Wayne Porter and USMC Colonel Mark 'Puck' Mykleby, argued that the United States needed to change its prevailing grand strategy discourse, and to develop a new national narrative that no longer overemphasized military power, and hyped a myriad of existential security threats endangering the country, but incorporated education, energy, and the environment as vital issues of the national interest in a holistic and comprehensive policy agenda of 'national security and prosperity.' The text stated: 'we want to become the strongest competitor and most influential player in a deeply inter-connected global system, which requires that we invest less in defense and more in sustainable prosperity and the tools of effective global engagement.'[88] Ideationally, Americans should not see themselves as 'the automatic leader of any bloc of nations,' but should stress the universalism of the values that underwrote American exceptionalism, reformulating American geopolitical identity toward a more cooperative and less hegemonic vision, again echoing a scenario of 'post American' geopolitics.[89]

Remarkably, this discursive intervention was undertaken by two officers that were working as special strategic assistants to the Chairman of the Joint Chiefs of Staff (CJCS), the highest echelon of the American military hierarchy. Under Obama, then, the idea of strategic sustainability had taken hold among the US military establishment, in particular in connection with the debate over America's fiscal deficit. As

Admiral Mullen, for example, had stated, the greatest threat to US national security was 'unsustainable debt.'[90] Mr Y.'s article then was an attempt to think outside-the-box of conventional wisdom from within the national security state, and to alter the threat-fixated grand strategy discourse in Washington DC, by focusing on several issues that were seen as vital concerns for the longterm prosperity of the country, but which could not be addressed by military means.

In terms of practical policy impact, the sustainability discourse and progressive expert ideas were in particular reflected in the *Quadrennial Diplomatic and Development Review* under Secretary Clinton, a process that was officially endorsed by CAP.[91] Clinton's Director of Policy Planning, Anne-Marie Slaughter, also had written the preface for the Mr. Y article, further stressing the significance of the sustainability leitmotif under the Obama administration. However, sustainability and cooperative security did not displace the central paradigm of hegemony, military supremacy, and existential threat from the center of national security discourse, and engagement as a grand strategy vision of global collective partnership did not supplant the key geopolitical imagination of American leadership and indispensability. As with offshore balancing and restraint, a vision of sustainable security remained too far outside the entrenched mainstream consensus on grand strategy to be of greater political significance and practical impact.

THE ROTATING DOOR: CNAS AND GRAND STRATEGY EXPERTISE IN THE OBAMA ADMINISTRATION

Part of the policy impact of think tanks stems from the fact that their individual experts have spent time as part of a presidential administration, offering valuable personal connections and practical experience, or will re-enter government at a later point, which allows them to transfer their knowledge and research expertise into their respective government functions. This 'rotating door' principle then directly connects the spheres of government and policy expertise, reinforcing intertextual links of converging discourses through the practical intersection of professional career paths in the national security establishment.

CNAS has enjoyed a particularly close connection to the Obama administration in this regard.[92] Several leading members of this think tank have occupied high-ranking policy positions for diplomacy and defense during Obama's first term in particular. The two co-founders of CNAS, for example, were Michèle Flournoy, who served as Under

Secretary of Defense for Policy, and Kurt Campbell, who as Assistant Secretary of State for East Asian and Pacific Affairs was one the leading architects behind Obama's 'pivot' of strategically rebalancing the United States to the Asia-Pacific region.[93] Frequently media reports remarked on the think tank's influential position on policymaking.[94] According to *The Washington Post*, for example: 'When CNAS talks, people listen.'[95] However, the closeness of CNAS to the military-industrial complex also provoked criticism and raised doubts over the independence and impartiality of its research. As the journalist Nathan Hodge commented: 'Institutions like CNAS are also heavily funded by major weapons manufacturers and Pentagon contractors, creating potential conflicts of interest rarely disclosed in the media.'[96]

The self-stated mission of CNAS was to 'develop strong, pragmatic and principled national security and defense policies that promote and protect American interests and values.'[97] Officially, a nonpartisan, independent think tank, the organization was described as 'a haven for hawkish Democrats,' and was particularly known for its outspoken support for an expansive military strategy of COIN in Afghanistan, supporting Gates and Clinton, and Generals David Petraeus and Stanley McChrystal against proponents of a more limited course of CT, as, for example, advocated by Vice-President Joe Biden.[98] Commenting on CNAS's role in shaping national security policy, Kelley Beaucar Vlahos wrote in *The American Conservative*: 'COIN today is the realm of CNAS, as if Frederick Kagan and AEI had never existed.'[99]

This observation again testifies to the intertextual crossover that linked Republicans and Democrats, conservative and centrist think tanks in supporting the militarized Washington consensus on hegemony. They 'all drank the Kool-Aid,' in the words of Andrew Bacevich.[100] Unlike the deviant elite voices of Cato and partially CAP, CNAS did not challenge conventional wisdom but was one of its leading proponents. Relating the elevated political position CNAS occupied in the Obama administration to the institution's views on national security and geopolitics makes this discursive link a further indicator of how in both ideational and practical terms the Washington establishment favored continuity over change, visions of leadership over ideas of restraint, and confidence in military power over reliance on diplomacy.

On grand strategy, CNAS accordingly formulated a vision of hegemonic engagement that focused on improving the effectiveness of US military power, but never questioned its indispensability for maintaining a liberal world order. In 2008, just before the presidential

election that would see Barack Obama defeat his Republican opponent John McCain, CNAS published a report, titled *Finding Our Way:
Debating American Grand Strategy*.[101] This text presented itself as a
repudiation of neoconservative primacy and pre-emptive warfare
and criticized the absence of a clear strategic vision in Washington
under George W. Bush. The report's authors, Shawn Brimley
and Michèle Flournoy, argued that the absence of grand strategy
under Bush had been reflected in the mismanagement of the Iraq
War.[102]

The report spelled out four distinctive grand strategy alternatives:
'Isolationism or restraint, selective engagement, cooperative security,
and primacy.'[103] Following the line of argumentation established by
mainstream conservative and centrist think tanks, 'isolationism' was
equated with offshore balancing and restraint, and the realist school
of IR, referring to Layne and Posen in particular.[104] Selective engagement was presented as 'hybrid strategy' that combined a 'forward posture' in security matters with general support for liberal goals of 'free
markets, human rights, and international openness.'[105] Cooperative
security was mainly characterized as a vision of liberal institutionalism,
naming Ikenberry as one of its main proponents.[106] Finally, primacy
and hegemony were used interchangeably to describe a grand strategy
that sought to perpetuate the 'unipolar moment' and ensure 'continued
global stability,' as endorsed for example by AEI and Kagan.[107]

CNAS itself proposed a grand strategy of 'sustainment' for the new
administration. This strategic 'long-term vision' essentially reproduced
the dominant establishment discourse of liberal hegemony, where the
United States, beyond defending its own homeland, promoted free trade,
guaranteed access to the 'global commons' of sea, air, and cyberspace,
maintained a global network of partnerships, alliances, and forwardly
deployed bases, and supported great power peace through its ability to
militarily dominate potential rivals.[108] While CNAS warned against the
dangers of overextension and exhaustion which resulted from a geopolitical vision of American primacy, it equally distanced itself from a view
of restraint, offshore balancing, or isolationism, where the United Sates
defined its national security simply along the lines of self-defense. In
terms of cooperative engagement, alliances and partnerships were seen
as a vital instrument of American power and influence in the world, but
not as a collective body of global governance that could ever replace
or supplant American leadership. CNAS emphasized that the United
States had to lead, but could not lead without support.[109]

The ultimate necessity of American world leadership was also the common thread running through the 2012 follow-up report named *America's Path: Grand Strategy for the Next Administration*.[110] Here, the central ideational paradigm of American hegemony extended far beyond the neoconservative experts' vision of primacy, and shaped policy ideas from 'selective engagement,' to 'network centrality,' and 'soft primacy.'[111] This convergence of geopolitical identity largely reduced the character of these grand strategies to mere variations of hegemony, instead of comprehensive alternatives for understanding America's role in the world. As CNAS itself remarked 'there is little that is fundamentally new in a strategy emphasizing the very theme and currents that lie deep within American history and the bipartisan exercise of statecraft over many decades.'[112]

This expert consensus only provided a limited bandwidth of opinion on American grand strategy alternatives, predominantly confirming American indispensability as a practical guide to orient security and defense policy. In October 2015, for example, AEI, Heritage, CNAS, and CSBA together with the libertarian Cato Institute were invited to testify on the topic of 'Alternative Approaches to Defense Strategy and Force Structure' before the US Senate Armed Services Committee. The statements and proposals by the invited think tanks again underlined how the grand strategy debate in Washington was a remarkably limited elite exchange over the better management of American hegemony and its military instruments.

The statement by Heritage's Senior Research Fellow for Defense Programs, Dakota Wood, for example, illustrated how American primacy and the ability to fight several conflicts simultaneously remained a *conditio sine quo non* for Washington's strategic community. Heritage argued for a capability standard of fighting a major war and sustaining 'large-scale commitments elsewhere' to size US forces, contrasting this with AEI, which argued for a three-theater standard, while the Brookings Institution supported a 1+2 construct, the ability to fight one large war and two smaller contingencies.[113] CNAS in turn urged Congress to recover America's 'military-technical advantage' as a 'foundational element of American defense strategy.'[114] According to CSBA, the United States should remain focused on 'preventing the rise of a hostile hegemonic power in the Far East.'[115] A notable exemption to this reconstitution of the hegemony discourse was again the Cato Institute. According to Cato, the role of the US military as the 'world's global constabulary' should end.[116]

In practical terms, the overwhelming expert consensus on liberal hegemony and American indispensability thus translated into political support for an expansive and offensive global security posture and military apparatus. It was in particular the reputation for pragmatism and technocratic expertise that had built the national security credentials of a think tank like CNAS and which had raised its political profile under the Obama administration.[117] This corresponded with many expert assessments of President Obama as pursuing an un-ideological, pragmatic course in foreign affairs, where grand visions were eschewed in exchange for workable solutions.[118] However, this alleged pragmatism nonetheless revolved around an item of faith in Washington's strategic community – the mantra of American indispensability.

CONCLUSION

Overall, the strategic community of think tanks in Washington DC acted less as an open forum for the exchange of competing ideas and more as an homogenous military-intellectual-complex, co-producing the geopolitical imagination of hegemony as expert opinion and common-sense knowledge. In a similar vein, the military-entertainment industry liaison regularly produced this vision as a product of popular culture and common-sense understandings.[119] Under Obama, the expert discourse on grand strategy then largely took place within a black box of limited imagination and acceptable mainstream opinion. Policy debates over US national security revolved around a sacrosanct imagination of American military superiority, global leadership, and exceptionalist indispensability.

It was the illusion of a debate, rather than an actual debate, that took place among the various national security experts. The think tanks' policy advice and research output was marked by constant repetition of self-reinforcing truisms. Beyond a neutral assessment of interests, means, and ends, American grand strategy constituted a worldview, or *weltanschauung*, where key discursive elements were not derived from empirical, scientific analysis, but merely imposed a priori as normative convictions of truth. The limits of imagination were delineated by the unthinkability of isolationism, resulting in most experts' negation of restraint. It seems questionable, indeed improbable, that fundamental change in American grand strategy under Obama could have been possible, when virtually all policy options discussed by the supposedly independent network of strate-

gic analysts operated within the same ideational and practical parameters of discourse.

The conventional wisdom that represented American leadership,
military supremacy, and global power projection as unshakable pillars
of US national security policy remained largely unchallenged inside the
Washington Beltway. The one true outlier to this expert consensus was
the libertarian Cato Institute which promoted a distinctive grand strategy alternative of restraint, offshore balancing, and military downsizing. Politically, Cato's vision was endorsed in particular by conservative
populists and libertarians, who themselves however were considered to
exist at the fringes of acceptable opinion on US foreign policy.

From the neoconservative American Enterprise Institute, to the various centrist and bipartisan think tanks, to the progressive CAP, restraint
was denounced as morally reprehensible isolationism. Cato's argument
for restraint thus constituted an attack on the hegemonic discourse
perpetuated by the elite establishment that was akin to heresy in its
questioning of the wisdom of American primacy. As such, the strategic
community was another powerful voice in defense of the status quo of
America's role in the world and responsible for perpetuating a militarized discourse and practice of US foreign policy.

NOTES

1. Carpenter, 'Delusions of Indispensability.'
2. Ó Tuathail and Agnew, 'Geopolitics and Discourse,' p. 193.
3. Stone, Capturing the Political Imagination, p. 3.
4. Brimley and Flournoy, 'Introduction,' p. 6.
5. For an in-depth analysis of the role of think tanks and policy experts in
   American public policy, see in particular Stone, *Capturing the Political
   Imagination*, Rich, *Think Tanks, Public Policy, and the Politics of Expertise*.
6. McGann, *Think Tanks and Policy Advice in the U.S.*, p. 3.
7. From the *2012 Global Go To Think Tanks Report and Policy Advice*
   (McGann), six think tanks have been selected for analysis, each one
   was considered to be the top-listed think tank in the respective category
   of conservative, libertarian, centrist, and progressive, pertaining to their
   basic political orientation and ideological foundation. In the centrist category there is a further sub-division of center-right, centrist, and center-
   left, see McGann, *Think Tanks and Policy Advice in the U.S.*, pp. 11–13,
   see also, Rich, *Think Tanks, Public Policy, and the Politics of Expertise*,
   pp. 18–20. In addition, CNAS has been selected due to its particular
   high profile under the Obama administration, see, for example, Draezen,

'Obama Dips into Think Tank for Talent,' Lozada, 'Setting Priorities for the Afghan War.'

8. Mazarr, 'The Risks of Ignoring Strategic Insolvency,' Carpenter, 'Delusions of Indispensability.'

9. Croft, *Culture, Crisis and America's War on Terror*, p. 235.

10. The Think Tanks and Civil Societies Program (TTCSP) of the University of Pennsylvania ranks the top 55 think tanks in the United States based on an annual global peer and expert survey of over 1,950 scholars, policymakers, journalists, and regional and subject area experts. The report states: 'The Rankings' primary objective is to recognize some of the world's leading public policy think tanks and highlight the notable contributions these institutions are making to governments and civil societies worldwide.' McGann, *2012 Global Go To Think Tanks Report and Policy Advice*, p. 11.

11. In a study on US force structure in Asia for the Pentagon, the CSIS, for example, concluded that 'the repositioning of forces in the region has strategic consequences that will shape the trajectory of the next three decades,' CSIS, *U.S. Force Posture Strategy in the Asia Pacific Region*, p. 3.

12. Said, *Orientalism* (preface, 2003), p. xvi.

13. These include: John R. Bolton, Under Secretary of State for Arms Control and International Security Affairs (2001–2005) and US Ambassador to the UN (2005–2006); Richard Perle, Chairman of the Defense Policy Board Advisory Committee (2001–2003); Paul Wolfowitz, Deputy Secretary of Defense (2001–2005) and 10th President of the World Bank (2005-2007), and John Yoo, Deputy Assistant Attorney General (2001–2003).

14. AEI, *Annual Report*, p. 12.

15. Kagan and Kristol, 'Statement of Principles', Project for the New American Century.

16. Ibid.

17. Krauthammer, 'The Bush Doctrine,' p. 42.

18. Krauthammer, 'How fractured is the GOP?' Krauthammer, a leading neoconservative intellectual, speaks in this context of a conflict between 'isolationist' and 'internationalist' tendencies in the Republican Party.

19. McGrath, 'The Movement,' DiMaggio, *The Rise of the Tea Party*. While there is some ideological overlap, the Tea Party and libertarian conservatism should not be conflated with each other, see Ball, 'Libertarians Are Not the Tea Party.' Libertarians combine fiscal conservatism, social liberalism, and skepticism toward the national-security state, while about half of Tea Party followers identify with the Christian Right and social conservatism. According to a 2013 survey of the Public Religion Research Institute, only 26 percent of Tea Party followers identified themselves as libertarians, see Ball, 'Libertarians Are Not the Tea Party.'

20. US DoD, Office of the Under Secretary of Defense, *National Defense*

Budget Estimates FY 2016, pp. 250, 265–266. The federal outlays for national defense (in 2009 constant dollars) increased from US$407 billion in 2000 to US$693 billion in 2011, an increase from 2.9 percent to 4.6 percent of US GDP. The National Defense budget function is comprised of DoD military, atomic energy defense activities, and defense-related activities (of other federal agencies).

21. AEI, *Defense Spending 101*.
22. Congressional Budget Office, Estimated Impact of Automatic Budget Enforcement Procedures Specified in the Budget Control Act.
23. US DoD, *Overview – FY 2013 Defense Budget*.
24. Eaglen, 'The Sequester is Here to Stay – Now the Military Needs to Get to Work.' In December 2013, a bipartisan budget deal was struck by House Budget Committee Chairman Paul Ryan (R) and Senate Budget Committee Chairwoman Patty Murray (D) on 'sequester relief,' erasing US$63 billion in across-the-board spending cuts for the federal budget in 2014 and 2015 (US$31.5 billion for the Pentagon), see Bennett, 'Senate OKs Sequester-Relief Budget Plan.' However, overall sequestration levels were kept in place, extended to 2023, see Congressional Budget Office, *Bipartisan Budget Act of 2013*.
25. Ibid.
26. The Foreign Policy Initiative, American Enterprise Institute, and The Heritage Foundation, *Defending Defense*.
27. Ibid., p. 9.
28. Mahnken, *Asia in the Balance*.
29. Ibid.
30. Such measures recommended by AEI included continued development of the 'Conventional Prompt Global Strike system,' consideration of development of a 'submarine-launched conventional ballistic missile,' and fielding of the 'Next-Generation Bomber' to provide a 'flexible, global strike capability.' Furthermore, the United States should consider whether continuing to 'abide by the Intermediate-Range Nuclear Forces Treaty's global ban on the deployment of conventional ballistic and cruise missiles of intermediate range (500–5,500 kilometers)' was in the best interests of the United States, Mahnken, *Asia in the Balance*, p. 16.
31. Mahnken, *Asia in the Balance*.
32. See also, Friedberg, *A Contest for Supremacy*.
33. AEI, *Defense Spending 101*, p. 8.
34. Logan, 'Rand Paul is No Isolationist.'
35. Quoted in Duss, 'The Isolationist are Coming!'
36. Mead, 'The Tea Party in American Foreign Policy,' p. 40.
37. Logan, 'Rand Paul is No Isolationist,' Purple, Ted Cruz's Fourth-Way Foreign Policy.'

38. Donald Trump would formulate a similar challenge by outlining a Republican foreign policy vision of non-interventionism, combining both the Jacksonian and Jeffersonian strands, see Rucker and Costa, 'Trump Questions Need for NATO, Outlines Noninterventionist Foreign Policy.'
39. Lieberman and Kyl, 'The Danger of Repeating the Cycle of American Isolationism.'
40. Ibid.
41. Keller, quoted in Fisher 'Our New Isolationism Just Hit a 50-Year High: Why That Matters.'
42. Cato Institute, 'Isolationism.'
43. Ibid.
44. Kagan, 'Superpowers Don't Get to Retire.'
45. Kagan, *The World America Made*.
46. Logan, *China, America, and the Pivot to Asia*, p. 22.
47. Ibid.
48. Friedman and Preble, *Budgetary Savings from Military Restraint*.
49. Ibid., p. 12.
50. AEI, 'The Pivot to Asia: Rhetoric isn't Enough.'
51. Logan, *China, America, and the Pivot to Asia*, p. 22.
52. Brookings was titled 'Think Tank of the Year 2012' and no. 1 of the top-ranking think tanks of the world in 2012, see McGann, *2012 Global Go To Think Tanks Report and Policy Advice*, p. 41. Established in 1916, it was the 'first private organization devoted to the fact-based study of national public policy issues.' Brookings, 'Brookings Institution History.' Available at http://www.brookings.edu/about/history (last accessed September 14, 2016).
53. Jones, Wright, and Esberg, *Reviving American Leadership*.
54. O'Hanlon, *A Moderate Plan for Additional Defense Cuts*.
55. Ibid., p. 31.
56. Ibid., pp. 30–31.
57. Ibid., p. 31.
58. Jones, Wright, and Esberg, *Reviving American Leadership*, p. 5.
59. Löfflmann, 'The Pivot between Containment, Engagement and Restraint.'
60. As, for example, in the pages of *Foreign Affairs*, see Drezner, 'Does Obama Have a Grand Strategy?'
61. Betts, 'What is Obamas "Grand" Foreign Policy Strategy.'
62. Green, *Rethinking U.S. Military Presence in Asia and the Pacific*, p. 20.
63. Ibid., p. 19.
64. CSIS, *U.S. Force Posture Strategy in the Asia Pacific Region*, p. 3.
65. Ibid., p. 4.
66. Bender, 'Many D.C. Think Tanks Now Players in Partisan Wars,' Hagel, 'Remarks by Secretary Hagel at the IISS Asia Security Summit.'
67. Bower, 'Engagement in the Indo-Pacific.'

68. Founded in 1921 to enhance knowledge about IR following America's involvement in World War 1, the think tank describes its mission as 'dedicated to being a resource for its members, government officials, business executives, journalists, educators and students, civic and religious leaders, and other interested citizens in order to help them better understand the world and the foreign policy choices facing the United States and other countries.' Council on Foreign Relations, 'Mission Statement.'
69. Among its members in 2013 were for example: Madeline Albright, Andrew Bacevich, James Baker, Bill Clinton, Robert Gates, John Mearsheimer, and Fareed Zakaria.
70. This entails, for example: creating or adapting international arrangements to manage the challenges and threats inherent in globalization; negotiating bilateral, regional and global trade, energy and climate pacts; invigorating alliances and partnerships; and dealing with the threats posed by an aggressive North Korea, a dangerous Iran and a failing Pakistan,' quoted in Haass, 'The Restoration Doctrine.'
71. Haass, 'America Can Take a Breather. And It Should.'
72. Ibid.
73. Haass, 'The Restoration Doctrine.'
74. Betts, 'What is Obama's "Grand" Foreign Policy Strategy?'
75. Haass, for example, assesses that neither 'democracy promotion,' nor 'humanitarianism,' 'integration,' or 'counter-terrorism' could provide an adequate label to provide an overarching foreign policy doctrine for the United States, see Haass, 'The Restoration Doctrine.'
76. CAP's president and chief executive officer, for example, Neera Tanden, served as director of domestic policy for the Obama-Biden presidential campaign and as policy director for the Hillary Clinton presidential campaign.
77. CAP, 'About Sustainable Security.'
78. CAP, *Sustainable Security 101*. According to the 1994 UN Development Program, 'human security' focuses on 'the legitimate concerns of ordinary people,' and is concerned with individual safety from threats such as hunger, disease, and repression, collective security addresses the joint management of common security threats, as, for example, in international organizations like the UN and NATO, see Payne, 'Cooperative Security,' pp. 617–623.
79. Mainly terrorism, money laundering, illicit trade, criminal and drug syndicates, and global warming, ibid., p. 1.
80. Ibid., pp. 3–4.
81. Korb, Rothman, and Hoffman, *$100 Billion in Politically Feasible Defense Cuts for a Budget Deal*. The report recommended, for example, the cancellation of the F-35C stealth strike fighter program for the US Navy, and reducing the personnel strength of the US Army to 487,000 and

the USMC to 175,000, below the figures of 490,000 and 189,00 as envisioned by the federal government, and to reduce the number of deployed nuclear weapons from 1,700 to 1,100 by 2022.

82. Ibid., p. 1.
83. Ibid., p. 8.
84. Podesta, 'U.S. Rebalance to Asia: Japan as the Key Partner.'
85. Cooperative security envisions a rethinking of security beyond the realist paradigm of state sovereignty, military power, and national interest, see Payne, 'Cooperative Security.' In addition, the premise of sustainable security also draws from ideas of 'soft power' and 'smart power,' as developed by Joseph Nye in that a comprehensive approach to US foreign policy should go beyond the use of military power to advance American interests in a globalized world, see, for example, Nye Jr., 'The War on Soft Power.'
86. Smith, *In Search of Sustainable Security*, p. 12.
87. Norris, 'The Y Article.' CNN Wire Staff, 'Mullen: Debt is Top National Security Threat.'
88. Mr. Y, 'A National Strategic Narrative,' p. 3.
89. Ibid., p. 4.
90. Quoted in ibid., p. 3.
91. Korb, Duggan, and Conley, *Integrating Security*, p. 1.
92. Although a relatively new think tank operating since 2007, originally with just 30 employees, CNAS is considered one of the top-ranking think tanks in the United States, specifically dealing with issues of national security. Of CNAS's board of advisors in 2008, Flournoy, Campbell, Susan Rice, Richard Danzig, Wendy Sherman, and James Steinberg joined the administration in high-ranking positions for national security, foreign policy, and defense.
93. Mazza, 'Asia's Four Big Questions for Obama's Second Term.' Flournoy was considered as a possible alternative to Chuck Hagel for Secretary of Defense, see Bengali and Gold Tribune, 'Policy Ace Michele Flournoy Could be First Female Defense Chief.'
94. See, for example, Draezen, 'Obama Dips into Think Tank for Talent,' Lozada, 'Setting Priorities for the Afghan War.'
95. Lozada, 'Setting Priorities for the Afghan War.'
96. Hodge, 'The Nation: Who Drives The Think Tanks.'
97. CNAS, 'Mission.'
98. Exum, 'CNAS Policy Brief Afghanistan 2011: Three Scenarios,' Lozada, 'Setting Priorities for the Afghan War,' Bengali and Gold Tribune, 'Policy Ace Michele Flournoy Could be First Female Defense Chief.' On the differing opinions on COIN and CT strategies for Afghanistan in the Obama White House, see also Woodward, *Obama's Wars*, and Mann, *The Obamians*.

99. Beaucar Vlahos, 'One-Sided COIN.'

100. Quoted in ibid.

101. Brimley and Flournoy (eds.), *Finding Our Way*.

102. Brimley and Flournoy, 'Introduction,' p. 5.

103. Brimley, 'Finding Our Way,' p. 17.

104. Ibid.

105. Ibid., p. 18. According to Art: 'it takes neither an isolationist, unilateralist path at one extreme nor a world policeman role on the other,' quoted in ibid.

106. Brimley, 'Finding Our Way,' pp. 18–19.

107. Ibid., p. 19.

108. Brimley and Flournoy, 'Making America Grand Again.'

109. Ibid., p. 148.

110. Fontaine and Lord (eds.), *America's Path: Grand Strategy for the Next Administration*.

111. Ibid.

112. Brimley and Flournoy, 'Making America Grand Again,' p. 138.

113. Wood, 'Testimony before the Senate Armed Services Committee.'

114. Brimley, 'Testimony before the Senate Armed Services Committee.'

115. Krepinevich Jr., 'Statement before the Senate Armed Services Committee on Defense Strategy.'

116. Preble, 'Testimony: U.S. National Security Strategy after Primacy: Resilience, Self-Reliance, and Restraint.'

117. Lozada, 'Setting Priorities for the Afghan War,' Bengali and Gold Tribune, 'Policy Ace Michele Flournoy Could be First Female Defense Chief,' Beaucar Vlahos, 'One-Sided COIN.'

118. Indyk, Lieberthal, and O'Hanlon, *Bending History*, Milne, 'Pragmatism or What?' Betts, 'What is Obama's "Grand" Foreign Policy Strategy,' Drezner, 'Does Obama Have a Grand Strategy?' Singh, *Barack Obama's Post-American Foreign Policy*.

119. Major US weapons manufacturers, such as Boeing, Lockheed Martin, or Raytheon count among the major donors of several influential think tanks investigated here, such as CNAS or CSIS, see Bender, 'Many D.C. Think Tanks Now Players in Partisan Wars,' Preble, 'The Revolving Door, Think Tanks and the MIC.'

Chapter 6

STRATEGIC VISION: NATIONAL SECURITY, DEFENSE POLICY, AND THE GEOPOLITICS OF MILITARY PRE-EMINENCE

The United States is the strongest and greatest nation on earth.

Robert M. Gates[1]

It is a discursive commonplace that the United States possesses outstanding military capabilities and an unmatched ability for global power projection. America's 'awesome military' provides the material foundation for the nation's exceptional status in world politics, and it dominates the thinking on US national security, while allowing US policymakers to project American power and strategic rationales around the globe.[2] The US military's global geopolitical reach – the ability to dominate geographical, outer and cyber space through force and its 'command of the commons' – Posen, for example, defined as an enduring foundation of US hegemony. Brooks saw this military singularity as material confirmation of America's continued exceptionalism under President Obama.[3] As Scheinmann and Cohen observed, 'securing the commons' was indeed an intertextual fixture of the national security dialogue in Washington.[4]

> One of the few points of agreement between President Obama's 2010 *National Security Strategy*, the 2010 *Quadrennial Defense Review*, the neoconservative Project for the New America's Century's 'Rebuilding American Defense' report, various NATO research papers, and numerous think tank publications is that they all emphasize the importance of 'safeguarding the global commons.'

In sustaining a global, militarized hegemony, both ideologically and materially, the political debate in turn was mostly about *how* America should lead, not *if*. In the minds of IR scholars, political commentators, media journalists, film producers, and policymakers, armed might represents a category that separated the United States from the rest of the world. Military power remained perhaps the most obvious and visible expression of American hegemony under Obama: a global icon of US power and American exceptionalism that permeated popular culture, academic analysis, and political discourse alike.

In practical terms, the US DoD acted as key producer of a grand strategy discourse that regularly translated geopolitical imaginations, threat assessments, and strategic narratives into concrete policy outcomes and security practices, from defense policy planning documents to the stationing of US troops and the conducting of military operations.[5] As Mamadouh and Dijkink have remarked, practical geopolitics is 'the domain of policy making and geopolitical reasoning justifying concrete foreign policy actions.'[6] High-level strategic documents published under Obama, such as the *Quadrennial Defense Review* reports or the *Defense Strategic Guidance* (*DSG*) were thus central elements in providing the 'big picture' of national security, both legitimizing and operationalizing American hegemony in the practical realm of defense policymaking. Official statements and media appearances by the Secretary of Defense and the CJCS, the President's 'principal defense policy advisor,' and 'senior military advisor' complemented this discourse from within the center of the national security state and the top level of the US military hierarchy.[7]

Under President Obama, however, several practical issues in defense policymaking and military planning were, at the same time, indicating a careful shift in the conceptualization and operation of American hegemony. Budget sequestration had a lasting impact on the overall size of the US military, while Obama's 'pivot to Asia' shifted its geopolitical and operational focus. This limitation, recalibration, and downsizing challenged a status quo of American primacy and global military supremacy that politicians, policy experts, and military officials had largely taken for granted since the end of the Cold War. A final point in assessing the practical dimension of security and defense was how the US military establishment adapted the thinking of grand strategy through its senior educational institutions, in particular the United States National War College (NWC). Here, grand strategy was taught to train future officers for leadership in the highest positions in the national security establishment, joint military command, and general staff functions.[8] The military's own academic studies complex provided a further important indicator for a momentum of transition and the adaption of strategic thinking. Unlike most think tank policy experts, America's future military leaders were increasingly in anticipation of a post-American world, with the United States no longer at the center, but still heavily engaged and invested in the success of a liberal world order.

Taken together, the various elements of defense policymaking, strategy planning, the development of military doctrine and operational concepts, and professional senior military education suggested a careful reframing of American hegemony in practical discourse under the Obama presidency, putting greater emphasis on cooperative engagement and restraint, while preserving the United States' ability to act with superior military force where it was deemed politically necessary in the pursuit of vital national security interests. The result was that, while still the most visible denominator of global leadership, US military pre-eminence was simultaneously downsized and recalibrated toward more regional prioritization, increased collaboration, greater financial sustainability, and less ambitious geopolitical goals in US national security policy.

US DEFENSE POLICY PLANNING AND AMERICAN LEADERSHIP IN A MULTIPOLAR SYSTEM

The US DoD has been described by Secretary Gates, who served at its head under both Presidents Bush and Obama, as the 'largest, most complex organization on the planet.'[9] In 2016, 1.3 million men and women served on active duty in the American military.[10] Another 810,000 Americans served in the National Guard and Reserve forces.[11] In addition, the Pentagon employed a civilian workforce of 718,000 people, making it the 'nation's largest employer.'[12] Under President Obama, the DoD operated an average annual budget in excess of US$500 billion – providing the US military with a globally unique technological and logistical profile – US$700 billion if accounting for the supplementary budgets to finance the wars in Iraq and Afghanistan, officially dubbed 'overseas contingency operations.' The DoD oversees operations and military installations in the entire world: an informal empire of hundreds of US bases in more than 150 countries, maintained by the US government in its global pursuit of national security and liberal hegemony.[13]

One of the first significant strategy documents on defense to be released under the Obama administration to provide strategic guidance to this behemoth was the *Quadrennial Defense Review Report* (QDR), submitted in February 2010. The *QDR* is a Congressionally mandated report, requiring the examination of defense strategy and priorities every four years by the DoD. The new *QDR* emphasized prioritizing America's current conflicts, the engagements in Iraq and Afghanistan, marked by asymmetric conflicts, COIN and CT operations, over planning for potential conflicts with 'near peer' rivals in conventional scenarios of war fighting. This conceptual shift resulted in the cancellation of several high-profile weapons programs primarily designed for such conflicts as part of the FY 2010 budget, such as the F-22 air superiority fighter, or the Army's Future Combat System.[14] The 2010 *QDR* also anticipated a global geopolitical diffusion of political, economic, and military power, in particular singling out the rise of India and China in this context. In this increasingly multipolar international system, the United States would 'remain the most powerful actor but must increasingly work with key allies and partners if it is to sustain stability and peace.'[15] The geopolitical assessment of the *QDR* was a direct reproduction of the popular analysis of multipolarity in Zakaria's best-seller, *The Post-American World*, and it reflected a liberal internationalist analysis of 'mutual indispensability' and 'network centrality' by such authors as Slaughter, Nye, and Gelb, as articulated, for example, in *Foreign Affairs*.

The conclusion that a geopolitical diffusion of power and influence was occurring and that it was modifying the established hegemony of the United States and its global leadership role represented an intra-governmental consensus among US defense planning and intelligence analysis. The NIC, for example, an internal government think tank located with the Office of the Director of National Intelligence (ODNI), and drawing experts from government, academia, and the private sector, published a report in 2008 titled *Global Trends 2025: A Transformed World*. In this text, the NIC concluded that a 'global multipolar system is emerging with the rise of China, India, and others.'[16]

According to its mission statement, the NIC was supposed to provide 'long-term strategic analysis' to the intelligence community of the United States and the Director of National Intelligence (DNI). The DNI in turn served as 'principal advisor' to the President and the National Security Council on intelligence matters related to national security. Compared to the Pentagon, the NIC's intelligence assessment was even more candid in its view of the relative decline of American economic and military power, and the future constraints of US policy options. Overall, the defense policy planning process under Obama began to internalize the idea that its current military superiority notwithstanding, the United States was facing the irreversible rise of a multipolar system.[17]

The text of the 2010 *QDR* subsequently moved away from the idea of a 'unipolar moment,' or the 'Global War on Terror' that had dominated under Bush and the neoconservative 'Vulcans,' and embraced cooperative engagement as way forward to secure American world leadership:[18] 'We must display a continued willingness to commit substantial effort to strengthen and reform the international order and, in concert with our allies and partners abroad, engage in cooperative, purposeful action in the pursuit of common interests.'[19] This rhetorical shift from primacy to engagement represented a cross-discursive intertextual link between political practice and formal expertise, connecting the Pentagon planning process to the expertise of influential Washington think tanks, leading geopolitical experts, and prominent IR scholars.

Intellectually, the move to reframe and reformulate American grand strategy from neoconservative primacy to hegemonic engagement had already been set up by the 2009 CNAS report, titled *Finding Our Way: Debating American Grand Strategy*, edited by Shawn Brimley and Michèle Flournoy.[20] Flournoy in particular would then be centrally involved in the formulation of the Pentagon's 2010 *QDR*; as Under Secretary of Defense for Policy, she was directly responsible for the development of this strategy document.[21] After the publication of the new *QDR*, the geopolitical vision outlined there was then flanked by prominent *Foreign Affairs* articles by both Clinton and Gates, who stressed a new era of 'building partner capacity' and 'smart power.' Finally, Mead, Ikenberry, and Brzezinski, also writing in *Foreign Affairs*, would all hail the Obama administration for its vision of 'engagement' that seemingly repudiated the unilateralism of the Bush administration.[22]

In comparison with key strategy documents of the Bush presidency such as the *National Security Strategy* of 2002 and 2006 or the *National Defense Strategy* of 2008, the 2010 *QDR* developed a vision of hegemonic engagement that put much greater emphasis on cooperative multilateralism to pursue US interests, detailed as 'security, prosperity, broad respect for universal values, and an international order that promotes cooperative action.'[23] The previous 2006 *QDR* under Donald Rumsfeld, for example, had singled out the United Kingdom and Australia and their military support role for the US-led military invasion of Iraq as, 'models for the breadth and depth of cooperation that the United States seeks to foster with other allies and partners around the world.'[24] Here, the strategic focus had predominantly been on fighting a 'long war' under American leadership, with America's allies as welcome auxiliaries in a globe spanning conflict: 'With its allies and partners, the United States must be prepared to wage this war in many locations simultaneously and for some years to come.'[25]

While both documents frequently mentioned 'allies' and 'partners' as the cornerstone and necessary foundation of US national security and defense, the Obama QDR described engagement in the context of a much broader geopolitical vision of global cooperation: 'The United States cannot sustain a stable international system alone. In an increasingly interdependent world, challenges to common interests are best addressed in concert with likeminded allies and partners who share responsibility for fostering peace and security.'[26] In the words of the NIC, 'the multiplicity of influential actors and distrust of vast power means less room for the U.S. to call the shots without the support of strong partnerships.'[27] At the same time, this shift toward greater cooperative engagement, compared to the Bush administration's emphasis on a US-led global agenda for promoting freedom and democracy, and the fight against terrorist extremism, did not signal a departure from American military pre-eminence as anchoring American grand strategy, as the QDR made clear:

> The United States remains the only nation able to project and sustain large-scale operations over extended distances. This unique position generates an obligation to be responsible stewards of the power and influence that history, determination, and circumstance have provided.[28]

Greater engagement as a key element of Obama's defense policy, then, was meant to reformulate American hegemony, not to replace it. This was also illustrated when Flournoy took a decisive stand against notions of restraint and retrenchment of US military power and global forward presence in the *Foreign Affairs* article she co-authored in 2012.[29] Far from a radical change, there was a strong continuity in defense policy planning and the way practical discourse framed the role of the United States and its military power in national security and world politics.

This practical rationale, however, was far from an isolated self-serving discourse produced by the top level of the military bureaucracy in the Pentagon. The equation of military pre-eminence, American hegemony, and its stated positive effects for regional stability, liberal democracy, and global prosperity was widely supported and contributed to by the formally independent expertise from IR scholars and Washington think tanks, which argued to varying degrees for the 'pre-eminence' of US military power as a stabilizing factor and deterrent of potential aggressors. In popular culture, the supremacy of the US military and its historic achievements provided one of the key arguments for Robert Kagan's popular tractate on America as the George Bailey of the international system, the sole thinkable guarantor of a liberal world order, its military power essential to 'shape its norms, uphold its institutions, defend the sinews of its economic system, and keep the peace.'[30] This vision of an American supremacy of power likewise underwrote the geopolitical best-sellers by Robert Kaplan or George Friedman and their neo-imperial fantasies of the US president as 'global emperor,' and America's 'voluntary Romanization.'[31] And with active support from the Pentagon, the various cinematic accounts of the US military heroically defending freedom and democracy against evil terrorists, alien invaders, and super villains firmly embedded the notion of military supremacy and US leadership in the popular imagination of Americans and their everyday encounters of geopolitics and national security.

Standing within this political and cultural continuity of a militarized geopolitical imagination, the 2010 *QDR* identified 'stewardship of the international system' as the enduring and necessary world political role of the United States and its military. This world political role description both represented yet another metaphor for hegemony and reflected an institutionalized continuity of strategic thinking, dating all the way back to America's emergence as a global superpower at the end of World War II. Representations of the global ambition and military reach of the United States, as outlined in the 2010 *QDR*, then, directly linked the grand strategy visions of George W. Bush and Barack Obama. The unique capability for global power projection remained the foundational claim around which the global leadership role of the United States was imagined. As the 2011 *Military Strategy of the United States*, published by the Joint Chiefs of Staff (JCS), and meant to complement the 2010 *QDR* described: 'Leadership is how we exercise the full spectrum of power to defend our national interests and advance international security and stability.'[32] And, as Obama declared in 2014 at the US Military Academy of West Point: 'The military . . . is, and always will be, the backbone of that leadership.'[33]

Ultimately, the ends of American grand strategy under Obama –

security, economic prosperity, a cooperative international order, and the promotion of liberal, democratic values – were all seen as advancing through continued American hegemony, with military supremacy as its indispensable foundation. At the same time, the global leadership role of the Unites States provided the rationale for the continued existence, maintenance, and exercise of that outstanding military power. The result was an argumentative tautology that reproduced itself in practical grand strategy discourse: because of the superior military power it possessed, the United States was able to lead; because it was an indispensable leader in world affairs, the United States required superior military power. Yet, while this military axiom continued to dominate strategic thinking on the level of identity discourse, the practical exercise of America's military superiority would occur in a much more restrained fashion under Obama.

SUPERPOWER UNDER RESTRAINT: SEQUESTRATION AND ITS IMPACT ON US DEFENSE POLICY

With the presentation of the 2012 *DSG* it became obvious that under Obama restraint would enter the highest level of defense policy planning, and would in turn modify the military definition of US hegemony. The *DSG* was released in January 2012 under Obama's second Secretary of Defense Leon Panetta, who described it as 'reflecting the President's strategic direction to the department.' The *DSG* officially adapted, for the first time since the end of the Cold War, the standard measure for the global power projection capability of the United States, defined as the ability to fight two wars simultaneously. Instead the standard was reduced to the ability to fight one major war and act defensively against the aggressive aspirations of another actor in a second conflict.[34] Whatever the actual practical value of the two-war standard, the official abandonment of this established discursive trope of American global hegemony constituted an important signifier indicating a more limited ambition and imagination of America's military role and geopolitical reach.

At the same time, it was announced that the United States would in future prioritize its military capabilities in the 'Asia-Pacific region.'[35] This announcement was part of the Obama administration's vaunted 'pivot to Asia,' that was promoted as key strategic priority to underwrite American leadership in a 'Pacific Century' by several prominent members of Obama's national security team in late 2011 and early 2012.[36]

According to then National Security Advisor Tom Donilon, the over-arching objective of the United States in the Asia-Pacific region was 'a stable security environment and a regional order rooted in economic openness, peaceful resolution of disputes, and respect for universal rights and freedoms,' in short a perpetuation of *Pax Americana* as the region's overall ordering principle.[37] Militarily, one of the key results of this strategic shift was that from 2020 onwards the US Navy would have 60 percent of its forces stationed in the Pacific, compared to a previous rough parity of forces between the Atlantic and the Pacific.[38]

Overall, the 'pivot to Asia' was framed as a geopolitical refocusing – a substantially increased investment of the United States, diplo-matically, militarily, and economically in the Asia-Pacific. The share of global GDP (measured in purchasing power parity terms), by Asia had increased from under 30 percent in 2000 to about 40 percent in 2014, with China projected to become the world's largest economy by 2025.[39] This dramatic shift marked the vital strategic and geo-economic importance of the region for envisioning the future of American grand strategy. The pivot was thus designed both to secure America's lasting engagement with Asia as a 'Pacific power,' and to reinvigorate the country's global leadership position, which had seemed in decline since the financial crisis of 2008 and US setbacks in Iraq and Afghanistan. During his speech to the Australian Parliament on November 17, 2011, President Obama thus clearly outlined the pivot as geopolitical transi-tion of America's strategic priorities from the post-9/11 environment toward a Pacific future: 'As we end today's wars, I have directed my national security team to make our presence and mission in the Asia Pacific a top priority.'[40]

To offset the impression that the United States was withdrawing, or pivoting away from the Middle East and Europe, the 'pivot' was soon after renamed 'rebalancing' in official US government statements.[41] This rhetorical rebranding notwithstanding, a retrenchment from regions deemed to be of decreasing strategic importance to the United States was clearly underway under Obama. In practical terms, this manifested, for example, in the removal of the US Army's last two heavy infan-try brigades and remaining main battle tanks from Germany in April 2013, the limited US involvement in the 2011 Libya intervention, and the absence of military action in response to Assad's chemical weap-ons attacks in Syria in September 2013.[42] Reinforcements of American troops in Europe in response to the Russian annexation of Crimea in March 2014 were in turn relatively small-scale and on a rotational basis, while the US-led military campaign against the Islamic State terror organization that began in September 2014 remained limited to air strikes, intelligence gathering, and training and equipment for Iraqi troops and Kurdish fighters, ruling out American 'boots on the ground.'[43]

With the 2012 *DSG*, the United States engaged in a geopolitical realignment, which clearly prioritized one particular region, the Asia-Pacific, over others in the long-term orientation of US national security policy. This strategic downsizing and recalibration documented that Obama's defense policy would to some degree redefine the meaning of US military pre-eminence and subsequently that of American global hegemony in general. This reorientation was primarily motivated by concerns over the sustainability of America's foreign and domestic commitments and the country's fiscal situation, with increased political efforts to reign in discretionary federal spending. In his opening remarks to the *DSG* document, Obama first focused on ending America's post-9/11 conflicts, ending the war in Iraq, putting 'al-Qa'ida on the path to defeat,' and the transition in Afghanistan to Afghan responsibility.[44] Directly after addressing this legacy of Bush, he referred to the BCA of 2011, and the need to reduce defense spending, in order to renew America's 'long-term economic strength.'[45] This cautious and limited military reduction produced a predictable, widespread outcry against President Obama's 'weakening' of US military power, his acceptance of incalculable risk in a dangerous world of ever growing threats, and the demise of America's historic primacy in conservative and Republican circles, and the wider foreign policy establishment.[46]

As an assessment by the Congressional Research Service (CRS) stated, the strategy review leading up to the *DSG* was initiated by the President in April 2011, in order to identify US$400 billion in additional savings in the defense budget as part of a broader effort to achieve US$4 trillion in deficit reduction over twelve years.[47] Changes to the size and trajectory of defense spending would thus affect the core of future strategy and defense planning and US national security practices under Obama. In the words of the CJCS, General Martin Dempsey: 'Cost has reemerged as an independent variable in the U.S. national security equation.'[48] In realist terms, defense spending provides the 'material base' for grand strategy, fiscally sustaining the military instrument of US hegemony and its global presence.[49] From a critical perspective, however, it was not primarily the correlation between financial and military resources that was most relevant. Rather it was how the representation of military cost, budgetary distributions, and debt projections affected the identity discourse of national security, and how it changed existing paradigms of grand strategy thinking. While even after sequester-induced reductions the United States would maintain by far the largest single defense budget in the world, well in excess of US$500 billion, spending more than three times as much as China with an officially reported defense budget of US$150 billion in 2015, the *DSG* was another signifier that an era of restraint would succeed the post-9/11 decade of ever-increasing defense expenditures and costly military interventions. In fact, the 2012 *DSG* itself did not yet account for the possibility of sequestration, which senior officials in the Pentagon claimed would 'break' the new defense strategy.[50] When it became clear that sequestration would in all likelihood become a political and fiscal reality, the DoD sought to further develop a strategic course of restraint that the 2012 *DSG* had set out.

A Strategic Choices and Management Review (SCMR) was conducted in 2013 under the new Secretary of Defense Chuck Hagel that would further explore options for cutting costs. The 2014 *QDR*, then, was designed to build upon and update the 2012 guideline, and its vision of American leadership in an 'age of austerity.'[51] As part of the Pentagon budget proposal for 2015, Hagel announced further cuts to American Armed Forces, bringing the US Army down to its 'smallest number of troops since before the Second World War,' as it was widely reported. As part of the Pentagon budget proposal for 2015, the US Army was to be cut from previous levels of 520,000 soldiers to between 450,000 and 440,000 soldiers, and the active-duty Marine Corps was to be reduced from 200,000 to 182,000.[52] Should sequestration levels stay in place after 2016, the numbers of the US Army and USMC were scheduled to drop further, to levels of 420,000 and 175,000 respectively, together with the retirement of an aircraft carrier, and further cuts to the numbers of US ships and airplanes.[53] While a two-year budget deal was reached in 2015, increasing the DoD base budget for fiscal year 2016 from sequestration levels of US$498 billion to US$522 billion, sequestration was ultimately scheduled to remain in place for 2018 and beyond.[54] The 2012 *DSG* also put a strong emphasis on cooperative engagement within the context of the sustainability of US national security. Calling repeatedly for continued efforts to work with allies, the document stressed that 'building partnership capacity elsewhere in the world also remains important for sharing the costs and responsibilities of global leadership.'[55] In his cover letter to the *DSG*, President Obama referred to military operations in Libya to illustrate this vision of military (and financial) 'burden sharing.'[56] As Obama also pointed out, however, any fiscal constraint on US military capabilities would not fundamentally question the established identity discourse:

> we will keep our Armed Forces the best-trained, best-led, best-equipped fighting force in history ... in a changing world that demands our leadership, the United States of America will remain the greatest force for freedom and security the world has ever known.[57]

As with the greater emphasis on cooperative engagement compared to Bush, restraint would modify US grand strategy in practical terms but not replace the militarized imagination that guided 'big picture' thinking in Washington. The highest civilian and military representatives of the United States regularly framed US military power as a unique force for good whose superiority was unparalleled in history, and whose necessity was beyond doubt in a world of ever-increasing risks, seen as beyond everything the United States had experienced in the past. As Hagel, generally considered a non-interventionist, stated during a Senate hearing about the future of defense spending in 2014: 'The United States of America possesses the most lethal, strongest, most powerful military today in the history of the world. We will continue to have that kind of a military. We need that kind of a military to protect our interests.[58] The DNI, James Clapper, perfectly illustrated the inflationary use of this rhetoric of geopolitical volatility, existential threat, and mounting risks during another Senate hearing on US intelligence: 'I have not experienced a time when we have been beset by more crises and threats around the globe.'[59] And, as General Dempsey informed the Senate Armed Service Committee: 'I will personally attest to the fact that [the world is] more dangerous than it has ever been.'[60] As Micah Zenko wryly summed up this statement: 'Dempsey argues that we are not merely living in the most dangerous moment since his birth in 1952, but since the earth was formed 4.54 billion years ago.'[61]

Given the real possibility of a global, thermo-nuclear war with the Soviet Union for more than fifty years alone, this institutionalized, hyperbolic rhetoric of threat and fear seemed predominantly motivated by bureaucratic interests, reflecting institutionalized establishment positions. While developments like Russian incursions in Syria and Ukraine, China's military build-up, or the rise of Islamic State might be viewed as morally reprehensible, regrettable, and detrimental to regional stability and international security, fundamentally they were not threatening the existence of the United States or posing a challenge comparable to that of the Cold War. The key aim of this 'threat inflation' was thus to secure the continued political influence and financial resources of the intelligence and military apparatus of the US national security state and to maintain a geopolitical vision of American hegemony as its basic rationale.

The practical reasoning that was supposedly rooted in a careful appreciation of facts, and the rational analysis of international trends by seasoned experts and strategists, reproduced a culturally deeply embedded Manichean worldview, a conviction of truth that established a simplistic dichotomy between US power and virtue and a Hobbesian world of chaos and upheaval. This militarized imagination of American exceptionalism fueled an entire political economy of national security, worth billions of dollars and securing hundreds of thousands of jobs in both the US government and the American economy, including weapons manufacturers, defense contractors, private intelligence analysts, think tank researchers, and even the entertainment industry. Only rarely was the validity of this imagination probed and questioned within the mainstream discourse of American grand strategy.[62]

As Robert Golan-Vilella has suggested, one of the results of this prevalent 'threat inflation' and mental militarization in American politics and culture was potentially that when polled on national security issues, Americans displayed a tendency to understate the military superiority of the United States, and to overstate risks and threats, for example expressing the belief that Iran was already in possession of nuclear weapons.[63] Yet, while winning the 'long War' against terrorism and extremism had dominated under George W. Bush, and the wars in Afghanistan and Iraq had still been at the forefront in 2010, in Obama's second term 'fiscal austerity' had become a prime focus of strategic planning at the Pentagon as Hagel made clear: 'the 2014 Quadrennial Defense Review (QDR) is principally focused on preparing for the future by rebalancing our defense efforts in a period of increasing fiscal constraint.'[64] As a result, there was a growing divide between the rhetoric and practice of American grand strategy. As a 2012 report by the CRS stated, Obama's *DSG* would underscore 'the unique global leadership role of the United States,' but not define the 'scope or scale' of this leadership.[65] The basic disconnect between continued hegemonic aspirations and increasingly limited means would be replicated on the operational level, where the 'pivot to Asia' would prove to be more rhetorical than practical.

FROM COIN TO AIR-SEA BATTLE: THE GEOPOLITICS OF MILITARY STRATEGY

In January 2012, Secretary of Defense Panetta remarked that the United States saw itself 'at a turning point after a decade of war';[66] a metaphor also frequently used by President Obama.[67] The American invasions of Afghanistan and Iraq had required hundreds of thousands of US soldiers and Marines to occupy and patrol foreign territory, leading to substantial and financially costly increases in the personnel strength of the US Army and USMC. This trajectory was reversed under Obama. From 2012 onwards, US forces would 'no longer be sized to conduct large-scale, prolonged stability operations.'[68] The United States was ending its decade-long, large-scale ground combat operations in the Middle East and Central Asia, and the experience of America engaging in militarily enforced regime change and COIN missions was not to be repeated under Obama. As Secretary Gates memorably summed up this strategic directive for greater caution at the United States Military Academy at West Point: 'In my opinion, any future defense secretary who advises the president to again send a big American land army into Asia or into the Middle East or Africa should have his head examined . . . .'[69]

This recalibration of US defense policy would have geopolitical, institutional, and operational implications. The US Army and USMC, the principal instruments of land warfare, were downsized, the US Navy and US Air Force were largely maintained at post-9/11 levels or modestly increased.[70] This reflected a renewed American interest in the Asia-Pacific, primarily a maritime theater, which, under the Pentagon's 'Unified Command Plan' was under the responsibility of United States Pacific Command (US PACOM). The United States military was leaving behind 'COIN' and the Middle East, and preparing for 'Air-Sea Battle' (ASB) in the Pacific. COIN was a comprehensive military strategy to achieve victory in asymmetrical conflicts. The doctrine rose to prominence under a group of so-called 'warrior scholars' that sought to redefine American war fighting in the post-9/11 environment.[71] One of the strategy's key texts was the 2006 US Army and USMC field manual FM 3-24, co-authored by US Army General David Petraeus and USMC General James F. Amos. COIN called for the military to concentrate not just on the elimination of enemies on the battlefield, but to follow a broader political, social, and economic approach toward defeating armed insurrection.[72] The protection of civilian populations to win 'hearts and minds,' the targeting of insurgency leaders, and support for a legitimate host-nation government were all counted as part of this comprehensive approach. As FM 3-24 declared: 'COIN operations always demand considerable expenditures of time and resources.'[73]

COIN later became largely synonymous with US military efforts in Iraq and Afghanistan, but also with the immense financial burden and considerable military and civilian resources necessary to undertake operations that were simultaneously aimed at providing security, economic assistance, and development to protect and support local populations in conflict zones.[74] And despite years of American efforts, a stable political environment would neither emerge in Afghanistan nor in Iraq, undermining the military's case for COIN. Two names in particular were associated with COIN under Obama. First, General Petraeus, who served as US commander in Iraq from 2007 to 2008 and later as combatant commander of US Central Command from 2008 to 2010, the military command in charge of all American forces in the Middle East and Central Asia. The second was General Stanley McChrystal, who served as NATO and US commander in Afghanistan from 2009 to 2010. Both defined COIN as the only possible strategy for the United States to win in Afghanistan, the conflict that would take center stage during Obama's first term.[75] Both Petraeus and McChrystal were later discredited, and so was COIN as a key military doctrine of the United States.[76] As *The Washington Post* remarked in an article in March 2014: 'In Washington, among policymakers, the Afghan war is increasingly discussed with exasperation, like a curse. It is the type of warfare the United States must avoid at all cost, President Obama argued during his State of the Union address.'[77]

According to many influential and congruent journalistic reports and insider accounts, like the memoirs of Secretary Gates, or *The New York Times* best-selling books written by the investigative *Washington Post* journalist Bob Woodward and the *Los Angeles Times* foreign affairs correspondent James Mann, President Obama felt frequently pressured by Petraeus, McChrystal, and the Pentagon's military leadership to endorse a COIN strategy for Afghanistan, and to agree to a significant American troop surge in the fall of 2009.[78] Obama would ultimately follow his military advisors and decide to send an additional 30,000 American troops to the country. The conflict over COIN, however, revealed an, at times, strenuous civil-military relationship and a deep rift between competing visions within Obama's national security team, where Gates and Clinton supported the more expansive COIN option and Biden and then Deputy National Security Advisor Donilon supported a more restrained approach of counter-terrorism.

COIN in Afghanistan, while officially endorsed by the President, was never framed by Obama as absolutely vital to US national security. Gates, for example, commented in his memoirs how Obama framed the Afghanistan conflict predominantly in terms of 'exit paths,' and 'drawdowns,' but far less in terms of victory or 'accomplishing the mission.'[79] The 'pivot to Asia' was, in comparison, a far more central element in President Obama's strategic vision for America's long-term interest and future geopolitical trajectory. Accordingly, the Air-Sea Battle concept became increasingly prominent in military and civilian expert circles involved in debating and planning America's next war-fighting doctrine.[80] ASB as an operational concept first entered the official grand strategy policy discourse with the *QDR* of 2010, which stated: 'The Air Force and Navy together are developing a new joint ASB concept for defeating adversaries across the range of military operations, including adversaries equipped with sophisticated anti-access and area denial capabilities.'[81] In August 2011, the Pentagon announced the establishment of an ASB Office to coordinate related policies.[82] ASB essentially envisioned a potential challenge to US hegemony in Asia, and to a lesser degree in the Middle East.[83] It assumed that the improvement and proliferation of advanced military technological capabilities, in particular conventional and nuclear submarines, satellites, stealth, drones, precision-guided ammunitions, and advanced ballistic missile and air defense systems could endanger US military installations and naval assets, and offset the traditional advantage conventional forces had enjoyed in the past.[84] These 'A2/AD' capabilities could prohibit American military access to and movement within a region, and were in particular attributed to the rising military profile of China in Asia.[85] As the *Military Strategy of the United States* explained in its segment on regional security in the Asia-Pacific:

> To safeguard U.S. and partner nation interests, we will be prepared to demonstrate the will and commit the resources needed to oppose any nation's actions that jeopardize access to and use of the global commons and cyberspace, or that threaten the security of our allies.[86]

Since the uninhibited projection of military power and command of the 'global commons' provided the essential foundation of America's global leadership role and cornerstone of its security and defense strategy, 'A2/AD' was perceived as a potential threat to vital US interests, and an unacceptable challenge to US hegemony. In response, ASB envisioned a range of counter-measures, ranging from a naval blockade targeting the Chinese economy to precision strikes on strategic Chinese targets.[87] As the CSBA defined 'Air-Sea Battle,' it should help set the conditions 'to sustain a stable, favorable conventional military balance throughout the Western Pacific region.'[88] One of the key figures behind ASB was the futurist Andrew Marshall who had developed the new operational concept for over twenty years at the Pentagon's Office of Net Assessment (ONA).[89] In essence, the ONA was the Pentagon's equivalent to the NIC, an internal research and analysis organization, tasked with developing a long-term strategic outlook for US national security and defense matters in support of political decision-making and operational planning. It enjoyed wide admiration for its grand strategy proficiency among the defense policy establishment, and in particular the Washington think tank scene, where it was seen as a much needed antithesis to the un-strategic, short-term crisis reaction mode associated with conventional decision-making in Washington.

Subsequently, grand strategy and security experts reacted with dismay to rumors that the organization might be closed by Obama and Hagel due to budget cuts.[90] The Chairman of the Armed Services Seapower Subcommittee, Randy Forbes, wrote to Secretary Hagel in October 2013 protesting the move: 'Given the critical contributions to U.S. national security made by the office during its forty-year history and its role as a central repository for long-range strategic thinking, we believe it would be a serious error to further consider its abolition.'[91] The admiration for Marshall and the ONA and its visionary abilities for strategic insight documented how, aside from the universal mantra of leadership, there existed something akin to a cult of grand strategy in Washington DC, where the elite discourse of national security and defense policy was fixated on the indispensability of strategy and the essential insights of the strategist in guiding the national interest over the long term.[92]

Marshall and the ONA were firmly embedded in the Washington foreign policy establishment and had created a wide network of supporters among the Pentagon, think tanks, Congress, and the defense industry for the operational ideas behind ASB.[93] A key supporter was

CSBA, which published its first report on the subject in 2010.[94] Andrew Krepinevich, the think tank's president, who authored the first report for CSBA on the subject, had previously worked under Marshall as a defense analyst in the Pentagon, and would later advocate ASB in several articles in *Foreign Affairs*.[95]

The framing of ASB between policymakers, military officials, and civilian experts as an operational concept of vital strategic importance for the long-term security of the United States perfectly illustrated the discursive machinery of hegemony in Washington DC. A new operational concept to secure the necessary military primacy of the United States in Asia was established as dominant knowledge and a generally accepted truth through the intertextual links between practical, formal, and popular discourses, interconnecting policy advice, academic expertise, and policymaking. In the movie *Battleship*, there was even a prominent popular reflection of US military power relating naval warfare in the Pacific to US national security and America's geopolitical identity as a 'Pacific Power.' In the relatively short time between 2010 and 2012, ASB emerged as a key feature of geopolitical imagination on US national security in military strategy documents, think tank reports, journal articles, press statements, conference presentations, public speeches, and even, it could be argued, a major Hollywood movie, exposing a self-reinforcing cycle of mutual confirmation and cross-discursive convergence in linking a hegemonic geopolitical imagination to a new practice of security to sustain American hegemony.

At the same time, as a military-operational element of grand strategy practice, ASB and the 'pivot to Asia' combined efforts to maintain the established liberal hegemony of the United States with elements of a realist offshore balancing approach. Obama's rebalancing did not result in a significant military build-up of the United States in Japan or South Korea, the traditional locations for the forward presence of US troops in the region. Instead, the United States sent two Littoral Combat Ships (LCSs) to Singapore, and announced the deployment of 2,500 Marines to Darwin in Australia on a rotational basis, 'off-shore' locations in the geopolitical calculation of neorealists.

This in turn gave rise to criticisms of the pivot as being mere 'rhetoric' from circles that envisioned a stronger US military presence in the region to confirm American primacy, as for example done by AEI. The Congressionally mandated and Pentagon-commissioned *Asia-Pacific Rebalance 2025* study by CSIS concluded that cuts to the defense budget from 2009–2015 had already limited the Pentagon's ability to pursue the rebalance, and that long-term budget uncertainty was creating a difficult environment for the future of the strategy.[96] Even General Dempsey acknowledged that from a military point of view: 'For now, this shift in focus is more about thinking than it is doing.'[97] Thus, ASB and the military implementation of the Asia rebalance under Obama entailed yet another articulation of the contradiction between hegemony and restraint in US national security policy.

'GROOMING FOR LEADERSHIP' – THE US MILITARY AND THE INSTITUTIONALIZATION OF GRAND STRATEGY THINKING IN SENIOR MILITARY EDUCATION

A final significant component when considering the practical discourse of American grand strategy and the role of the Pentagon and the Armed Forces in articulating and executing this vision is the realm of professional military education (PME). Leadership is one of the most important qualities that the United States military values in its members, and in particular in its officers. At the same time, leadership on a global level is viewed as vital to American security interests, with America's military establishment charged with sustaining and carrying out that vision. As General Dempsey has remarked in context with the 2012 *DSG*: 'The real test of this strategy is not in the choices we made, but in putting the choices to work. I am confident that we will pass this test for one simple reason—leadership.'[98]

Leadership as a professional military skill and a mark of personal character is being developed throughout the career of an officer in the US military in several educational institutions. At the beginning stands officer cadet training, either at the individual service academies, most famous among them being the United States Military Academy at West Point and the United States Naval Academy in Annapolis, in reserve officer training courses (ROTC) at regular US colleges and universities, or at the military's officer candidate schools (OCSs). These stand at the beginning of a lifelong system of PME, where the development of military skills and knowledge is being developed in hierarchical stages of progress, designed so that upon successful completion, American officers are able to take on ever-greater responsibilities for command, from the tactical to the operational, and finally at the strategic level.[99]

In the context of grand strategy, the most important of these institutions and programs are those which train future flag-rank and general staff officers for the highest military command positions and other high-profile assignments in the national security and defense establish-ment. At this level, the senior education of military leadership at war colleges incorporates the teaching of grand strategy, IR theory, and geo-politics, deemed essential professional knowledge for maintaining the global leadership role of the United States. American military power, then, also manifests as a Foucauldian nexus of power/knowledge and the particular production of strategic knowledge that underwrites mili-tary practices. A CSIS report exemplary related the PME in geopolitical and strategic knowledge to the practice of grand strategy: 'They [the officers of the US military] represent the human capital that will sustain the global leadership of the United States and secure its role as the world's sole remaining superpower into the twenty-first century.'[100]

One of the most important institutions for the teaching of grand strat-egy is the National Defense University (NDU), located in Washington DC, and the NDU's National War College. [101] According to its website:

> The mission of the National War College is to educate future leaders of the Armed Forces, State Department, and other civilian agencies for high-level policy, command, and staff responsibilities by conducting a senior-level course of study in national security strategy.[102]

Designed to introduce the key concepts and issues at the highest level of strategic thought, the syllabus of the NWC's core curriculum empha-sizes the practice of grand strategy over abstract theory. Classical think-ers and practitioners of war, military power, and geopolitics, such as Machiavelli, Clausewitz, and Mahan, are emphasized for study and critical examination about the assumptions that underpin strategic thinking.[103] By considering the 'highest level of strategic thought,' the past and contemporary debates and choices of American grand strategy, military, and non-military sources of national power, and the domestic and global context of US national security, students are sup-posed to 'free their minds from ingrained habits of reasoning and begin to appreciate the subtle and complex relationships among the elements of strategic thought.'[104]

A further element at this highest level of PME is the assignment of senior officers as students at regular graduate schools at national and international universities, or as research fellows with prominent think tanks, further stressing the intellectual and intertextual exchange between military thinking and civilian expertise, between formal and practical discourses in the production of grand strategy knowledge. Remarkably, though, in the military education of strategy, the US military does not define strategy as strictly scientific knowledge, and purely rationalist-technological calculation of means and ends, as the majority of positivist IR literature suggests. Instead the creative dimension of strategic thinking is emphasized, the interplay of means, ends, and ways, and how 'strategy is an art.'[105] The *US Army War College Guide to National Security*, published by the college's Institute for Strategic Studies, for example, explicitly relates the operation of grand strategy to the underlying geopolitical imagination of the country: 'At the grand strategic level, the ways and means to achieve U.S. core national interests are based on the national leadership's strategic vision of America's role in the world.'[106] Furthermore, the text relates the successful political formulation of grand strategy and its discursive authority to its intertextual connectivity and recognition in the popular realm:

> To be effective, each new administration has had to express a vision for the U.S. role in the world that does not outpace the experience of the American people, and thus lose the decisive authority or domestic consensus to implement the strategic vision. Is the vision, in other words, suitable and acceptable?[107]

As the Mr. Y article has documented, there was a growing awareness in military circles that the political-military leadership faced the challenge to develop a new strategic narrative that resonated with the American public and that could bring the imagination of American leadership in line with changing geopolitical dynamics in the twenty-first century. Here, the aim was to develop a grand strategy focused on promoting sustainability and common security interests with other countries, rather than one focused on an exclusive concentration on threats and military primacy alone. Apparently, in the realm of PME of national security, a similar shift toward greater cooperative engagement and military restraint in formulating grand strategy took place. In 2012, the author and journalist Edward Luce described an annual grand strategy exercise at the NDU, undertaken by high-ranking military officers and civilian officials, which concluded that 'America still had enough power to help shape the kind of world it wanted to see. By 2021 that moment would have passed.'[108] One officer involved in the exercise explained: 'The window on America's hegemony is closing.'[109] He continued by outlining a clear vision of restraint and offshore balancing for the United

States, suggesting a deliberate downsizing of its worldwide military profile: 'The country should sharply reduce its "global footprint" by winding up all wars, notably in Afghanistan, and by closing peacetime military bases in Germany, South Korea, the UK, and elsewhere.' The military's grand strategy exercise resulted in a call to end American primacy, and to embrace cooperative engagement and military restraint as way to 'restore America's economic vitality.'[110] Both at the top level and in its future leadership personnel, the US military seemed to be adapting the premise of American leadership and military pre-eminence to a grand strategy vision that was both more dependent on allies and partners, and less willing to accept the costs of global hegemony.

CONCLUSION

The practical discourse on national security and defense in the Pentagon and the Armed Forces illustrates how ideas of continued American hegemony and global military pre-eminence coexisted, and were in fact developed jointly with geopolitical visions of increased cooperation, greater restraint, and more limited geopolitical ambitions. Such flexibility and pragmatism in the design of grand strategy clearly frustrated purists, such as the neoconservative experts populating Washington's think tanks, who blended visions of American grand strategy with firmly entrenched ideological predispositions toward security and defense. Yet the US military, which defined grand strategy predominantly as a creative exercise, was more willing to accept such pragmatic solutions in the complex interplay of ways, means, and ends that defined the long-term pursuit of the national interest.

At the same time, however, this pragmatism came into conflict with the established mantra of American indispensability in political, media, and expert circles, where the absence of American leadership and military resolve were the cause for increased global instability and heightened risk, from the continued Syrian civil war, to Chinese assertiveness in the Pacific, and the resurgence of Putin's Russia. As such, neither the ASB concept with its limited practical implications and mixed messages concerning the perception and future threat projection of China, nor the ever-growing focus on sustainability in the Pentagon's *QDR* reports were designed to reinvigorate American military supremacy to levels seen under the George W. Bush administration. Under Obama, US defense policy had to adapt to shrinking – or at best flat-lining – resources, reflecting the president's emphasis on an era where the 'tide of war has receded,' at least as far as large-scale US military interventions were concerned.

With the end of the wars in Iraq and Afghanistan and the onset of sequestration, then, a focus on restraint took on ever-greater practical and discursive significance for US national security and defense policy over the course of the Obama presidency. While this development did not signal that the United States was willing to relinquish its global military leadership role, nor that there was an overall reframing of geopolitical identity, it clearly shifted the main focus of security and defense planning away from the open-ended Global War on Terror toward a concern with national security and sustainability. The 'pivot to Asia' and sequestration, although both discursively linked to a continued vision of American hegemony, reflected a United States that had to adapt the make-up of its national security to an age of austerity and unprecedented limitations of US actions that was likely to endure for the foreseeable future. At the same time, this documented a growing rift between the hegemonic imagination of the United States and its role in the world – marked by notions of leadership, exceptionalism, indispensability, and unparalleled military power – and political practices that downsized and recalibrated America's Armed Forces.

NOTES

1. Gates, 'A Balanced Strategy,' p. 39.
2. O'Hanlon and Petraeus, 'America's Awesome Military.'
3. Posen, 'Command of the Commons,' Brooks, *American Exceptionalism in the Age of Obama*.
4. Scheinmann and Cohen, 'The Myth of "Securing the Commons,"' p. 115. In fact, there is a strong intellectual congruence between the idea of US military control of the global commons, and classic geopolitical conceptualizations of spatial domination, such as Mackinder's' 'Heartland,' or Spykman's 'Rimland' theory.
5. Ó Tuathail, for example, classified the 1995 *National Military Strategy of the United States*, published by the Joint Chiefs, as 'geo-strategic doctrine' that established 'overseas presence' and 'power projection' as key elements of America's strategic outlook of geopolitical primacy, see Ó Tuathail, 'Postmodern Geopolitics?' p. 32.
6. Mamadouh and Dijkink, 'Geopolitics, International Relations and Political Geography,' p. 355.
7. US DoD, 'About the Department of Defense.' Available at http://www.

defense.gov/about/ (last accessed September 19). Both the Secretary of Defense and the CJCS are also mandatory members of the National Security Council that was established through the National Security Act of 1947. The role of the JCS chairman was further strengthened through the Goldwater-Nichols Act of 1986, which elevated his position compared to the individual service chiefs of the Air Force, Navy, Army and Marine Corps, in order to 'present the president a prompt, single, unified military position' on security and defense issues, see Sapolsky, Gholz, and Talmadge, *U.S. Defense Politics*, p. 54.

8. Rourke, 'Military Education for the New Age.'
9. Gates, *Duty*, p. 577.
10. US DoD, 'Department of Defense (DoD) Releases Fiscal Year 2017 President's Budget Proposal.'
11. Ibid.
12. US DoD, 'About the Department of Defense.' Available at http://www.defense.gov/about/ (last accessed September 19, 2016).
13. Vine, 'The United States Probably Has More Foreign Military Bases Than Any Other People, Nation, or Empire in History.'
14. Gates, *Duty*, pp. 311–322.
15. US DoD, *Quadrennial Defense Review Report (2010)*, p. iii.
16. NIC, *Global Trends 2025*, p. iv.
17. Ibid., p. 93.
18. Mann and Mann, *Rise of the Vulcans*. In March 2009 the DoD officially changed the name from 'Global War on Terror' to 'Overseas Contingency Operation' (OCO) to designate its CT activities, see Wilson and Kamen, '"Global War on Terror" is Given a New Name.'
19. US DoD, *Quadrennial Defense Review Report (2010)*, p. 5.
20. Brimley and Flournoy (eds.), *Finding Our Way*.
21. Thompson, 'Michèle Flournoy Departs.'
22. Ibid.
23. US DoD, *Quadrennial Defense Review Report* (2010), p. iv; where the Rumsfeld *QDR* of 2006 for example mentioned 'allies' fifty-seven times, the Gates *QDR* of 2010 nearly doubled this number, mentioning 'allies' 107 times; 'engagement' on the other hand was counted as a strategic priority for defense planning and security cooperation under Rumsfeld, while it featured prominently in the 2010 *QDR*.
24. US DoD, *Quadrennial Defense Review Report (2006)*, p. 7.
25. Ibid., p. 1.
26. US DoD, *Quadrennial Defense Review Report (2010)*, p. 57.
27. NIC, *Global Trends 2025*, p. xi.
28. US DoD, *Quadrennial Defense Review Report (2010)*, p. v.
29. Flournoy and Davidson, 'Obama's New Global Posture.'
30. Kagan, *The World America Made*, p. 139.

31. Friedman, *The Next Decade*, p. 14; Kaplan, *The Revenge of Geography*, pp. 342–344.
32. Joint Chiefs of Staff, *The National Military Strategy of the United States*, p. 1.
33. White House, 'Remarks by the President at the United States Military Academy Commencement Ceremony,' May 28, 2014.
34. US DoD, *Sustaining U.S. Global Leadership*, p. 4. The former assistant secretary of defense in the Reagan administration and senior fellow at the CAP, Lawrence J. Korb, and the journalist, Mark Thompson, have pointed out that the 'two-war' standard has always been a construct, as demonstrated for example by the inability of the American Armed Forces to simultaneously prioritize Afghanistan and Iraq, see Korb, 'The Right Cuts,' Thompson, 'The Two-MRC Strategy.'
35. Ibid., p. 2.
36. Clinton, 'America's Pacific Century,' Donilon, 'America is Back in the Pacific and Will Uphold the Rules,' White House, 'Remarks By President Obama to the Australian Parliament.'
37. White House, 'Remarks By Tom Donilon, National Security Advisor to the President.' In order to achieve this outcome, the Obama administration aimed to implement a 'a comprehensive, multidimensional strategy,' focused on five key areas: the strengthening of existing alliances; deepening partnerships with emerging powers; development of a stable, constructive relationship with China; the empowering of regional institutions; and helping to build a regional economic architecture to sustain shared prosperity.
38. Further military components of the 'pivot' included increased training exercises of the United States with allies and strategic partners, such as Japan, South Korea, Vietnam, Thailand, Singapore, and the Philippines.
39. See, for example, IMF, *Regional Economic Outlook*, NIC, *Global Trends 2025*.
40. White House, 'Remarks By President Obama to the Australian Parliament.'
41. Brewster, '"Asian Pivot" is really an "Asian Re-balance."'
42. In this context, see also the analysis by Carpenter, 'U.S. Security Retrenchment,' and Metz, 'A Receding Presence.'
43. Obama, 'Transcript: President Obama's Speech Outlining Strategy to Defeat Islamic State.'
44. US DoD, Sustaining U.S. Global Leadership, cover letter.
45. Ibid.
46. Zakheim, 'A Budget Strategy that Courts Disaster,' Herman, 'America's Disarmed Future,' Schmitt and Donnelly, 'No Superpower Here.'
47. Dale and Towell, *In Brief*, p. 2.
48. Dempsey, 'From the Chairman,' (3rd quarter 2012), p. 2.

49. Stuart Kaufman, 'US National Strategy from Bush to Obama,' p. 13.
50. Quoted in Dale and Towell, *In Brief*, p. 1.
51. Dale, *The 2014 Quadrennial Defense Review (QDR) and Defense Strategy.*
52. Marshall, 'DoD Budget Request Adapts to Fiscal Realities, Hagel says,' Alexander, 'Big Budget Cuts Pose "Tough, Tough Choices" for Pentagon: Hagel.'
53. Korb, Hoffman, and Blakeley, 'A User's Guide to the Fiscal Year 2015 Defense Budget.' Sequestration was ultimately opposed by the Pentagon and the Obama administration as damaging to US national security.
54. Pellerin, 'DoD Comptroller: Budget Deal Offers Relief, Uncertainty.'
55. US DoD, *Sustaining U.S. Global Leadership*, p. 3.
56. Ibid., cover letter.
57. Ibid.
58. Quoted in US Senate Committee on Armed Services, Department of Defense Authorization of Appropriations for Fiscal Year 2015 and the Future Years Defense Program, p. 61.
59. *Washington Post*, 'Transcript: Senate Intelligence Hearing on National Security Threats.'
60. Quoted in Zenko, 'Most. Dangerous. World. Ever.'
61. Ibid.
62. Zenko and Cohen, 'Clear and Present Safety.'
63. Golan-Vilella, 'The Results of Threat Inflation.' A 2010 CNN poll, for example, found that 71 percent of Americans believed that Iran already had nuclear weapons at its disposal; a separate CNN poll in 2012 indicated that Americans believed that the threat from Iran was on par with the one presented by the Soviet Union in the mid-1980s, see ibid.
64. US DoD, *Quadrennial Defense Review Report (2014)*, p. iv.
65. Dale and Towell, *In Brief*, p. 3.
66. Panetta, 'Statement on Defense Strategic Guidance.'
67. 'The tide of war is receding' was an image President Obama used, for example, in a speech to the UN General Assembly in New York on September 21, 2011, referring to the drawdown of US forces in Iraq and Afghanistan, see Mills, 'Obama.' During his second inaugural address on January 21, 2013 Obama explained that 'a decade of war is now ending'; White House, 'Inaugural Address by President Barack Obama.'
68. US DoD, *Sustaining U.S. Global Leadership*, p. 6.
69. Quoted in Shanker, 'Warning Against Wars Like Iraq and Afghanistan.'
70. US DoD, 'Department of Defense (DoD) Releases Fiscal Year 2017 President's Budget Proposal.' As part of FY 2017, the Pentagon budget would fund an Army of 460,000 and a Marine Corps of 182,000 active-duty Marines. For the Navy, the budget grew the fleet from 280 ships to 308 ships. The budget also supported an Air Force of 491,700 active-duty,

Reserve and National Guard Airmen with fifty-five tactical fighter squadrons.

71. See, for example, Entous and Stewart, 'Exclusive: The Warrior-Scholar Versus the Taliban.'
72. US Army/US Marine Corps, *Counter-Insurgency Field Manual.*
73. Ibid., p. 24.
74. Ikenberry, 'The Limits of Counter-Insurgency in Afghanistan.'
75. Woodward, *Obama's Wars.*
76. Petraeus had to resign as CIA director in 2012 over an extramarital affair, which was discovered in the course of an FBI investigation. McChrystal was fired as ISAF commander by President Obama in 2010 due to derogatory comments members of McChrystal's staff had made about members of Obama's national security team, in particular Vice-President Biden, in an article that appeared in *Rolling Stone* magazine; see Hastings, 'The Runaway General.' This had been the first time a President had relieved a sitting wartime commander of his duty since President Truman had fired General Douglas MacArthur for insubordination during the Korean War.
77. Londoño, 'The Last Casualties.'
78. Gates, *Duty*, Woodward, *Obama's Wars*, Mann, *The Obamians*, see also, Sanger, *Confront and Conceal*, Landler, *Alter Egos.*
79. Gates, *Duty*, pp. 298–299.
80. Jaffe, 'U.S. Model for a Future War Fans Tensions with China and Inside Pentagon.'
81. US DoD, *Quadrennial Defense Review Report (2010).*
82. The office was closed in 2015 and at the time of writing a successor to ASB was still in development, the Joint Concept for Access and Maneuver in the Global Commons (JAM-GC). Where ASB had emphasized US naval and air power, JAM-GC sought greater operational integration of US ground forces.
83. Krepinevich, *Why AirSea Battle?*
84. Ibid.
85. Ibid., pp. 13–25.
86. Joint Chiefs of Staff, *National Military Strategy of the United States*, p. 13.
87. Work, 'AirSea Battle,' p. 26.
88. van Tol et al., *AirSea Battle*, p. xi.
89. Jaffe, 'U.S. Model for a Future War Fans Tensions with China and Inside Pentagon.'
90. Singer, 'Bad Idea for the Pentagon's Idea Shop.'
91. Quoted in Weisgerber and Bennett, 'Pentagon Determining Fate of Revered Net Assessment Office.'
92. See in this context also, Edelstein and Krebs, 'Delusions of Grand Strategy.'

93. Jaffe, 'U.S. Model for a Future War Fans Tensions with China and Inside Pentagon.'
94. Krepinevich, *Why AirSea Battle?*, van Tol et al., *AirSea Battle.*
95. Krepinevich, 'The Pentagon's Wasting Assets,' Krepinevich, 'Strategy in a Time of Austerity.'
96. Green, Hicks, and Cancian, *Asia-Pacific Rebalance 2025*, p. 4.
97. Dempsey, 'From the Chairman,' p. 3.
98. Ibid.
99. For a detailed description of PME and its various stages of officer training, see CSIS, 'Professional Military Education.'
100. Ibid., p. 302.
101. The senior service colleges, like the US Army War College, the US Naval War College, the US Air War College, and the USMC War College operate below the level of the NDU and NWC, and train selected officers (minimum 16–22 years of service) to train for future leadership positions, focusing on the 'macro-realm of national security strategy' and teaching students 'how to think as opposed to what to think.' CSIS, 'Professional Military Education,' p. 312.
102. US National War College, 'Mission.' Available at http://www.ndu.edu /Academics/CollegesCenters/NationalWarCollege.aspx (last accessed September 18, 2016).
103. US National War College, 'Curriculum Overview.' Available at http://nwc. ndu.edu/Academics/Curriculum-Overview/ (last accessed September 21, 2016), see also *Course 1, Syllabus – Block A: Philosophies of Statecraft* (Year: 1999–2000). Available at http://www.resdal.org/Archivo/syl1-a.htm (last accessed September 18, 2016), and Kurth Cronin, 'National Security Education: A User's Manual.'
104. Course 1, Syllabus – Block A: Philosophies of Statecraft.
105. Bartholomees Jr. (ed.), 'Appendix. Guidelines for Strategy Formulation,' p. 413.
106. Ibid., p. 414. The text identifies four distinctive grand strategy visions: 'isolationism' (pre-World War II), 'global engagement' (World War II), 'containment' (Cold War), and 'American primacy' (post-Cold War-era), ibid.
107. Ibid.
108. Luce, *Time to Start Thinking*, p. 9.
109. Ibid.
110. Ibid., pp. 8–11.

Chapter 7

THE 'OBAMA DOCTRINE' – VISION FOR CHANGE?

═══════

Don't do stupid shit.

Barack Obama[1]

The President of the United States functions as both the source and focal point of the national debate on American grand strategy, and the country's future direction in world politics. As President of the United States, Barack Obama was in a constant exchange with both political opponents and diverging voices within his own administration over defining America's world political role and the purpose behind American power. Through the constitutional role as head of state and government, and commander-in-chief of the Armed Forces, the President occupies a privileged position in shaping the national narrative and framing political discourse; at the same time, the President is a highly symbolic figure, invested with the vestiges and icons of American power, from the Oval Office to Air Force One.

As Ó Tuathail and Agnew have remarked on the discursive role of the President: 'He is the chief *bricoleur* of American political life, a combination of storyteller and tribal shaman.'[2] Obama's strategic vision thus not only informed the political debate and determined policy, but also represented the central hub in an intertextual network of grand strategy discourses, providing the focus for the policy advice and criticism of Washington think tanks, the reporting and commentary of the media, and the intellectual attention of academic researchers interested in the study of US foreign and security policy. This exalted position in American public life also makes the President a particular fixture of popular culture, from satirical ridicule by *The Simpsons* to filmic reflections of presidential power and determined resolve, ranging from *The West Wing* (1999–2006) and *24* (2001–2010) to *Independence Day* (1996) and

White House Down (2013).[3] Finally, the direction the President charts in guiding the nation's role in world politics also constantly reverberates in public opinion polls, adding a further dimension of popular confirmation or contestation of the geopolitical vision originating from the White House.

Under the Obama presidency, American exceptionalism, global leadership, and military pre-eminence remained central tenets around which a geopolitical imagination of America's preferred role and position in the world were constructed in political-practical discourse. In the foreword to the *National Security Strategy* (*NSS*) of 2015, for example, Obama reiterated: 'Strong and sustained American leadership is essential to a rules-based international order . . . The question is not whether America should lead, but how we lead.'[4] Obama also declared on several occasions that the United States was 'objectively' exceptional in several ways, singling out the size of its economy, unmatched military capability, and constitutionally enshrined democratic values.[5] By invoking American exceptionalism, Obama thus connected with a dominant political-cultural framework of reference for US foreign policy and grand strategy that stressed the enduring singularity and superiority of American geopolitical identity and its unique role in international affairs and world history.[6]

Yet, from the onset of his presidency Obama also attempted to reconcile singular representations of the United States as 'exceptional' and 'indispensable' with a strategic course of cooperative engagement and 'burden sharing,' highlighting the limitations of US power and influence. This challenged the existing identity-policy link in practical grand strategy discourse that translated exceptionalist sentiments about American identity at home into regular calls for the use of force abroad. Obama's opening letter to the 2015 *National Security Strategy* again revealed this contradictory tension. While the document described America's global leadership role as 'indispensable,' it stated that American resources and influence were not infinite and that the United States should not 'attempt to dictate the trajectory of all unfolding events around the world.'[7] The lessons of the failed military interventions in Iraq and Afghanistan were translated by Obama into a political maxim that the United States should avoid making 'stupid' mistakes, resulting from moral absolutism, exceptionalist hubris, and a misguided faith in military solutions to complex political problems. In articulating this grand strategy vision, Obama thus reconfirmed a national and bipartisan consensus – the ideational dimension of American exceptionalism, liberal hegemony, and military supremacy – while simultaneously linking this hegemonic, geopolitical identity of the United States to a pragmatic policy course of cooperative engagement and military restraint that large segments of the Washington establishment rejected for challenging the elite consensus on liberal hegemony.

THE OBAMA DOCTRINE AND THE ELITE CHALLENGE TO THE WASHINGTON CONSENSUS FROM WITHIN

On a trip to Asia in April 2014, President Obama employed a uniquely American baseball analogy to contrast the popular reflection of his foreign policy in Washington with his own definition of the 'Obama Doctrine':

> You hit singles, you hit doubles; every once in a while we may be able to hit a home run. That may not always be sexy. That may not always attract a lot of attention, and it doesn't make for good argument on Sunday morning shows. But we steadily advance the interests of the American people and our partnership with folks around the world.[8]

This careful appreciation for the scope and limitations of American power and influence in the world by the President of the United States renewed once more a virulent debate about Obama's grand strategy in American media and the US foreign policy establishment.[9] In fact, shortly after his Asia trip, and after an even more offhand description of his basic foreign policy premise had become prominent, Obama announced a final drawdown of US forces from Afghanistan until 2016. This was supposed to end America's longest running war by the time the President would leave office in 2017, yet it also provided his critics with further evidence that a policy of geopolitical retrenchment lay at the heart of Obama's grand strategy.[10] Partly to counter this prevalent criticism of his administration's retreat from American leadership, Obama presented a much anticipated declaration of the 'Obama Doctrine' on May 28, 2014 before the graduation class of the US Military Academy at West Point, the same location where he had announced a substantial troop increase to Afghanistan five years earlier. As announced by the White House, the President would now, after having wound up the legacy of the Bush wars, finally offer his own strategic vision of national security.[11]

Far from a new or original interpretation of America's role in the world, however, Obama used his West Point speech to reiterate a series of familiar themes that were prevalent in his formulation of grand strategy ever since he took office in January 2009: the continued indispensability of American world leadership; a strong emphasis on cooperative engagement, and increased burden sharing with allies and partners in support of a liberal international order; the end of America's decade of war, a more limited national security focus on counter-terrorism; and finally a prioritization of America's domestic renewal and greater concern with military restraint and the prudent use of American power abroad.[12] As Obama explained at West Point:

> America must always lead on the world stage. If we don't, no one else will. The military ... is, and always will be, the backbone of that leadership. But U.S. military action cannot be the only, or even primary, component of our leadership in every instance. Just because we have the best hammer does not mean that every problem is a nail.[13]

Far from a coherent strategic vision, the West Point speech revealed once more the inherent tension between the established hegemonic imagination of American exceptionalism and its foundation in military pre-eminence, and countering discourses of 'nation-building at home,' and 'leading from behind.' Unable and unwilling to artificially dissolve this tension, Obama thus formulated a grand strategy that failed to deliver the coherent rationale and consistent narrative that most experts and commentators demanded of the 'big picture' of America's role in the world.[14] Obama's presentation at West Point and the controversial reaction to it in American media and expert circles, from *CNN* and *The New York Times* to *Foreign Affairs* and *The National Interest*, once again confirmed the intertextual connectivity but also the hybridity and ideational complexity of the President's geopolitical vision, which Obama himself had placed between the contradictory impulses of 'isolationism' and 'interventionism.'[15]

As William Martel has argued, the difficulty of formulating a coherent and consistent American grand strategy after the end of the Cold War – while missing a clearly defined primary adversary like the Soviet Union – was encountered by all American presidents, and the much coveted and sought after elegance of containment critics and foreign policy experts regularly demanded, historically represented 'the exception rather than the norm.'[16] As Obama himself acknowledged, his grand strategy was not always 'sexy.' Nor, apparently could it fit on a bumper sticker.[17] In fact, Ben Rhodes, one of the President's closest national security advisers, perfectly illustrated this tension between a geopolitical complexity as framed by the Obama White House and the reductionist demands for an American grand strategy as succinct as containment:

> If you were to boil it all down to a bumper sticker, it's 'Wind down these two wars, reestablish American standing and leadership in the world, and focus on a broader set of priorities, from Asia and the global economy to a nuclear-nonproliferation regime'.[18]

As such, each post-Cold War American President would not only face the historic legacy of containment, which constituted a mythologized ideal of visionary thinking and long-term strategic planning in US foreign policy circles, but the challenge to reconcile contradictory impulses emerging from America's main foreign policy traditions. As identified by Walter Russell Mead: a Hamiltonian emphasis on international commerce and free trade; a Jeffersonian focus on perfecting American democracy at home; Jacksonian unilateral nationalism; and the transformative impetus of Wilsonian liberal idealism. All were frequently reproduced as guiding principles in official rhetoric and intellectual expertise.[19] Yet on an ideational level of identity construction, all post-Cold War American grand strategies – from George H. W. Bush's 'New World Order' and Bill Clinton's 'Engagement and Enlargement' strategy to George W. Bush's emphasis on unilateralism and pre-emption – represented mere variations of the theme of liberal hegemony, securing and expanding US leadership and national security within an international system defined by democracy and capitalism.

Within this continuity, Obama's grand strategy of hegemonic restraint and limited engagement presented the greatest challenge to the status quo to date, and the criticism by US foreign policy experts about it lacking coherence and consistency was more vehement than under his predecessors, as it signaled a significant departure from the Washington consensus in both discourse and practice. Both conservative and liberal proponents of the Washington consensus on hegemony reacted negatively to Obama's vision for America's role in the world. They criticized a mood of national decline, an era of shrinkage, and a strategy of global retrenchment and restraint to have taken hold under the Obama presidency: signs of weakness they believed responsible for dangerously undermining a liberal world order of American origin.[20]

This was particularly the case for conservative critics and Obama's opponents in the Republican Party, who attacked Obama's supposed lack of vigor and lack of faith in American exceptionalism. Charles Krauthammer expressed this deep-seated conservative frustration and exasperation with Obama's grand strategy: 'As with the West Point speech itself, as with the President's entire foreign policy of retreat, one can only marvel at the smallness of it all.'[21] Kagan in turn had criticized Obama's retreat from the world and a national mood of inward-looking passivity in a lengthy tractate for *New Republic* titled 'Superpowers Don't Get to Retire.' Other critics of US foreign and security policy, such as Oliver Stone or Andrew Bacevich, in turn charged Obama not for a lack of leadership resolve, but for continuing on the misguided path of American Empire.[22]

In April 2016, then, the American magazine *The Atlantic* featured the 'Obama Doctrine' as its cover title. President Obama used this popular media outlet to once more place his foreign policy course between 'internationalism' and 'realism,' laying out an American grand strategy of engaged multilateralism and military restraint. At the same time, Obama declared that in 2013 over Syria, he had finally thrown out a 'Washington playbook' of intervening militarily to demonstrate American resolve to the world. The American President pointedly criticized the US foreign policy establishment and Washington think tank scene for fetishizing American credibility abroad and militarizing US policy responses.[23] The criticism of the 'Obama Doctrine' by large segments of that same Washington establishment in turn reached a highpoint over the aborted plan to launch US air strikes against the Assad regime, and the caveated 'no boots on the ground' intervention against the Islamic State terror organization that began in September 2014.[24] Prominent media pundits, foreign policy experts, neoconservative hawks, and liberal interventionists accused Obama of following a vision that led the United States into retreat.[25]

Obama's geopolitical vision and conduct of national security policy responded to what the President defined as a heightened complexity of world politics at the beginning of the twenty-first century. Here, various economic, social, and political dynamics did not allow for coherent but overly simplistic narratives, supposed to capture a nation's imagination and give purpose to its power. While not quite post-American, the 'Obama Doctrine' was characterized by a multiplicity of discourses and the fluidity of meaning that was rejected by Obama's many critics on both the left and right. The 'Obama Doctrine' disappointed demands for a strategic course correction by critics of the Washington consensus, yet at the same time Obama did not fully subscribe to the elite accord of liberal hegemony, resulting in the contradictory character of the Obama Doctrine that oscillated between hegemony, engagement and restraint.

LEADING THROUGH ENGAGEMENT IN A POST-AMERICAN WORLD

Obama made it clear from the onset of his presidency that his vision for America's role in the world was intended to depart significantly from that of his predecessor, which had been marked by a preference for unilateralism, a doctrine of pre-emptive warfare, and a simplistic, Manichean rhetoric of 'you're either with us or against us' that expected fellowship and support rather than inviting mutual consultation and collaboration. Against this unapologetic display of American primacy by the George W. Bush administration, in particular during Bush's first term, Obama contrasted a geopolitical vision of engagement and cooperation for the United States. In 2009, in his first State of the Union address, Obama announced this shift of perspective for US foreign policy that seemed to correspond with his central campaign message of 'hope' and 'change':

> In words and deeds, we are showing the world that a new era of engagement has begun. For we know that America cannot meet the threats of this century alone, but the world cannot meet them without America.[26]

A policy of engagement and Obama's rhetoric of mutual respect were meant to restore the credibility and international legitimacy of the United States and its policies, which under Bush had reached a dramatic low point in many parts of the world.[27] According to a Pew research poll, released in July 2009, this campaign was initially successful: 'The image of the United States has improved markedly in most parts of the world, reflecting global confidence in Barack Obama.'[28] While Obama's approval ratings abroad went down in subsequent years, in part due to his controversial signature counter-terrorism policy of drone strikes, they never reached the lows of his predecessor.[29] A central point in Obama's speeches and statements was that the United States was strongest when it could lead through the power of its example, not alone the example of its power.[30]

This key idea also entered the text of the *National Security Strategy* of 2010, which stated: 'Our moral leadership is grounded principally in the power of our example—not through an effort to impose our system on other peoples.'[31] The idea that American leadership and moral authority in the world could be restored and renewed through a collaborative network of allies and partners represented a long-standing political belief of Obama's. While still a US Senator, he had formulated a distinct vision for a different set of domestic and foreign policies in his best-selling book *The Audacity of Hope*. Here, he displayed a clear preference for principled multilateralism: 'Acting multilaterally means . . . engaging in the hard diplomatic work of obtaining most of the world's support for our actions, and making sure our actions serve to further recognize international norms.'[32] In his speeches and statements on multilateralism and a collaborative foreign policy, President Obama primarily connected with an established liberal discourse of hegemonic engagement. However, where Obama's geopolitical vision of cooperation went further than established notions of multilateral leadership was that he demonstrated a willingness early on to engage with states considered America's adversaries, like Iran, Russia, or Cuba, without fixed preconditions or political demands to the other side.[33]

During the Democratic, primaries Hillary Clinton, Obama's main inner-party opponent, would exploit this relatively open stand vis-à-vis countries considered to be America's rivals to attack his inexperience in foreign policy.[34] John McCain later accused his Democratic opponent of being naive in the face of grievous threats to the nation.[35] This conservative charge against Obama's supposed weakness, lack of leadership credibility, and missing conviction in American power would re-emerge in the 2012 campaign, when Obama's Republican challenger Mitt Romney attacked President Obama for constantly 'apologizing' for America, and not believing in American exceptionalism.[36]

Obama's rhetoric and invitation to dialogue with members of Bush's infamous 'axis of evil' further underlined his promise of a policy change in Washington; a break with the usual 'threat inflation' and the political class's hyperbole, just as Obama's vote against the Iraq War had set him apart from establishment figures like McCain and Clinton, who had both supported the decision to go to war. As *The New York Times* journalist David Sanger observed, Obama promised to restore American engagement by talking and listening to America's most troubling and reluctant partners.[37] Obama documented this willingness for a new era of cooperative engagement on several occasions. One of the most visible examples was his presidential speech at the University of Cairo in June 2009, meant as 'a new beginning' between the United States and the Muslim world, based on 'mutual interest and mutual respect.'[38]

Here, Obama also invited discussions between the United States and the Islamic Republic of Iran, again 'without preconditions on the basis of mutual respect.'[39] However, on Iran, the Obama administration actually pursued a two-pronged strategy of diplomatic engagement and economic sanctions, meant to dissuade the country from developing nuclear weapons – a strategy that would ultimately prove successful in July 2015 with the conclusion of the Iran nuclear framework agreement. At the same time, Obama had frequently declared that the United States considered a nuclear armed Iran 'unacceptable,' and that military solutions would be 'on the table' in dealing with such an obvious threat to US national security.[40] The Iran example illustrates how cooperative engagement and multilateral diplomacy were not an exclusive grand strategy in itself, but merely one element in Obama's pursuit of national security and foreign policy.

In many ways Obama's pursuit of US national security, then, represented not a break with the previous Bush administration and its policies, but a continuation, and in the case of drone strikes, even an escalation. This continuity between Bush and Obama was particularly pronounced in counter-terrorism policy.[41] While Obama, for example, suspended the use of 'enhanced interrogation techniques' by the CIA, such as the infamous water boarding, and replaced the 'War on Terror' terminology with the less martial sounding phrase 'countering violent extremism,' he at the same time intensified the use of surveillance technologies and covert military operations, in particular the use of unmanned aerial vehicles (UAVs) to identify, target, and eliminate suspected terrorists, expanding US operations in Yemen and Pakistan, while simultaneously withdrawing American ground troops from Iraq.[42] The 2009 'surge' of US troops in Afghanistan, undertaken to implement a comprehensive COIN strategy in the country, was likewise modeled after the troop increase authorized by Bush in 2007 in Iraq. Leading political and military figures like Gates, Petraeus, and McChrystal, who had already served under Obama's predecessor, strongly advocated the intensification of US military engagement.

As such, Obama rejected some of the more bellicose, Manichean rhetoric and unilateral impulses of the Bush administration, but he did not engage in a fundamental reorientation of US policy, nor ultimately questioned the preventive logic of a militarized US counter-terrorism policy that sought to eliminate terrorist threats abroad before they could materialize on the US homeland. The hegemonic discourse of the 'War on Terror' which had been institutionalized and normalized under Bush stayed largely intact, even if the very phrase was no longer in use.[43] Obama's public announcement to close down the Guantanamo prison camp within a year after he took office was thus undertaken primarily to restore America's moral standing in the world, as was the rhetorical shift away from the 'War on Terror' and the presidential ban on torture. However, Obama failed to deliver on this promise in the face of Congressional opposition and negative public opinion, and continued the indefinite incarceration of 'enemy combatants,' held in an ambiguous legal status in one of the most notorious sites associated with America's global 'War on Terror.' As Matthew Waxman, senior fellow for law and foreign policy at the conservative Hoover Institution has argued: 'While it decries Guantanamo as contrary to American values, the Obama administration has convinced courts of Guantanamo's legal validity.'[44] Thus, while frequently mobilizing the foundation of America's liberal values and stressing a departure from Bush in rhetorical style, Obama tacitly acknowledged or even openly endorsed security practices that represented the substance of Bush's policies, and that directly challenged this vaunted liberal identity. This contradictory stance led to a persistent criticism of Obama's policies by the American left and international human rights organizations, with the civilian casualties produced by US drone strikes serving as a focal point of that criticism.[45]

The charge against Obama's naiveté in wanting to engage countries like Iran or Russia in turn, and to not clearly label them as enemies or adversaries of the United States, formed part of a larger discourse in expert circles, elite media, and American politics that questioned the conduct of US foreign and security policy under Obama, not for the contradiction between liberal identity and illiberal security practices, but because it did not fully comply with the dominant mainstream consensus on American hegemony. Both neoconservative and liberal internationalist critics accused Obama's grand strategy of 'weakness' and 'retreat.'[46] Here, Obama appeared as both weak in the face of great power aggression – as with Russian incursions into Ukraine, or China's territorial claims in the South China Sea – and as passive and aloof from the concerns for human rights, opposing, for example, the establishment of a no-fly zone in Syria.

To the various neoconservative and liberal proponents of the hegemony discourse, 'American leadership,' usually a standard metaphor meaning the use of force by the United States, was the universal answer to international crises as regionally and topically varied as Russia's resurgence under Putin, the rise of China, and the advance of Islamic State in the Middle East. Obama's lack of leadership in turn, i.e. his reluctance to use or consider the use of hard power, thus had supposedly provoked the outbreak of these crises in the first place, or exaggerated their negative effects. This criticism of the 'Obama Doctrine' displayed an intellectual fixation with an America-centric, militarized unipolarity that was fundamentally at odds with the geopolitics of interdependence, to which Obama regularly referred to in his foreign policy speeches. Here, world politics was shaped less through the effects of military power and less clearly defined along the lines of Manichean dichotomies of friendship or enmity with the United States. As Obama explained at West Point, while the United States was and remained 'the one indispensable nation,' the world had changed:[47] 'From Brazil to India, rising middle classes compete with us, and governments seek a greater say in global forums.'[48]

Obama's grand strategy vision, and in particular his emphasis on engagement, were reflecting America's changing role in a post-American world, in which the diffusion of power and the 'rise of the rest' were ending an era of American unipolar primacy, and where relative decline would mean that the United States was still the most influential, but no longer the sole, dominant power in the international system.[49] Now, more countries than ever before demanded a voice in global governance, and required attention, respect, and consultation. Military power was no longer the sole determinant of global influence in this world, and the efficacy of military solutions was seriously in doubt after the Iraq and Afghanistan experiences. As Obama remarked during a G-20 summit in London, the world had changed: 'If it's just Roosevelt and Churchill sitting in a room with brandy . . . that's an easier negotiation. But that's not the world we live in.'[50]

Obama was famously photographed on the campaign trail holding a copy of Zakaria's best-seller that had firmly established the notion of a 'post-American world' in American geopolitical discourse.[51] Yet, despite the sometimes more outspoken, sometimes more tacit, acknowledgement of post-American dynamics and geopolitical scenarios of relative decline, as, for example, in Obama's speeches, the NIC's strategic forecasts, or the Pentagon's *QDR* reports, the underlying assumption among Washington elites was that other countries still 'anticipated, expected and demanded' American leadership of the international community.[52] The politically widely shared and culturally deeply embedded discourse of hegemony framed American leadership not only as resulting from superior economic and military resources, and the attractiveness of American values, but also as stemming from the clear demand of other nations.

However, the regular professions by American elites on how foreign countries instinctively turned to the United States for guidance and leadership clearly only reflected a partial reality of American influence in a globalized and increasingly multipolar world. This was evident, for example, in Germany's refusal to follow American demands for larger fiscal stimulus packages for the Eurozone, the unwillingness of most NATO allies to substantially increase their military commitments to the US-led Afghanistan mission, or China's reluctance to accommodate the United States by raising the exchange rate of its currency. As remarked by US government officials, when Obama came to office he and his administration did not face a 'rising India and China,' these countries had already risen.[53] In the words of Robert Singh, when Obama entered the White House 'many nations and peoples were simply not looking to Washington any longer.'[54]

In fact, the Gallup Global Leadership Track, the largest global public opinion study of views about American leadership, concluded in 2013 that the image of US leadership had weakened over the course of the Obama presidency:

> Obama and new Secretary of State John Kerry may not find global audiences as receptive to advancing the U.S. agenda as they have in the past. In fact, they may even find audiences increasingly critical — even in key partner countries.[55]

Yet, presidential rhetoric, expert opinion, and popular sentiment regularly intersected in supporting and perpetuating a worldview of exceptionalist singularity and global superiority. The American foreign policy establishment displayed traits of something akin to hegemonic narcissism, when the rest of the world was perceived almost exclusively through the prism of America's own vaunted leadership role. Not only was the world 'made in America,' it was also the only positive world imaginable.[56] However, the notion of a post-American world, and US policies that seemed to fall in line with such sentiments, represented a prevailing counter-influence in American grand strategy discourse. Obama's efforts for enhanced 'burden sharing' with allies and partners and engagement with adversaries counteracted the Washington consensus on hegemony and the perceived uniqueness of America's world political role. As Zakaria commented in *The Washington Post* on this tension between established notions of past American primacy and the post-American future tacitly outlined by Obama:

> Washington's elites — politicians and intellectuals — miss the old days as well. They wish for the world in which the United States was utterly dominant over its friends, its foes were to be shunned entirely and the challenges were stark, moral and vital.[57]

In the interdependent world President Obama described, American leadership was less, not more important than before, and the perception of American power and influence by others was not static, as usually implied in American grand strategy discourse, but constantly changing and adapting, in part due to developments, like the 'rise of China,' entirely outside of American control, again suggesting less, not more, global influence for the United States. Although the discourse of engagement promoted by Obama was meant to serve as a bridge, this fundamental tension between the perception of an increasingly post-American world and the continued profession of America's indispensable leadership role remained unresolved in Obama's strategic vision.

NATION-BUILDING AT HOME, COVERT OPERATIONS ABROAD

Engagement under Obama was also meant to correct an over-reliance on military force, the fixation on national security threats, and a pervasive polarization of foreign policy and national security issues that had dominated under Bush and that continued to inform the Washington consensus on hegemony. As Deputy National Security Adviser Ben Rhodes, one of Obama's speechwriters and closest foreign policy advisors, described this shift against established opinion in the strategic vision of the Obama administration:

> What's notable in some of the debate is how much U.S. engagement abroad is viewed through the prism of whether or not we're taking military action, almost up to the point that if you're not

using the military you're not dealing with issues . . . We're seeking to reorient that to show that you can use diplomacy to try to resolve conflicts like we're doing in the Middle East.[58]

Together with his emphasis on engagement, President Obama reformulated the use of American military power for the pursuit of US national security in significant ways, and by doing so partially redefined the meaning of America's global military pre-eminence in grand strategy discourse. When Obama entered the White House he inherited two ongoing wars. The war in Iraq he had always opposed, and characterized as the 'dumb war.'[59] On February 27, 2009, Obama fulfilled one of his central campaign promises, when he announced that all US forces would leave Iraq by the end of 2011.

Afghanistan, however, Obama had referred to as a 'war of necessity' that had been under-resourced by the Bush administration, because of the distraction of Iraq.[60] Obama intended to change this. Shortly after his inauguration in January 2009, he authorized a troop increase in Afghanistan of 17,000 soldiers in response to an urgent request by the local commander of US forces, General McKiernan, and while an initial sixty-day review of the war launched by the White House was still underway.[61] As *The New York Times* observed, the war in Afghanistan would from now on carry 'Obama's stamp.'[62] At the end of an initial sixty-day review, President Obama agreed to dispatch another 4,000 soldiers to Afghanistan to implement a COIN strategy, and to 'disrupt, dismantle and defeat' Al Qaeda.[63] This review had also included Flournoy, who together with the Center for a New American Security had been a staunch supporter of COIN operations from the outset. As James Mann reported: 'Flournoy returned again and again to core COIN concepts.'[64] As with the preparation of the 2010 *QDR*, the implementation of a strategy of COIN for Afghanistan by the Obama White House was also the result of an institutionalized exchange in the production of strategic knowledge via Washington's 'rotating door', linking the policy advice of think tanks and the policymaking of defense officials and security experts.

As a result of a more comprehensive three-month Afghanistan review Obama then agreed to send an additional 30,000 troops to Afghanistan in November 2009, bringing the total American troop strength there to just under 100,000. However, with the decision to 'surge' in Afghanistan, announced at West Point on December 1, 2009, Obama, at the same time changed gear and set new priorities for the war, including a fixed date for the withdrawal of the American military presence there. As Obama declared:

> We have been at war now for eight years, at enormous cost in lives and resources . . . And having just experienced the worst economic crisis since the Great Depression, the American people are understandably focused on rebuilding our economy and putting people to work here at home.[65]

Instead of victory through an open-ended COIN operation, Obama focused on an exit strategy that would allow the United States to start withdrawing its troops from Afghanistan from July 2011 onwards. After the end of 2014, US troops would no longer serve in an active combat role, apart from a residual presence meant for CT operations to keep a check on the remnants of the Al Qaeda network in Afghanistan and Pakistan. As with US withdrawal from Iraq, however, Obama would later have to partially reverse his decision, declaring in July 2016 that up to 8,400 American troops (instead of 5,500 as originally planned) would remain in Afghanistan for the remainder of his presidency to train Afghan forces and support operations against Al Qaeda and other armed groups, including Islamic State.[66]

Overall, however, Obama switched to a strategy of 'good enough' in Afghanistan.[67] This shift in priorities was supposed to finally allow the United States to focus on 'nation-building at home.'[68] As Obama declared during his 2012 State of the Union address: 'Take the money we're no longer spending at war, use half of it to pay down our debt, and use the rest to do some nation-building right here at home.'[69] Over the course of his presidency, and in particular in his second term in office, Obama would continue to emphasize his focus on ending America's wars, not to start new ones, and to weigh his commitment to American national security against his domestic priorities of reforming healthcare, revitalizing the economy, and putting the federal budget on a sustainable path. During the 2014 State of the Union address Obama declared: 'We must fight the battles that need to be fought, not those that terrorists prefer from us – large-scale deployments that drain our strength and may ultimately feed extremism.'[70] Obama's emphasis on military restraint, and the need to rebuild American strength at home, then, were directly linked to key arguments presented by prominent critics of the Washington consensus on liberal hegemony. As Walt, for example, explained: 'That strategy – which would eschew nation-building and large onshore ground and air deployments – would both increase our freedom of action and dampen anti-Americanism in a number of key areas.'[71]

As Cato would put it: 'We should reduce our military power in order to be more secure.'[72] When in September 2014 Obama announced a new US-led offensive against the Islamic State terror organization, which had conquered large swaths of territory in Iraq and Syria, he made it clear that above all else he wanted to avoid getting sucked back into the quagmire of Iraq.[73] While Obama declared a prolonged campaign to destroy Islamic State, including the formation of an international coalition to that effect, and announced US air strikes in Syria, Obama over the coming months vehemently and repeatedly ruled out American 'boots on the ground.'[74] Obama thus ruled out an active ground combat role for the US military, yet thousands of US soldiers would indeed return to the country. In presenting his strategy against Islamic State, Obama also reiterated the theme of burden sharing that would allow the United States once again to lead from behind: '. . . this is not our fight alone. American power can make a decisive difference, but we cannot do for Iraqis what they must do for themselves, nor can we take the place of Arab partners in securing their region.'[75]

The strong intertextuality between Obama's rhetoric and political course of action and libertarian and realist arguments for restraint and offshore balancing, again demonstrated that the practical grand strategy discourse under Obama could not be reduced to liberal ideas of cooperative engagement and multilateralism. At the same time, Obama was by no means an isolationist or pacifist, and demonstrated a willingness to use military force unilaterally, when deemed necessary for the vital security interests of the United States, as with the violation of Pakistani sovereignty in the bin Laden raid. As Obama had declared in his Nobel Peace Prize acceptance speech in December 2009: 'Negotiations cannot convince al Qaeda's leaders to lay down their arms. To say that force may sometimes be necessary is not a call to cynicism – it is a recognition of history; the imperfections of man and the limits of reason.'[76]

President Obama's strategic vision, then, incorporated significant elements of realpolitik thinking and a realist concern for conserving America's financial, economic, and military strength, while voicing fundamental doubts over the efficacy of military interventions. This strong emphasis on restraint in Obama's strategic thinking was also reflected in his frequently stated admiration for Reinhold Niebuhr, a Protestant theologian, who had warned against Americans' penchant for assuming a stance of moral superiority and their own innocence in conducting foreign affairs, instead advocating a course of moderation and humility.[77]

Besides attempting to end the wars in Iraq and Afghanistan, Obama also followed a course of greater military restraint when he initiated the profound rhetorical and operational shift away from the strategic focus on Bush's 'War on Terror.' During a speech at the NDU in May 2013, one of the nation's prime locations for the senior military education of grand strategy, Obama declared a change in American counter-terrorism strategy that was widely perceived as an unofficial announcement of an end to the conflict.[78] As Obama explained in his speech, 'every war must come to an end':

> Neither I, nor any President can promise the total defeat of terror . . . Targeted actions against terrorists, effective partnerships, diplomatic engagement and assistance – through such a comprehensive strategy we can significantly reduce the chances of large-scale attacks on the homeland and mitigate threats to Americans overseas.[79]

The President redefined Bush's global war into a strategy to manage an existing but not existential threat to the United States.[80] The NDU speech, at the same time, implied that the United States would continue to rely on one particular instrument in America's counter-terrorism arsenal: drones. As outlined earlier in the chapter, under Obama there had been a marked increase in drone strikes against suspected terrorist targets in Afghanistan, Pakistan, and other countries, such as Yemen and Somalia.[81] These attacks with guided bombs and missiles on suspected terrorist targets, launched from remote-controlled, unmanned aerial vehicles, were credited by US officials for having seriously 'disrupted and degraded' Al Qaeda and affiliated groups and their operational capacity. In the words of Obama: 'Dozens of highly skilled Al Qaeda commanders, trainers, bomb makers and operatives have been taken off the battlefield.'[82]

At NDU, Obama presented several criteria under which the United States was supposed to operate in relation to drone strikes and counter-terrorism policy. These included an existing agreement of cooperation between the US and the country above whose territory the drones operated, the use of drones only where the insertion of special operations troops was not feasible, and the use of drones without host nation consent, only if a government was either incapable, or unwilling, to operate against suspected terrorists. Yet, the fact remained that the use of drones and other covert operations represented a powerful, if largely invisible, expression of American primacy.

Violating the territorial integrity and sovereignty of other nations was fundamentally at odds with notions of cooperative engagement and mutual respect. The outrage the bin Laden raid had produced in Pakistan over the covert infiltration of Pakistani territory in 2011 had triggered a political fallout that had never been fully resolved.[83] Furthermore, as McCrisken and Phythian have pointed out, Obama's use of drones raised questions over the 'morality, legitimacy, accountability, and proportionality' of targeted killings and US counterterrorism policy in general.[84] At the same time, drones were a stopgap measure, a tactical, technological solution to the symptoms of terrorism and violent extremism, but not a long-term strategy to combat its root causes. According to Dennis Blair, the former DNI, Obama's signature counter-terrorism policy was politically advantageous: 'low cost, no U.S. casualties, gives the appearance of toughness. It plays well domestically, and it is unpopular only in other countries.'[85]

In combination with Obama's use of Special Forces – as highlighted by the successful raid on Osama bin Laden by US Navy SEALs on May 2, 2011, the suspected use of cyber technologies against Iran's nuclear program, such as the 'stuxnet' computer virus, or the comprehensive surveillance activities by the NSA, revealed by the agency's former contractor Edward Snowden – the use of American power by President Obama reformulated the exercise of US hegemony in surprising ways.[86] This also found a particular echo in American popular culture, from the Pentagon-supported and Navy-produced *Act of Valor*, to the immensely successful *Call of Duty* video game franchise, which regularly featured the use of drones and US special operations soldiers in global counter-terrorism campaigns. A prominent example was also Katherine Bigelow's *Zero Dark Thirty* (2012) on the CIA's ten-year hunt for Osama bin Laden.[87]

Yet, Obama's aggressive counter-terrorism policy also counteracted his pledge to seek a 'new beginning' with Muslim counties. According to opinion polls, in the Middle East hostility toward the United States was higher in 2013 than when Obama became President. Aside from assurances by US officials, inducing the President that US actions were 'effective,' and 'legal,' and that drone targets would be carefully selected and 'collateral damage' kept to a minimum, no fundamental change of policy was likely to occur under Obama. Remarkably, President Obama was directly involved in approving the individual targets of drone strikes, a personal participation of an American President in the details of military operations not seen since President Lyndon B. Johnson personally approved targets for US air strikes over North Vietnam.

Where President Obama's vision of engagement attempted to balance a tacit appreciation for what has been dubbed the 'post-American world' with the continued emphasis on American leadership, a similar tension in grand strategy discourse existed in the President's repeated insistencies that the 'tide of war' was turning and in the increased covert use of American military power and secret intelligence assets abroad. While the era of large-scale American COIN operations in Iraq and Afghanistan was ending, the United States continued to wage a war from the shadows against suspected terrorists and their networks. These covert tools of American primacy demonstrated a continued reliance on unilateralism, and the global projection of military power in the pursuit of US national security, but with almost no risk of American casualties, and far fewer financial resources required. Practically, the use of these covert instruments of American power did fall in line with Obama's verdict that US national security should be pursued more cost-effectively, with less direct military involvement on the ground, and less burden on the American taxpayer. Obama, then, reoriented and recalibrated the use of force by the United States, switching from expansive ground combat operations to a more limited application of military power, primarily air power, while simultaneously perpetuating a condition of permanent war under which the United States operated in the post-9/11 environment.

Discursively, however, SEAL Team 6, stuxnet, and the NSA represented a 'black hole' at the center of the 'Obama Doctrine.'[88] As *The New York Times* reporters Joe Becker and Scott Shane remarked: His [President Obama's] actions have often remained inscrutable, obscured by awkward secrecy rules, polarized political commentary and the President's own deep reserve.[89] What was occasionally referred to as the 'light footprint' of the 'Obama Doctrine' by administration officials in fact appeared as the dark side of Obama's policy of military restraint that only rarely entered the spotlight of presidential rhetoric, or publicly available government documents.[90] Obama's use of drones and Special Forces was an integral part of a strategic vision that attempted to reconcile 'nation-building at home' with pursuit of a preventive, militarized counter-terrorism policy across the globe. Discursively, this fundamental tension in the execution of American power under Obama, between hegemony and restraint, would find maybe its most accurate expression in the phrase 'leading from behind.'

LEADING FROM BEHIND

The end of America's wars in Iraq and Afghanistan notwithstanding, global leadership and military pre-eminence remained the basic tenet of the dominant American grand strategy discourse in Washington: a lens of geopolitical indispensability, national exceptionalism, and military singularity through which America's global role was constructed in the eyes of elites and the public. A 2011 Pew research poll, for example, found that nine out of ten Americans, across party lines, stated that the United States either stood above all other countries in the world (38 percent) or was one of the greatest along with some others (53 percent).[91] At the same time, however, the geopolitical ambition and scope of the American leadership role were being scaled back under Obama, adding a further dimension of tension and inconsistency in grand strategy discourse. Aside from the end of the wars in Iraq and Afghanistan, and the abandonment of COIN as a military strategy of choice, this was most visible in Obama's 'leading from behind' approach in the Libyan crisis, and his response to the use of chemical weapons in Syria.

According to several congruent media reports, it was due to substantial pressure from some of the key members within his own administration that Obama gave his approval for American military support of the Libyan rebels fighting Gaddafi in March 2011.[92] In publicly advocating America's involvement in Libya, the President then once again invoked the image of American indispensability:

> To brush aside America's responsibility as a leader and — more profoundly — our responsibilities to our fellow human beings under such circumstances would have been a betrayal of who we are. Some nations may be able to turn a blind eye to atrocities in other countries. The United States of America is different.[93]

The United States however, soon withdrew from the frontlines and let NATO, especially France and the United Kingdom, take the lead in operating militarily against Gaddafi.[94] This new, more cooperative, and at the same time more limited and restrained approach would become famous as 'leading from behind.' The term was attributed to an unknown member of Obama's national security staff, and found a wide media echo, in particular after it featured prominently in an article published in *The New Yorker*.[95]

The political and public reaction to 'leading from behind' was so strong because the term seemed to encapsulate a new geopolitical vision, a new way in which the United States exercised its power, and understood its hegemonic position in world politics. As Ryan Lizza, the author of *The New Yorker* article, put it: 'at the heart of the idea of leading from behind is the empowerment of other actors to do your bidding . . . .'[96] At the same time, as the advisor who coined the phrase admitted, this approach counteracted the dominant, popular imagination of America's world role and basic understanding of who the country was and how it acted: 'It's so at odds with the John Wayne expectation for what America is in the world.'[97] Under Obama, the global sheriff was looking for deputies. To Republicans 'leading from behind' represented further proof that Obama's vision consisted of diminishing American power in the world, and accepting American decline.[98] Although Obama never used the term 'leading from behind' himself, it seemed to fit with the geopolitical vision of America's changed role in a more interdependent world that he had laid out in successive statements and speeches. At the same time, the popular reaction to 'leading from behind,' revealed the American public's great ambivalence over changes in the identity discourse.

There was a growing popular sentiment in the United States, which questioned the country's extensive foreign commitments, and which demanded greater focus on domestic concerns. A much reported Pew research poll in 2013, for example, found that 52 percent of Americans were of the opinion that the United States should 'mind its own business internationally and let other countries get along the best they can on their own' – the first time since 1964 that more than half the public held that view.[99] This result and similar polls like it were promptly denounced as a sign of a dangerously increasing mood of 'isolationism' among the American people by proponents of the hegemony discourse in an attempt to discredit views suggesting greater American restraint on the world stage.[100]

This included key elite media outlets like *The Washington Post, The New York Times*, or *The Wall Street Journal*.[101] As such, the public's endorsement of 'leading from behind' and policies of greater restraint also revealed a widening rift between the foreign policy establishment, including the media, and the popular sentiment of a majority of ordinary Americans. This rift would culminate in the candidacy and

eventual election of Donald Trump to the presidency. Trump had formulated his populist vision of economic protectionism, nativist nationalism, and isolationism as a direct attack on the status quo favored by
the Washington establishment and his Democratic opponent Hillary
Clinton.

In trying to differentiate a policy of non-interventionism and military
restraint from the stigma of isolationism employed by neoconservative
primacists and liberal hegemonists, Obama was again reproducing key
arguments forwarded by proponents of the restraint discourse. As Cato,
for example, commented: 'the public is neither isolationist nor misguided when it comes to foreign policy. Americans do not want to
withdraw from the world; they just prefer not to try to run it with their
military.'[102] Obama made his case for greater restraint at West Point
like this:

> Since World War II, some of our most costly mistakes came not
> from our restraint but from our willingness to rush into military
> adventures without thinking through the consequences, with-
> out building international support and legitimacy for our action,
> without leveling with the American people about the sacrifices
> required.[103]

Obama's careful shift in perspective about the possibilities of America's
role in the world, and the more limited meaning of military force, however, seemed also to correspond with a certain generational change in
popular attitudes toward American exceptionalism. A 2011 Pew poll
found that only 32 percent of the Millennials' generation in the United
States thought their country was 'the greatest in the world' — compared
to 72 percent of those between the ages of 76–83 years.[104]

Even more striking when considering the established mainstream
consensus on US foreign policy were poll results about popular sentiments of Americans toward American leadership in the world, the
sacrosanct mantra of the grand strategy discourse in Washington that
Obama too was unwilling to breach. As Pew reported in August 2014,
about 70 percent of Americans favored a 'shared leadership role in
the world.'[105] Despite the majority of popular, formal, and practical
discourses that overwhelmingly stressed the exceptionalism and indispensability of American leadership in the world, and the paramount
importance of US military pre-eminence for peace, prosperity, and
freedom, a clear majority of Americans seemed willing to accept a more

restrained and less hegemonic role of their country in world politics. As an article in *Time* magazine concluded: 'Simply put, Obama has given the people the foreign policy they want—one in which America "mind[s] its own business."'[106] Obama himself acknowledged this national mood of retrenchment and restraint, when he directly quoted from a veteran's letter addressed to him, during his nationally televised address on Syria on September 10, 2013: 'This nation is sick and tired of war.'[107]

But while in his Syria speech Obama reemphasized his focus to end America's wars, not to start new ones, and to focus on rebuilding the nation at home, he did invoke the image of American exceptionalism as a special responsibility for the United States to act abroad when its unique values where violated, as with the gas attacks attributed to the Assad regime in Syria. Yet, Obama also went to great lengths to distinguish a possible military intervention in Syria from the wars in Iraq and Afghanistan, from the beginning ruling out the possibilities of ground invasion, regime change, or even a prolonged air campaign along the lines of the Kosovo or Libya examples. This caveated, limited, and cautious link between American exceptionalism and the use of force that Obama demonstrated in his speech was ultimately completely severed, when Obama postponed seeking an authorization for military strikes from Congress, a vote he was likely to have lost. Instead, Obama opted for a diplomatic solution in accordance with Russia to get rid of Assad's chemical weapons. Obama had closed his remarks on Syria with the following:

> America is not the world's policeman. Terrible things happen across the globe, and it is beyond our means to right every wrong. But when, with modest effort and risk, we can stop children from being gassed to death . . . I believe we should act. That's what makes America different. That's what makes us exceptional.[108]

The image of American exceptionalism in Obama's speech implied a special responsibility of the United States to commit its outstanding military assets when its liberal values were violated; however, a policy that would demonstrate this failed to materialize. While President Obama had worked toward redefining American grand strategy toward restraint, engagement, and multilateral cooperation, the country's geopolitical identity remained firmly linked to an image of American leadership and military pre-eminence: the use of force in defense of

American values and national interests. On Libya, Obama could reconcile this tension, encapsulated in the phrase 'leading from behind.'[109] On Syria, however, the implied consequences for crossing the 'red lines' Obama set up in his speech did not result in military actions by the United States, and 'red lines' subsequently became a symbol for the perceived weakness of the United States under Obama among conservative critics, foreign policy experts, and the media alike.[110] And even though a majority of Americans had favored a diplomatic solution in Syria, the dominant impression was that Obama and the United States had been diplomatically outmaneuvered by Russia.[111] A CBS/*New York Times* poll, for example, released on September 25, 2013, found that just 37 percent of Americans approved of President Obama's handling of the Syrian crisis.

The controversy over Syria indicated a fundamental tension prevailing in American grand strategy discourse on all levels, between an emphasis on engagement and restraint and policies reflecting this strategic vision, and a hegemonic imagination that continued to represent the country as the world's indispensable and exceptional leader. This political rhetoric of American hegemony in turn produced expectations among elites and the public that Obama's political actions would reflect this ideational paradigm. Yet the somewhat schizophrenic split in Obama's grand strategy – between continued American primacy and greater restraint in a post-American world – was also present within the American population, which according to polls favored diplomatic engagement, and was weary of further military entanglements abroad, but was also critical of the perceived lack of American leadership and resolve on the world stage. 'Leading from behind' seemed quite accurately to describe the mood of a majority of Americans when it came to their country's preferred role in the world, but the implication of a diminished status of the United States was resented at the same time.

CONCLUSION

Obama's vision of American grand strategy combined hegemony, engagement, and restraint, incorporating a set of competing and mutually exclusive discourses. Obama's simultaneous confirmation and contestation of such diverse discursive strands as multilateral hegemony, liberal internationalism, realist offshore balancing, military primacy, and American exceptionalism made it impossible to assign the President's geopolitical vision a clear and distinctive label that would correspond to the narrative cohesiveness and clarity of purpose geopolitical strategists, foreign policy experts, and media pundits expected of an American grand strategy. The dominant voices behind the Washington consensus on hegemony demanded clarity of vision and confirmation of American leadership, not the pragmatic management of relative decline, nor the tacit reorientation toward a more complex and interdependent world of multiple centers of global power and influence in a post-American world.

Obama's grand strategy managed to disappoint the expectations of neoconservative primacists, humanitarian interventionists, realist offshore-balancers, and progressive critics of American imperialism in equal measure. Yet, while Obama did not holistically reorient the United States toward a grand strategy of offshore balancing, he incorporated key elements of the restraint discourse in his strategic vision. In fact, over the course of his presidency restraint took on ever-greater significance, both rhetorically and practically. Obama thus increasingly positioned himself against the Washington establishment, and formulated a direct challenge to the elite consensus on American grand strategy from within.

Obama did not act as a President who was already operating in a post-American world, but he formulated a strategic vision that pointed the way into a future where American leadership would be less distinctive, more contingent on outside support, and ultimately less in control of the shaping of outside events and processes. To a foreign policy establishment that constantly professed that this world and its established order were a product of American leadership, this careful reframing of American grand strategy discourse presented a disconcerting iconoclasm. Obama, however, seemed largely in tune with an American public that was increasingly weary of the country's foreign commitments. Yet, Americans also welcomed the substance of a more restrained US foreign policy, rather than the cautious style and caveated prose with which it was delivered.

Obama used the image of American exceptionalism and hegemony to advance policies actually designed to lessen the burden of American leadership, and to divert resources, both economic and intellectual, for domestic priorities, thus inverting the conventional linkage of exceptionalist rhetoric and hegemonic practices expressed through foreign interventionism and the use of force. Yet, as the Syria episode illustrated, the identity of America as a leader in world politics and policies, which counteracted this identity, could not be bridged indefinitely within the existing paradigm of geopolitical identity. This conflict between the hegemonic imagination of American leadership and the practice of cooperative engagement and military restraint under Obama thus raised the question about the limits of reframing American grand strategy without also changing its underlying identity discourse, and the potential future breaking point of the existing discourse.

NOTES

1. Quoted in Rotkopf, 'Obama's "Don't Do Stupid Shit" Foreign Policy.' President Obama used this explicit in a background conversation with journalists aboard *Air Force One* to describe his overriding foreign policy maxim – to avoid further military entanglements of the United States – while also voicing his objecting to the fetishization of grand strategy in general, see Parsons and Hennessy, 'Obama will Explain "Interventionist" Foreign Policy at West Point.' Subsequently, the phrase gained wide media circulation and public attention.
2. Ó Tuathail and Agnew, 'Geopolitics and Discourse,' p. 195.
3. Under Obama, two Hollywood action movies, *Olympus Has Fallen* (2013) and *White House Down* (2013), have shown the President, the embodiment of US national security, under attack by terrorists in the White House. These films not only documented the continued relevance of the terrorist threat in the popular imagination in the United States, but also the highly symbolic nature of the President's role in defending the nation.
4. White House, *National Security Strategy* (2015).
5. White House, 'Remarks by the President in Address to the Nation on the Way Forward in Afghanistan and Pakistan,' White House, 'Remarks by the President in Address to the Nation on Syria,' White House, 'Statement by the President on ISIL,' White House, *National Security Strategy* (2015).
6. McCrisken, *American Exceptionalism*.
7. White House, *National Security Strategy (2015)*.
8. Landler, 'Ending Asia Trip, Obama Defends His Foreign Policy.' As one op-ed columnist for *The New York Times* commented: 'It doesn't feel like leadership. It doesn't feel like you're in command of your world . . . What happened to crushing it and swinging for the fences? Where have you gone, Babe Ruth?' Dowd, 'Is Barry Whiffing?'
9. For some prominent examples of this debate in Obama's second term, see Slaughter, 'Does Obama Have a Grand Strategy for his Second Term?' Bremmer, 'The Tragic Decline of American Foreign Policy,' Bonicelli, 'Five Years is Long Enough to Wait for an Obama Grand Strategy.'

10. *Washington Post* Editorial Board, 'President Obama continues his retreat from Afghanistan.'
11. Baker, 'Rebutting Critics,' Cassidy, 'A Reluctant Realist at West Point.'
12. In the 2010 *National Security Strategy* Obama had already broadly described this vision, see White House, *National Security Strategy*, p. 1.
13. *New York Times*, 'Transcript of President Obama's Commencement Address at West Point,' May 28, 2014.
14. As *The New York Times* commented: 'The address did not match the hype, was largely uninspiring, lacked strategic sweep and is unlikely to quiet his detractors, on the right or the left.' *New York Times* Editorial Board, 'President Obama Misses a Chance on Foreign Affairs.'
15. See also the discussion of Obama's speech in Bergen, 'Obama Says Goodbye to American Hubris,' Heilbrunn, 'Barack Obama Misfires at West Point,' O'Hanlon, 'The Obama Defense,' Drezner, 'Five Things I Think I Think about U.S. foreign policy after Obama's West Point speech.'
16. Martel, *Grand Strategy in Theory and Practice*, p. 301.
17. Chait, 'Liberalism's Bumper Sticker Problem.'
18. Quoted in Lizza, 'The Consequentialist. How the Arab Spring Remade Obama's Foreign Policy.'
19. Ibid., Mead, *Special Providence*.
20. Kagan, 'Superpowers Don't Get to Retire.' According to *The New York Times* some of Obama's remarks during his West Point speech were formulated as a direct rebuttal to Kagan's charge, see Baker, 'Rebutting Critics.'
21. Krauthammer, 'Krauthammer: Obama Doctrine Forged in Retreat.'
22. Stone and Kuznick, *The Untold History of the United States*, pp. 549–615, Bacevich, *Washington Rules*, pp. 19–20.
23. Goldberg, 'The Obama Doctrine.'
24. Cohen, 'Obama's Flawed Realism,' Dueck, *The Obama Doctrine*, Gerson, 'Obama's Foreign Policy and the Risks of Retreat,' Lieber, *Retreat and its Consequences*.
25. Krauthammer, 'Krauthammer: Obama Doctrine Forged in Retreat,' Judis, 'Speak Loudly and Carry a Small Stick.'
26. White House, 'Remarks of President Barack Obama – As Prepared for Delivery Address to Joint Session of Congress,' February 24, 2009.
27. Singh, *Barack Obama's Post-American Foreign Policy*, p. 16.
28. Pew Research Center, 'Confidence in Obama Lifts U.S. Image Around the World.'
29. Pew Research Center, 'America's Global Image Remains More Positive than China's.'
30. White House, 'Remarks by the President in State of the Union address,' January 27, 2010.

31. White House, *National Security Strategy* (2010), p. 10.
32. Obama, *The Audacity of Hope*, p. 309.
33. Mann, The Obamians, p. 194; Singh, Barack Obama's Post-American Foreign Policy, p. 24.
34. Associated Press, 'Clinton: Obama 'Naive' on Foreign Policy.'
35. Michael Cooper, 'McCain Sharpens his Foreign Policy Attacks on Obama.'
36. Wilson, 'Obama, Romney Differ on U.S. Exceptionalism.'
37. Sanger, *Confront and Conceal*, p. xvi.
38. White House, 'Remarks by the President on a New Beginning.'
39. Ibid. Obama also set himself apart by referring to Iran by its official name and acknowledging the role the United States had played in overthrowing the country's democratically elected government in the 1950s.
40. Landler, 'Obama Says Iran Strike is an Option, but Warns Israel.' In October 2012, *The Atlantic* listed more than twenty statements of President Obama to that effect, see Goldberg, 'Obama's Crystal-Clear Promise to Stop Iran From Getting a Nuclear Weapon.'
41. Dueck, *The Obama Doctrine*, pp. 48–57.
42. Ibid., p. 49.
43. Jackson, 'Culture, Identity and Hegemony,' p. 401.
44. Waxman, 'Obama's Guantanamo Legacy.'
45. Whitlock, 'Drone Strikes Killing More Civilians than U.S. Admits, Human Rights Groups Say.'
46. Krauthammer, 'Krauthammer: Obama Doctrine Forged in Retreat,' Judis, 'Speak Loudly and Carry a Small Stick.'
47. White House, 'Remarks by the President at the United States Military Academy Commencement Ceremony.'
48. Ibid.
49. See also, Mann, *The Obamians*, p. 252; Singh, *Barack Obama's Post-American Foreign Policy*.
50. Quoted in Cooper, 'On the World Stage, Obama Issues an Overture.'
51. Zakaria, *The Post-American World*.
52. Singh, *Barack Obama's Post-American Foreign Policy*, p. 7.
53. Mann, *The Obamians*, p. 72.
54. Singh, *Barack Obama's Post-American Foreign Policy*, p. 8.
55. The Gallup Global Leadership Track is part of the U.S.-Global Leadership Project, a joint effort between the Meridian International Center and Gallup to 'provide a comprehensive assessment of how world residents view U.S. leadership.' Gallup, *The U.S.-Global Leadership Project*, p. 2.
56. Kagan, *The World America Made*, Friedman and Mandelbaum, *That Used To Be Us*, Brooks and Wohlforth, 'The Once and Future Superpower.'
57. Zakaria, 'Obama's Leadership is Right for Today.'

58. Quoted in Kuhnhenn, 'Obama Faces "New Chapter" Of American Foreign Policy.'
59. Obama, 'Transcript: Obama's Speech Against The Iraq War.'
60. Stolberg, 'Obama Defends Strategy in Afghanistan.'
61. Cooper, 'Putting Stamp on Afghan War.'
62. Ibid.
63. Mann, *The Obamians*, pp. 127–128.
64. Ibid., p. 126.
65. White House, 'Remarks by the President in Address to the Nation on the Way Forward in Afghanistan and Pakistan.'
66. *Al Jazeera*, 'Obama to Slow Pace of Afghanistan Troop Withdrawal.'
67. Sanger, *Confront and Conceal*, pp. 15–58.
68. White House, 'Remarks by the President in State of the Union address,' January 24, 2012.
69. Ibid.
70. White House, 'President Barack Obama's State of the Union address,' January 28, 2014.
71. Walt, 'Offshore Balancing.'
72. Preble, *The Power Problem*.
73. Obama, 'Transcript: President Obama's Speech Outlining Strategy to Defeat Islamic State.'
74. Shear, 'Obama Insists U.S. Will Not Get Drawn into Ground War in Iraq,' Rubin, 'Obama is the War-Weary One.' At the time of writing (September 2016), ca. 4,000 US troops were present in Iraq, acting as advisors, protecting US diplomatic personnel and American citizens and facilities in the country, and conducting special operations against Islamic State in both Iraq and Syria.
75. Obama, 'Transcript: President Obama's Speech Outlining Strategy to Defeat Islamic State.'
76. White House, 'Remarks by the President at the Acceptance of the Nobel Peace Prize.'
77. Douthat, 'Obama the Theologian.' Niebuhr's most relevant work in this regard is the *Irony of American History* in which he advised that the United States should accept the responsibilities of power balanced by humility, patience, and charity, see also Clausen and Nurnus, 'Obama, Grand Strategy and Reinhold Niebuhr,' Niebuhr, *The Irony of American History*.
78. Baker, 'Pivoting From a War Footing,' Zengerle and Spetalnick, 'Obama Wants to End "War on Terror" but Congress Balks.'
79. White House, 'Remarks by the President at the National Defense University.'
80. As part of this realignment of CT policy, Obama renewed his promise to close down the Guantanamo Bay prison camp, and pointed to the

release of a Presidential Policy Guidance on the use of force against terrorists, including drone strikes. Finally, he formulated his personal goal to 'refine, and ultimately repeal,' the Authorization to Use Military Force (AUMF) mandate that was passed by Congress after 9/11 and allowed the US President to use all 'necessary and appropriate force' against those deemed responsible for planning, authorizing, committing or aiding in the September 11th attacks, ibid.

81. See, in particular, Sanger *Confront and Conceal*, pp. 243–273. According to *The New York Times*, in Pakistan these attacks approved by Obama included both 'personality' strikes aimed at named, 'high-value' terrorists, and 'signature' strikes that were targeted at training camps and suspicious compounds in areas controlled by militants, see Becker and Shane, 'Secret "Kill List" Proves a Test of Obama's Principles and Will.'

82. White House, 'Remarks by the President at the National Defense University.'

83. Sanger, *Confront and Conceal*, pp. 243–273.

84. McCrisken and Phythian, 'The Offensive Turn,' p. 189.

85. Quoted in Becker and Shane, 'Secret "Kill List" Proves a Test of Obama's Principles and Will.' These targeted assassinations have led to criticism of Obama both domestically and abroad for the violation of international law and the civilian casualties associated with US drone strikes. See on this issue, Human Rights Watch, 'Targeted Killings and Drones,' Whitlock, 'Drone Strikes Killing More Civilians than U.S. Admits, Human Rights Groups Say.'

86. On Obama's foreign and security policy and the use of cyber technologies, such as stuxnet, see Sanger, *Confront and Conceal*, pp.188–225; on the bin Laden mission, see Gans Jr., '"This is 50-50,"' on the NSA revelations, see, in particular, the website by *The Guardian*, 'The NSA Files.'

87. Bigelow apparently had substantial support from the White House in acquiring unprecedented access to classified information and intelligence material for producing the filmic adaptation of what is widely considered one of Obama's lasting achievements in national security policy, see Judicial Watch, 'Judicial Watch Obtains Department of Defense and CIA Records Detailing Meetings with bin Laden Raid Filmmakers.' This cooperation outraged Republicans, who accused the White House of instrumentalizing Hollywood for Obama's re-election campaign, see Child, 'Kathryn Bigelow Denies White House Favouritism over Bin Laden Film.'

88. Sanger, *Confront and Conceal*, p. 245.

89. Becker and Shane, 'Secret "Kill List" Proves a Test of Obama's Principles and Will.'

90. Ibid., p. 243.

91. Pew Research Center, 'Beyond Red vs. Blue.'

92. Most notably among those were Secretary of State Clinton, national

security staff member Samantha Power, and the US ambassador to the UN Susan Rice, all considered either humanitarian interventionists, or liberal hawks, see Cooper, 'Obama Takes Hard Line with Libya after Shift by Clinton.'

93. Quoted in Wilson, 'On Syria, Obama's Past Words Collide with National Security Implications.'

94. From an initial discussion to establish a no-fly zone, Obama and the United States ultimately pressed for a UN Security Council resolution that would authorize all measures to protect civilians on the ground. Essentially, the Libya intervention, which took place in the context of the 'responsibility to protect' doctrine (R2P), was interpreted by the United States and its NATO allies in terms of regime change, i.e. to remove Gaddafi from power.

95. Lizza, 'Leading from Behind,' Krauthammer, 'The Obama doctrine: Leading from behind, Boyle, 'Obama: 'leading from behind' on Libya, Steinmetz, 'Top 10 Buzzwords: 10. *Leading from Behind.*'

96. Lizza, 'Leading from Behind.''

97. Quoted in Lizza, 'The Consequentialist. How the Arab Spring Remade Obama's Foreign Policy.'

98. Krauthammer, 'The Obama Doctrine,' see also Cohen, 'Leading from Behind.'

99. Drake, 'Obama Charts a New Foreign Policy Course for a Public that Wants the Focus to be at Home.'

100. Three-Brennan, 'Poll Shows Isolationist Streak in Americans.'

101. Walt, 'Sloppy Journalism at the *New York Times,*' Fisher, 'Our New Isolationism Just Hit a 50-Year High: Why That Matters,' Lieberman and Kyl, 'The Danger of Repeating the Cycle of American Isolationism.'

102. Friedman and Preble, 'Americans Favor Not Isolationism But Restraint.'

103. *New York Times*, 'Transcript of President Obama's Commencement Address at West Point,' May 28, 2014.

104. Pew Research Center, 'Generational Divide Over American Exceptionalism.'

105. Drake, 'Obama Charts a New Foreign Policy Course for a Public that Wants the Focus to be at Home.'

106. Crowley, 'This May Be the Real Obama Doctrine.'

107. White House, 'Remarks by the President in Address to the Nation on Syria.'

108. Ibid.

109. Gelb, 'In Defense of Leading from Behind.'

110. Spetalnick, 'Obama's Syria "Red Line" has Echoes in his Warning to Ukraine.'

111. Balz and Craighill, 'Poll: Americans Strongly Back Diplomatic Solution on Syria but Give Obama Low Marks.'

CONCLUSION

Prominent media pundits, foreign policy experts, neoconservative hawks, and liberal interventionists repeatedly attacked President Obama for following a vision that led the United States into retreat, and undermined a liberal, international order of American origin. Robert Kagan accused Obama of presiding over 'an inward turn by the United States that threatened the global order and broke with more than 70 years of American presidents and precedence' in a much-read essay in the *New Republic*, which appeared on May 26, 2014.[1] Speaking only two days later at West Point, Obama countered:

> [. . .] by most measures, America has rarely been stronger relative to the rest of the world. Those who argue otherwise – who suggest that America is in decline, or has seen its global leadership slip away – are either misreading history or engaged in partisan politics.[2]

Ironically, only two years earlier Obama had embraced Kagan's argument for American hegemony in his 2012 State of the Union address, reconfirming the enduring role of the United States as the world's 'indispensable nation.' Yet, while Obama continued to invoke the rhetoric of American exceptionalism and indispensability, which underwrote the bipartisan consensus on hegemony, his practice of foreign and security policy, emphasizing military restraint and the limits of American power and influence, was increasingly seen as a contradiction of that consensus by large segments of the Washington establishment. The controversy over the 'Obama Doctrine' highlighted the deep divisions that had opened up under the Obama presidency between competing discourses of hegemony, engagement, and restraint.

Grand strategy functions both as a guideline for national security policy and as an internal, hegemonic discourse that reconfirms established notions of geopolitical identity. Under Obama, the dominant ideational paradigm underwriting elite opinion linked an ideology of political and economic liberalism and the mythologized identity construct of American exceptionalism to an activist foreign and security policy, and maintaining the global supremacy of US military power. This grand strategy vision of liberal hegemony in support of a world order 'made in America' represented a broad consensus among elite producers of geopolitical discourses, resulting in a marked congruence of opinion between neoconservative intellectuals, liberal media outlets, and centrist think tanks in their recommendations for America's preferred world political role.

From Hollywood blockbusters to popular best-sellers, expert debates, scholarly analysis, and political rhetoric, Americans continued to be socialized in and informed by a mainstream discourse that reproduced the geopolitical reality of a hegemonic United States, reflecting a narrative of historic continuity. Here, the mantra of American leadership was a vital component for confirming the exceptionalist self-image of the United States in the geopolitical imagination of elites and the public. In practical terms, however, American leadership under Obama seemed to be less distinct, more dependent on outside support, and overall less in control of outside events and developments, whether in Afghanistan, the Middle East, or the global economy.

Under the Obama presidency, there was no single, dominant American grand strategy that actually functioned as the coherent narrative and supreme guideline for the national interest that foreign policy experts, media pundits, and strategists themselves postulated and demanded from the White House. There was no longer a national consensus on America's role in the world that linked identity and policy, discourse and practice. Liberal internationalists and neoconservative primacists defended an increasingly tenuous status quo of unipolarity, liberal hegemony, and military supremacy against calls for substantial change by libertarian conservatives, populists, progressive critics, and realists, which all demanded a strategic course correction and greater restraint in the conduct of American foreign and security policy, and in particular in the use of force.

While a grand strategy of restraint lacked the intertextual embeddedness and discursive authority of the expansive-exceptionalist and liberal-hegemonic definition of America's world political role, the policy proposals by Cato or the presidential candidacy and eventual election of Donald Trump testified to its political influence beyond the academic debate and growing significance under the Obama presidency. Most importantly, Obama himself adopted some of the key arguments of the restraint discourse, as displayed in several of his key foreign policy decisions, and in particular with respect to his use of force, resulting in the complex and contradictory nature of the Obama Doctrine, which constantly oscillated between an America-centric, hegemonic identity discourse and a post-American practice of hegemony.

The dominant American grand strategy discourse aimed to de-politicize issues of national security policy and geopolitics by establishing an exclusive reality of American leadership, exceptionalism, and military supremacy as beyond legitimate debate. The de-legitimization of libertarian and realist concepts of restraint as 'isolationism' by proponents of the Washington consensus demonstrated this genealogical construction of the hegemony discourse. Neoconservatives and liberals from AEI and Charles Krauthammer to Brookings and President Obama declared a geopolitical vision of strict non-interventionism and greatly reduced military expenditures to stand outside acceptable opinion, by linking it to the historic narrative of isolationism and its catastrophic consequences. The worldview of liberal hegemony, on the other hand, was underwritten by an America-centric perspective of world history and international relations, where American victories in World War II and the Cold War created an international system of freedom, democracy, economic prosperity, and the rule of law, deemed unable to function without US military protection.

While supposedly offering a rationalist analysis of external threats and how to counter them, the use of these narratives and discourses demonstrates how grand strategy actually operates as a decidedly political worldview that divides world politics into legitimate and illegitimate concepts of security and power, identity and order. In drawing the 'big picture,' grand strategy is never neutral, but is always highly politicized. The majority of American grand strategy thinking under Obama was retrospective, conservative, and reluctant to accept changing geopolitical realties, greater complexity, and less certainty in international affairs. Both a non-interventionist United States which practiced restraint and offshore balancing, and a 'post-American world' of multiple centers of global power and influence in which America existed as only one of many hubs, clashed directly with the established continuity of strategic thinking that wanted to perpetuate America's historic hegemony and exceptional status.

Grand strategy visions of engagement and restraint offered more complexity and uncertainty for orienting the future role of the United Sates, not less. In the dominant grand strategy discourse promoted by the Washington consensus, however, the 'big picture' was supposed to be clear, coherent, and focused. Realties that seemed to question long-held beliefs, assumptions, and convictions of identity were being rejected when they questioned the hegemonic premise of American leadership. The political debate about Congressional sequestration and cuts to the Pentagon budget also occurred in such virulent form, because these practical policy issues touched on entrenched ideas about the geopolitical identity of the United States as an unchallenged, global superpower, and the political-military and fiscal practice necessary to sustain this status.

In an era marked by geopolitical uncertainty, where changes to the status quo were predominantly seen as increased risk and threat, from the Arab Spring to the rise of China and Russian revisionism, an American grand strategy was expected to provide national self-confirmation. The discourse of hegemony served an identity building and identity stabilizing function, meant to assure the continued premier status of the United States in the international system and the liberal values it supported. In the words of President Obama, the United States was and remained the one indispensable nation, both in the 'century passed' and 'for the century to come.'[3]

Yet, the global financial crisis and US failures in Iraq and Afghanistan had also seriously undermined the premise of a 'unipolar moment,' and the American claim to undisputed world leadership seemed more tenuous than maybe at any point since the end of the Cold War. At the same time, discounting a few outliers within the engagement and restraint discourses, global leadership, American exceptionalism, and indispensability remained the prism through which the most influential discursive producers in the United States perceived, and in turn reconstructed, America's world political role. It was a question of *how* the United States should lead, not *if*. This in turn lead to a persistent militarization of US policy responses, where the outbreak of international crises, from the annexation of Crimea to the Syrian civil war, resulted in the habitual calls for military action by Washington.

Issues of identity and practice were not separate, but intrinsically linked and mutually reinforcing each other in constituting grand strategy as a dominant worldview. This intertextual and cross-discursive linkage in constituting the establishment consensus on liberal hegemony manifested in multiple ways that went beyond the strict confines of US national security and foreign policy: The provision of military goods and services by the Pentagon to Hollywood film productions which popularized a 'good war' narrative of American military heroism. A researcher of the CSIS think tank anonymously drafting a speech by Secretary of Defense Chuck Hagel, confirming America's status as a 'Pacific power.' The hiring of leading members of the Center for a New American Century think tank by the Obama White House into senior positions for foreign policy and defense. Secretary Gates presenting the Pentagon's new 'partner-building' initiative in the pages of *Foreign Affairs*. The political endorsement of Hillary Clinton, a 'liberal hawk,' by Robert Kagan, a staunch, neoconservative hegemonist in *The New York Times*.[4] These are only some of the examples of how the geopolitical vision of American leadership was being maintained and reinforced in Washington DC through an intertextuality that connected popular, formal, and practical discourses, reconfirming it as a product of common-sense knowledge, practical reasoning, and intellectual expertise. As such, the reproduction of the grand strategy discourse of hegemony also represented a self-reinforcing cycle of conventional wisdom and elite opinion that rewarded the perpetuation of the status quo, rather than outside-the-box thinking, or progressive ideas for change.

In fact, the geopolitical imagination of global leadership, military supremacy, and an interventionist foreign policy in support of a liberal, international order maintained and reproduced by the elite class of the US national security and foreign policy establishment, was responsible for an entire political economy of hegemony. The strategic consensus of the Washington establishment also materialized in the multitude of US national security think tank research projects, multi-billion US-dollar weapons programs, university study courses, and a prolific publishing enterprise running under the grand strategy label, all designed to maintain, forward, and advance American leadership. The American grand strategy debate in Washington thus largely existed within a self-contained and self-replicated political reality of reiterated clichés, normative convictions, and historic genealogies. This interlinkage of conventional wisdom, research expertise, and political reasoning stretched from the sacrosanct mantra of 'leadership' to the frequent labeling of any alternative to all-out hegemony as dangerous and irresponsible 'isolationism.'[5] A singularity of thinking impeded the ability for political change and ideational transformation. From combating climate change to concluding the Middle East Peace Process, and the safeguarding of regional stability in the Asia-Pacific, the United States was regularly referred to as the single, most decisive factor in world politics. American foreign policy experts perceived the rest of the world almost exclusively through the prism of America's own vaunted leadership role. Not only was the world 'made in America,' it was also the only positive world imaginable.

There certainly was continued and outspoken demand for a leading role from the United States, for example by countries that sought American security guarantees, such as Japan and Poland vis-à-vis China and Russia, or by groups that asked for American military intervention on behalf of their own political goals, like rebel forces fighting in Libya or Syria. Oftentimes, however, the demands and needs for American leadership by others were simply postulated as self-evident reality by key members of America's strategic community. Like the argument for necessary singular US control of the 'global commons,' the idea that something besides unmitigated American hegemony could provide a feasible solution to global political challenges simply did not enter the mainstream discourse on American grand strategy. Here, foreign opinions and initiatives could at best augment US hegemony, but never replace it, or claim equal status.

Obama's nuanced vision of leadership, however, was more caveated, more appreciative of the complexity of international relations, and less simplistic in its characterization of American power, especially military power, and what it could achieve on the world stage. This alone set him apart from large parts of the political establishment in Washington, not just from the conservative proponents of unmitigated American primacy found in Republican circles, but also from the representatives of the liberal vision of hegemonic engagement in the Democratic party, Hillary Clinton first among them. Here, the often-postulated equation of unipolar stability, military supremacy, and global security was almost unanimously accepted as self-evident truth.

Given the negative record of past US military interventions in Afghanistan, Iraq, and Libya, however, the usefulness, efficacy, and validity of military power in determining political outcomes was severely in doubt. An uncertainty reflected in Obama's more restrained use of force, and his publicly voiced criticism that conclusions about the use of military power by the United States should be probed extensively for each individual case, and not reduced to knee-jerk reactions about American credibility and Western resolve. As such, Obama as commander-in-chief directly challenged the use of force on grounds of identity: the practice of military intervention to reinforce the dominant self-perception of American leadership among the political class, media pundits, and policy experts. In throwing out the 'Washington playbook,' Obama thus attempted to decouple exceptionalist rhetoric and representations of indispensability from the militarized practice of national security in the hegemony discourse.

Ultimately, President Obama acted not as a transformative figure but as a transitional figure in reorienting US foreign and security policy. Obama hinted at new realities influencing the role and position of the United States in world politics: fewer resources, more limited ambitions, and a more careful and restricted use of American military power. The competing discourses of grand strategy simultaneously employed by the President – as expressed in his frequent use of such key formulations as 'indispensable nation,' 'American leadership,' 'restraint,' and 'nation-building at home' – revealed a complexity of contemporary world politics, which was not easily subsumed under one central narrative, unitary threat perception, or single-minded prioritization of national resources that an American grand strategy was supposed to deliver.

As The Washington Post remarked, ending wars, nation-building at home, and the pivot to Asia were 'popular and attractive slogans,' but not a grand strategy.[6] Yet, while according to polls Americans in general favored a focus on 'nation-building at home' and 'leading from behind,' the geopolitical image of exceptionalism, leadership, and indispensability had also been a source of national pride and self-confirmation.[7] 'Leading from behind' was ultimately not able to dissolve this conundrum of having to inspire the geopolitical imagination of the nation through policies aimed at limiting costs and risks. American grand strategy under Obama, then, did not provide a stringent blueprint for political and military action, but primarily served as an attempt to reconfirm the hegemonic identity of the United States of America in a time where this identity seemed to come more and more under pressure, due to the diffusion of power and the rise of a multipolar system as indicated in several US government reports, intelligence assessments, and presidential statements. The worldview of American grand strategy, then, which up to the presidency of George W. Bush represented a dominant consensus for more than seven decades, was fracturing at the very center of mainstream discourse.

The geopolitical vision of a more restrained leadership role and more cautious global engagement as formulated by President Obama reflected the post-American future, rather than the hegemonic past of America's role in world politics. Most influential scholars, pundits, and policymakers, however, remained embedded in the Washington consensus on hegemony and mired in a unipolar worldview. They seemed unable or unwilling to move beyond an established historic narrative of the United States as triumphant victor of World War II and the Cold War, and the ideational paradigm of America as global defender of freedom and democracy, rooted in national exceptionalism and a unique sense of mission. Obama's grand strategy vision of 'leading from behind,' however, seemed to match the national mood, where a majority of the American people wanted the United States to 'mind its own business.' Yet Americans also seemed to welcome the substance of a more restrained American role in the world more than the cautious style and caveated rhetoric with which Obama presented this policy.

This in turn pointed to a further fracturing of the grand strategy consensus between elite opinion and the foreign policy establishment denouncing 'isolationist' tendencies, and an American public increasingly in favor of non-interventionism and in acceptance of a less singular hegemonic role. This conflict was also encapsulated in the contest for Obama's succession between Hillary Clinton, a quintessential Washington insider and firm believer in America's role as the world's indispensable nation, and Donald Trump, an anti-establishment populist who had aggressively questioned the elite consensus on US foreign and economic policy.

Oscillating between competing visions of unipolar primacy, cooperative engagement, and restraint, Obama neither changed course nor did he provide a fundamental reinterpretation of America's role in the world. As grand strategy, it was neither an embrace of isolationism nor an acceptance of American decline, but mostly a pragmatic response to maintain American leadership in an anticipated, but not yet fully realized post-American world. In its multidimensional complexity, however, and its contradictory linkage of identity discourse and foreign policy, the 'Obama Doctrine' was unable to forge a new consensus on America's role in the world.

NOTES

1. Horowitz, 'Events in Iraq Open Door for Interventionist Revival, Historian Says,' Kagan, 'Superpowers Don't Get to Retire.'

2. *New York Times*, 'Transcript of President Obama's Commencement Address at West Point,' May 28, 2014.
3. Ibid.
4. Horowitz, 'Events in Iraq Open Door for Interventionist Revival, Historian Says.'
5. Saunders, 'The Five Most Abused Foreign-Policy Cliches,' Larison, 'The Cliches of "Leadership" and "Resolve."'
6. *Washington Post* Editorial Board, 'President Obama Continues His Retreat From Afghanistan.'
7. Kagan, 'President Obama's Foreign Policy Paradox.'

APPENDIX

Table A.1 List of films surveyed (2009–2015)

Year	Title	US box office/ production cost (estimated US$)	Ranking	Threat scenario
2009	Avatar	749,766,139 237,000,000	1	Alien invasion
2009	Transformers: Revenge of the Fallen	402,111,870 200,00,000	2	Alien invasion
2009	G.I. Joe: The Rise of Cobra	150,201,498 175,000,000	18	Terrorism/WMD attack
2009	Inglourious Basterds	120,540,719 70,000,000	25	World War II/foreign enemy
2009	The Messenger	1,109,660 6,500,000	196	Iraq War/foreign enemy
2010	Iron Man 2	312,433,331 200,000,000	3	Domestic crime/ foreign infiltration
2010	Salt	118,311,368 110,000,000	22	Foreign infiltration
2010	RED	90,380,162 58,000,000	28	Rogue CIA operation
2010	The A-Team	77,222,099 110,000,000	44	Rogue CIA operation
2010	Knight and Day	76,423,035 117,000,000	45	Rogue CIA operation
2011	Transformers: Dark of the Moon	352,390,543 195,000,000	2	Alien invasion
2011	Mission: Impossible - Ghost Protocol	209,397,903 145,000,000	7	Terrorism/WMD attack
2011	Captain America: The First Avenger	176,654,505 140,000,000	12	Foreign enemy/WMD attack

Table A.1 *continued*

Year	Title	US box office/ production cost (estimated US$)	Ranking	Threat scenario
2011	X-Men: First Class	146,408,305 160,000,000	17	Cold War/foreign infiltration
2011	Battle: Los Angeles	83,552,429 70,000,000	37	Alien invasion
2012	Marvel's The Avengers	623,357,910 220,000,000	1	Alien invasion
2012	The Dark Knight Rises	446,894,498 250,000,000	2	Terrorism/WMD attack
2012	The Bourne Legacy	112,870,105 125,000,000	18	Rogue military operation
2012	Act of Valor	70,012,847 12,000,000	27	Terrorism
2012	Battleship	65,233,400 209,000,000	30	Alien invasion
2012	The Expendables 2	85,028,192 92,000,00	32	WMD proliferation
2013	Iron Man 3	409,013,994 200,000,000	2	Domestic crime/ terrorism
2013	Man of Steel	291,045,518 225,000,000	5	Alien invasion
2013	Lone Survivor	125,095,601 40,000,000	24	Afghanistan War/ foreign enemy
2013	G.I. Joe: Retaliation	122,523,060 130,000,000	25	Terrorism
2013	Captain Phillips	107,100,855 55,000,000	32	Piracy
2013	Olympus Has Fallen	98,925,640 70,000,000	36	Terrorism/foreign enemy
2013	White House Down	73,103,784 150,000,000	46	Terrorism
2014	American Sniper	350,126,37 58,800,000	1	Iraq War/terrorism
2014	Captain America: The Winter Soldier	259,766,572 170,000,000	4	Rogue intelligence operation
2014	Transformers: Age of Extinction	245,439,076 210,000,000	7	Alien invasion
2014	X-Men: Days of Future Past	233,921,534 200,000,000	9	Terrorism
2014	Godzilla	200,676,069 160,000,000	13	Alien invasion

Table A.1 *continued*

Year	Title	US box office/ production cost (estimated US$)	Ranking	Threat scenario
2014	*Edge of Tomorrow*	100,206,256 178,000,000	33	Alien invasion
2014	*Fury*	85,817,906 68,000,000	39	World War II/foreign enemy
2015	*Avengers: Age of Ultron*	459,005,868 250,000,000	3	Terrorism
2015	*Mission: Impossible – Rogue Nation*	195,042,377 150,000,000	11	Organized crime/ WMDs

Table A.2 Thompson Reuters Journal Citation Reports 2009–2015: Top 10 International Relations journals ranked by impact factor

Rank	Journal title	Total cites	Impact factor	5-year impact factor
2009				
1	*International Security*	2075	3.243	5.303
2	*Foreign Affairs*	2598	3.155	2.869
3	*Journal of Peace Research*	1529	2.468	2.677
4	*World Politics*	2134	2.114	2.815
5	*International Organization*	3465	2	4.4
6	*Space Policy*	241	1.707	1.454
7	*Biosecurity and Bioterrorism*	250	1.644	1.519
8	*International Studies Quarterly*	1363	1.625	2.459
9	*Journal of Conflict Resolution*	2410	1.507	3.015
10	*Security Dialogue*	390	1.49	1.807
2010				
1	*International Organization*	3641	3.551	5.059
2	*International Security*	1525	3.444	4.214
3	*World Politics*	2011	2.889	3.903
4	*Foreign Affairs*	1775	2.557	2.263
5	*Common Market Law Review*	702	2.194	2.071
6	*Marine Policy*	1524	2.053	1.961
7	*Journal of Conflict Resolution*	2562	1.883	3.165
8	*International Journal of Transitional Justice*	139	1.756	1.923
9	*Security Dialogue*	372	1.6	1.51
10	*International Studies Quarterly*	1690	1.523	2.427
2011				
1	*World Politics*	2134	3.025	3.489
2	*International Organization*	3441	2.98	4.377
3	*Common Market Law Review*	602	2.422	1.845

Table A.2 *continued*

Rank	Journal title	Total cites	Impact factor	5-year impact factor
4	International Security	1557	2.333	3.529
5	Journal of Conflict Resolution	2426	2.237	2.922
6	Foreign Affairs	1645	2.034	2.103
7	Journal of Peace Research	1522	1.98	2.152
8	Biosecurity and Bioterrorism	284	1.939	1.504
9	Marine Policy	1741	1.865	1.986
10	International Political Sociology	140	1.381	1.663
2012				
1	Common Market Law Review	765	3	2.074
2	International Security	1729	2.739	3.359
3	International Organization	3968	2.49	4.643
4	World Politics	2159	2.308	3.716
5	Marine Policy	2320	2.23	2.407
6	Journal of Peace Research	1782	2.191	2.526
7	Foreign Affairs	1684	2.09	2.055
8	New Political Economy	427	1.93	1.493
9	International Journal of Transitional Justice	209	1.791	1.88
10	Journal of Conflict Resolution	2620	1.701	2.885
2013				
1	Foreign Affairs	1839	3.347	2.447
2	International Security	1452	2.975	3.010
3	Maritime Policy	3283	2.621	2.948
4	International Organization	3803	2.600	3.984
5	Journal of Peace Research	1907	2.280	2.643
6	Common Market Law Review	506	2.043	1.672
7	Security Dialogue	521	1.952	2.007
8	New Political Economy	450	1.656	1.766
9	World Politics	2252	1.650	3.274
10	Biosecurity and Bioterrorism	334	1.618	1.532
2014				
1	International Security	1759	3.868	3.712
2	Journal of Peace Research	2358	3.387	3.549
3	International Organization	4733	3.019	4.922
4	Maritime Policy	3805	2.610	2.768
5	World Politics	2590	2.450	4.020
6	Foreign Affairs	1820	2.009	1.951
7	European Journal of International Relations	1055	1.972	2.541
8	Review of International Political Economy	1030	1.875	1.929
9	JCMS-Journal of Common Market Studies	1778	1.855	1.814
10	Common Market Law Review	606	1.795	1.686
2015				
1	International Organization	4818	3.213	4.09

Table A.2 *continued*

Rank	Journal title	Total cites	Impact factor	5-year impact factor
2	*World Politics*	2912	3.125	4.242
3	*International Security*	1914	2.911	3.573
4	*European Journal of International Relations*	1137	2.465	2.453
5	*Maritime Policy*	4796	2.453	2.715
6	*Review of International Organizations*	311	2.444	2.207
7	*Review of International Political Economy*	1164	2.414	2.395
8	*Foreign Affairs*	2135	2.295	2.330
9	*Journal of Peace Research*	2564	2.153	3.283
10	*International Studies Quarterly*	2409	1.943	2.298

Table A.3 List of think tanks examined[1]

American Enterprise Institute (AEI)	Conservative
Cato Institute	Libertarian
Center for Strategic and International Studies (CSIS)	Center-right
Council on Foreign Relations (CFR)	Centrist
Center for a New American Security (CNAS)	Centrist
Brookings Institution	Center-left
Center for American Progress (CAP)	Progressive

Note:
1. McGann, *2012 Global Go To Think Tanks Report and Policy Advice.*

BIBLIOGRAPHY

Ackerman, Spencer, 'Pentagon Quit the Avengers Because of its "Unreality,"' *Wired*, May 7, 2012, <http://www.wired.com/dangerroom/2012/05/avengers-military/> (last accessed September 12, 2016).

Adler, Emanuel, 'Seizing the Middle Ground: Constructivism in World Politics,' *European Journal of International Relations* 3, no. 3 (1997), pp. 319–363.

Agnew, John, 'An Excess of "National Exceptionalism": Towards a New Political Geography of American Foreign Policy,' *Political Geography Quarterly* 2, no. 2 (1983), pp. 151–166.

Agnew, John and Stuart Corbridge, *Mastering Space: Hegemony, Territory and International Political Economy* (London: Routledge, 1995).

Al Jazeera, 'Empire: Hollywood and the War Machine,' August 9, 2012, <http://www.aljazeera.com/programmes/empire/2010/12/2010121681345363793.html> (last accessed September 12, 2016).

Al Jazeera,' Obama to Slow Pace of Afghanistan Troop Withdrawal,' July 7, 2016, <http://www.aljazeera.com/news/2016/07/obama-leave-8400-troops-afghanistan-160706144621883.html> (last accessed February 26, 2017).

Alexander, David, 'Big Budget Cuts Pose "Tough, Tough Choices" for Pentagon: Hagel,' *Reuters*, March 6, 2014, <http://www.reuters.com/article/2014/03/06/us-usa-defense-budget-idU.S.BREA2500W20140306> (last accessed September 19, 2016).

Altman, Roger C., 'A Geopolitical Setback for the West,' *Foreign Affairs* 88, no. 1 (2009), pp. 2–14.

American Enterprise Institute, *Annual Report* (Washington DC: AEI, 2012).

American Enterprise Institute, *Defense Spending 101* (Washington DC: AEI, 2012).

American Enterprise Institute, 'The Pivot to Asia: Rhetoric isn't Enough,' July 29, 2015, <https://www.aei.org/events/the-pivot-to-asia-rhetoric-isnt-enough-2/> (last accessed February 25, 2017).

Anderegg, Michael, *Inventing Vietnam: The War in Film and Television* (Philadelphia: Temple University Press, 1991).

Appelman Williams, William, *The Tragedy of American* Diplomacy (New York: W. W. Norton & Company, 1972).

'Appendix. Guidelines for Strategy Formulation,' in J. Boone Bartholomees Jr. (ed.), *US Army War College Guide to National Security Issues. Vol. II. National Security Policy and Strategy* (Carlisle: Strategic Studies Institute, 2012), pp. 413–418.

Art, Robert J., *A Grand Strategy for America* (Ithaca: Cornell University Press, 2003).

Art, Robert J. (ed.), *America's Grand Strategy and World Politics* (New York: Routledge, 2009).

Art, Robert J., 'Geopolitics Updated: The Strategy of Selective Engagement,' *International Security* 23, no. 3 (1998), pp. 79–113.

Art, Robert J., 'Selective Engagement in the Era of Austerity,' in Richard Fontaine and Kristin M. Lord (eds.), *America's Path: Grand Strategy for the Next Administration* (Washington DC: CNAS, 2012), pp. 13–28.

Ashley, Richard, 'The Achievements of Post-Structuralism,' in Steve Smith, Ken Booth, and Marysia Zalewski (eds.), *International Theory: Positivism and Beyond* (Cambridge: Cambridge University Press, 1996), pp. 240–253.

Associated Press, 'Clinton: Obama "Naive" on Foreign Policy,' *NBC News*, July 24, 2007, <http://www.nbcnews.com/id/19933710/ns/politics-the_debates/t/clinton-obama-naive-foreign-policy/#.U5bxLBYdsoE> (last accessed September 10, 2016).

Axe, David, 'Pentagon, Hollywood Pair up for Transformers Sequel,' *Wired*, December 29, 2008, <http://www.wired.com/dangerroom/2008/12/pentagon-holl-1/> (last accessed September 21, 2016).

Bacevich, Andrew J., *American Empire* (Cambridge, MA: Harvard University Press, 2009).

Bacevich, Andrew J., 'Ending Endless War,' *Foreign Affairs* 95, no. 5 (2016), pp. 36–45.

Bacevich, Andrew J., '70 Years of "New Isolationism,"' *American Conservative*, October 24, 2013, < http://www.theamericanconservative.com/articles/70-years-of-new-isolationism/> (last accessed February 17, 2017).

Bacevich, Andrew J., *The Limits of Power: The End of American Exceptionalism* (New York: Metropolitan Books, 2008).

Bacevich, Andrew J., *The Short American Century* (Cambridge, MA: Harvard University Press, 2012).

Bacevich, Andrew J., *Washington Rules* (New York: Metropolitan Books, 2010).

Bacevich, Andrew J., 'We're Just Not That Special,' *Politico*, March 5, 2014, <http://www.politico.com/magazine/story/2014/03/american-exceptionalism-russia-ukraine-104318.html#.U43LExZJpOd> (last accessed September 3, 2016).

Baker, Peter, 'Pivoting From a War Footing, Obama Acts to Curtail Drones,' *New York Times*, May 23, 2013, <http://www.nytimes.com/2013/05/24/

us/politics/pivoting-from-a-war-footing-obama-acts-to-curtail-drones. html?_r=0> (last accessed September 12, 2016).

Baker, Peter, 'Rebutting Critics, Obama Seeks Higher Bar for Military Action,' *New York Times*, May 28, 2014, < http://www.nytimes.com/2014/05/29/ us/politics/rebutting-critics-obama-seeks-higher-bar-for-military-action. html?rref=politics&module=Ribbon&version=context&region=Header&ac tion=click&contentCollection=Politics&pgtype=article> (last accessed September 12, 2016).

Ball, Molly, 'Libertarians are Not the Tea Party,' *Atlantic*, October 29, 2013, <http://www.theatlantic.com/politics/archive/2013/10/libertarians-are-not-the-tea-party/280976/> (last accessed September 21, 2016).

Balz, Dan and Peyton M. Craighill, 'Poll: Americans Strongly Back Diplomatic Solution on Syria But Give Obama Low Marks,' *Washington Post*, September 17, 2013, <http://articles.washingtonpost.com/2013-09-17/poli tics/42124841_1_chemical-weapons-61-percent-47-percent> (last accessed September 28, 2016).

Barber, Nicholas, 'White House Down: Obama Gets his Big-Screen Moment,' *Guardian*, September 13, 2013, < https://www.theguardian.com/film/film blog/2013/sep/13/white-house-down-obama-foxx> (last accessed February 24, 2017).

Barnes, Julian E., Ned Parker, and John Horn, 'The Hurt Locker Sets Off Conflict,' *Los Angeles Times*, February 25, 2010, <http://articles.latimes.com/ 2010/feb/25/entertainment/la-et-hurt-locker26-2010feb26> (last accessed September 13, 2016).

Barron, Lisa, 'Zbigniew Brzezinski: The Man Behind Obama's Foreign Policy,' *Mint Press News*, February 28, 2012, <http://www.mintpressnews.com/ zbigniew-brzezinski-the-man-behind-obamas-foreign-policy/21369/> (last accessed September 29, 2016).

Bartlett, Henry C. and Paul G. Holman, 'Grand Strategy and the Structure of U.S. Military Forces,' *Strategic Review* 20 (Spring 1992), pp. 39–51.

Bass, Gary J., 'Endless War,' *The Sunday Book Review*, September 3, 2010.

Beaucar Vlahos, Kelley, 'One-Sided COIN,' *American Conservative*, August 1, 2009, <http://www.amconmag.com/article/2009/aug/01/00038/> (last accessed September 19, 2016).

Becker, Joe and Scott Shane, 'Secret "Kill List" Proves a Test of Obama's Principles and Will,' *New York Times*, May 29, 2012, <http://www.nytimes. com/2012/05/29/world/obamas-leadership-in-war-on-al-qaeda.html?page wanted=all&_r=0> (last accessed September 19, 2016).

Bender, Bryan, 'Many D.C. Think Tanks Now Players in Partisan Wars,' *Boston Globe*, August 11, 2013, <http://www.bostonglobe.com/news/nation/2013/ 08/10/brain-trust-for-sale-the-growing-footprint-washington-think-tank-industrial-complex/7ZifHfrLPlbz0bSeVOZHdI/story.html> (last accessed September 19, 2016).

Bengali, Shashank and Matea Gold Tribune, 'Policy Ace Michele Flournoy Could Be First Female Defense Chief,' *Stars and Stripes*, January 4, 2013, <http://www.stripes.com/news/us/policy-ace-michele-flournoy-could-be-first-female-pentagon-chief-1.202861> (last accessed September 18, 2016).

Bennett, John T. 'Senate OKs Sequester-Relief Budget Plan,' *Defense News*, December 18, 2013, <http://www.defensenews.com/article/20131218/DEFREG02/312180031/Senate-OKs-Sequester-Relief-Budget-Plan> (last accessed September 20, 2016).

Bergen, Peter, 'Obama Says Goodbye to American Hubris,' *CNN*, May 28, 2014, <http://edition.cnn.com/2014/05/28/opinion/bergen-obama-doctrine-smart-power/> (last accessed September 19, 2016).

Betts, Richard K, 'What is Obama's "Grand" Foreign Policy Strategy?' Council on Foreign Relations, April 16, 2013, <http://www.cfr.org/grand-strategy/obamas-grand-foreign-policy-strategy/p30457> (last accessed September 19, 2016).

Biersteker, Thomas J. 'Theory and Practice in International Security Studies,' *Security Dialogue* 41, no. 6 (2010), pp. 599–608.

Birdsall, Nancy and Francis Fukuyama, 'The Post-Washington Consensus,' *Foreign Affairs* 90, no. 2 (2011), pp. 45–53.

Blake, Aaron, 'The Republican Party Likes Rand Paul's Foreign Policy – At Least For Now,' *Washington Post*, 23 June 2014, <http://www.washingtonpost.com/blogs/the-fix/wp/2014/06/23/how-big-is-the-rand-paul-foreign-policy-wing-of-the-gop/> (last accessed September 19, 2016).

Blake, Aaron and Sean Sullivan, 'Team America No Longer Wants to be the World's Police,' *Washington Post*, September 13, 2013, <http://www.washingtonpost.com/blogs/the-fix/wp/2013/09/13/team-america-no-longer-wants-to-be-the-worlds-police/> (last accessed September 18, 2016).

Bonicelli, Paul, 'Five Years is Long Enough to Wait for An Obama Grand Strategy,' *Foreign Policy*, May 6, 2013, <http://shadow.foreignpolicy.com/posts/2013/05/06/five_years_is_long_enough_to_wait_for_an_obama_grand_strategy> (last accessed September 18, 2016).

Boot, Max, 'Think Again: Neocons,' *Foreign Policy*, January/February 2004, <http://www.cfr.org/united-states/think-again-neocons/p7592> (last accessed September 19, 2016).

Bower, Ernest Z, 'Engagement in the Indo-Pacific: The Pentagon Leads by Example,' CSIS, August 22, 2013, <http://csis.org/publication/engagement-indo-pacific-pentagon-leads-example> (last accessed September 19, 2016).

Boyd-Barrett, Oliver, David Herrera, and Jim Baumann, *Hollywood and the CIA: Cinema, Defence, and Subversion* (London: Routledge, 2011).

Boyle, Michael, 'Obama: "Leading from Behind" on Libya,' *Guardian*, August 27, 2011, <http://www.theguardian.com/commentisfree/cifamerica/2011/aug/27/obama-libya-leadership-nato> (last accessed September 19, 2016).

Brands, Hal, *What Good is Grand Strategy: Power and Purpose in American Statecraft From Harry S. Truman to George W. Bush* (Ithaca and London: Cornell University Press, 2014).

Bremmer, Ian, *Every Nation For Itself: What Happens When No One Leads the World* (London: Penguin, 2012).

Bremmer, Ian, 'The Tragic Decline of American Foreign Policy,' *National Interest*, April 16, 2014, <http://nationalinterest.org/feature/the-tragic-dec line-american-foreign-policy-10264> (last accessed September 19, 2016).

Brewster, David, '"Asian Pivot" Is Really An "Asian Re-balance,"' *The Interpreter*, June 22, 2013, <http://www.lowyinterpreter.org/post/2012/06/22/asian-piv ot-is-really-an-asian-rebalance.aspx?COLLCC=3789963749&> (last acc essed September 19, 2016).

Brimley, Shawn, 'Finding Our Way,' in Shawn Brimely and Michèle A. Flournoy (eds.), *Finding Our Way: Debating American Grand Strategy* (Washington DC: CNAS, 2008), pp. 9–22.

Brimley, Shawn, 'Testimony before the Senate Armed Services Committee: Arresting the Erosion of America's Military Edge,' October 29, 2015, < http://www.armed-services.senate.gov/download/brimley_10-29-15> (last accessed September 30, 2016).

Brimley, Shawn and Michèle A. Flournoy (eds.), *Finding Our Way: Debating American Grand Strategy* (Washington DC: CNAS, 2008).

Brimley, Shawn and Michèle A. Flournoy, 'Introduction,' in Shawn Brimley and Michèle A. Flournoy (eds.), *Finding Our Way: Debating American Grand Strategy* (Washington DC: CNAS, 2008), pp. 5–8.

Brimley, Shawn and Michèle A. Flournoy, 'Making America Grand Again,' in Shawn Brimley and Michèle A. Flournoy (eds.), *Finding Our Way* (Washington DC: CNAS, 2008), pp. 125–148.

Brooks, Stephen G., *American Exceptionalism in the Age of Obama* (New York: Routledge, 2012).

Brooks, Stephen G. and William C. Wohlforth, 'Reshaping the World Order,' *Foreign Affairs* 88, no. 2 (2009), pp. 49–63.

Brooks, Stephen and William C. Wohlforth, 'The Once and Future Superpower,' *Foreign Affairs* 95, no. 3 (2016), pp. 91–104.

Brooks, Stephen G. and William C. Wohlforth, *World Out of Balance: International Relations and the Challenge of American Primacy* (Princeton: Princeton University Press, 2008).

Brooks, Stephen, G. John Ikenberry, and William C. Wohlforth, 'Don't Come Home, America: The Case Against Retrenchment,' *International Security* 37, no. 3 (2012), pp. 7–51.

Brooks, Stephen, G. John Ikenberry, and William C. Wohlforth, 'Lean Forward: In Defense of American Engagement,' *Foreign Affairs* 92, no. 1 (2013), pp. 130–142.

Bruni, Frank, 'America the Shrunken,' *New York Times*, May 3, 2014, <http://

www.nytimes.com/2014/05/04/opinion/sunday/bruni-america-the-shru
nken.html?_r=0> (last accessed September 19, 2016).

Brzezinski, Zbigniew, 'An Agenda for NATO,' *Foreign Affairs* 88, no. 5 (2009),
pp. 2–20.

Brzezinski, Zbigniew, 'From Hope to Audacity,' *Foreign Affairs* 89, no. 1 (2010),
pp. 16–30.

Brzezinski, Zbigniew, *Strategic Vision* (New York: Basic Books, 2012).

Brzezinski, Zbigniew, 'Toward a Global Realignment,' *American Interest* 11,
no. 6, April 17, 2016, < http://www.the-american-interest.com/2016/04/17/
toward-a-global-realignment/> (last accessed September 1, 2016).

Buchanan, Patrick J, *Suicide of a Superpower: Will America Survive to 2025?* (New
York: Thomas Dunne Books, 2011).

Bumiller, Elisabeth, 'Obama Team Defends Policy on Afghanistan,' *New York
Times*, December 2, 2009, <http://www.nytimes.com/2009/12/03/world/
asia/03policy.html> (last accessed September 19, 2016).

Campbell, David, 'Beyond Choice: The Onto-politics of Critique,' *International
Relations* 19, no. 1 (2005), pp. 127–134.

Campbell, David, *Writing Security: United States Foreign Policy and the Politics of
Identity* (Minneapolis: University of Minnesota Press, 1992, revised edition,
1998).

Carpenter, Ted Galen, 'Delusions of Indispensability,' *National Interest*, no. 124
(March/April 2013), pp. 47–55.

Carpenter, Ted Galen, 'U.S. Security Retrenchment: The First Effects of a
Modest Shift,' CATO Institute, March 17, 2014, <http://www.cato.org/
publications/commentary/us-security-retrenchment-first-effects-modest-
shift> (last accessed September 19, 2016).

Cassidy, John, 'A Reluctant Realist at West Point,' *New Yorker*, May 29, 2014,
<http://www.newyorker.com/online/blogs/johncassidy/2014/05/a-reluc
tant-realist-at-west-point.html> (last accessed September 19, 2016).

Cato Institute, 'Isolationism,' <https://www.cato.org/pages/isolationism> (last
accessed February 25, 2017).

Center for American Progress, 'About sustainable security,' <https://www.
americanprogress.org/about/ss-about/> (last accessed February 25,
2017).

Center for American Progress, 'Neera Tanden,' <http://www.americanpro
gress.org/about/staff/tanden-neera/bio/> (last accessed September 19,
2016).

Center for American Progress, *Sustainable Security 101* (Washington DC: CAP,
2009).

Center for a New American Security, 'Mission,' <https://www.cnas.org/mis
sion> (last accessed February 25, 2017).

Center for Strategic and International Studies, 'Professional Military Education:
An Asset for Peace and Progress,' in Paul J. Bolt, Damon V. Coletta, and

Collins G. Shackelford Jr. (eds.), *American Defense Policy* (Baltimore and London: Johns Hopkins University Press, 2005), pp. 302–314.

Center for Strategic and International Studies, 'The Emerging Anti-Access/Area-Denial Challenge,' <http://csis.org/publication/emerging-anti-accessarea-denial-challenge> (last accessed September 13, 2016).

Center for Strategic and International Studies, *U.S. Force Posture Strategy in the Asia Pacific Region: An Independent Assessment* (Washington DC: CSIS, 2012).

Chait, Jonathan, 'Liberalism's Bumper Sticker Problem,' *New Republic*, April 28, 2011, <http://www.newrepublic.com/blog/jonathan-chait/87553/liberalisms-bumper-sticker-problem> (last accessed September 19, 2016).

Cheney, Dick and Liz Cheney, *Exceptional: Why the World Needs a Powerful America* (New York: Simon & Schuster, 2015).

Child, Ben, 'Kathryn Bigelow Denies White House Favouritism over Bin Laden Film,' *Guardian*, August 11, 2013, <http://www.theguardian.com/film/2011/aug/11/kathryn-bigelow-bin-laden-film> (last accessed September 19, 2016).

Chotiner, Isaac, 'The Surprisingly Left-Wing Politics of "White House Down,"' *New Republic*, June 28, 2013, <http://www.newrepublic.com/article/113668/white-house-down-reviewed-isaac-chotiner> (last accessed September 19, 2016).

Clark, Ian, *Hegemony in International Society* (Oxford: Oxford University Press, 2011).

Clausen, Daniel and Nurnus, Max, 'Obama, Grand Strategy and Reinhold Niebuhr,' *Diplomat*, March 24, 2015, <http://thediplomat.com/2015/03/obama-grand-strategy-and-reinhold-neibuhr/> (last accessed September 30, 2016).

Clinton, Hillary, 'America's Pacific Century,' *Foreign Policy*, October 11, 2011, <http://www.foreignpolicy.com/articles/2011/10/11/americas_pacific_century> (last accessed September 19, 2016).

Clinton, Hillary, 'Leading Through Civilian Power,' *Foreign Affairs* 89, no. 3 (2010), pp. 13–24.

CNN Wire Staff, 'Mullen: Debt is Top National Security Threat,' *CNN*, August 27, 2010, <http://edition.cnn.com/2010/U.S./08/27/debt.security.mullen/> (last accessed September 19, 2016).

Cohen, Michael, 'America Stands Accused of Retreat from its Global Duties. Nonsense,' *Guardian*, April 12, 2014, <http://www.theguardian.com/commentisfree/2014/apr/12/us-foreign-policy-retreatism-obama-accused-weakness> (last accessed September 19, 2016).

Cohen, Roger, 'Leading from Behind,' *New York Times*, October 31, 2011, <http://www.nytimes.com/2011/11/01/opinion/01iht-edcohen01.html> (last accessed September 19, 2016).

Cohen, Roger, 'Obama's Flawed Realism,' *New York Times*, March 18, 2016, <https://www.nytimes.com/2016/03/19/opinion/obamas-flawed-realism.html?_r=0> (last accessed February 26, 2017).

Cohen, Roger, 'Putin's Crimea Crime,' *New York Times*, March 3, 2014, <http://www.nytimes.com/2014/03/04/opinion/putins-crimean-crime.html?_r=0> (last accessed September 19, 2016).

Colby, Elbridge and Paul Lettow, 'Have We Hit Peak America?' *Foreign Policy*, July/August 2014, <http://www.foreignpolicy.com/articles/2014/07/03/have_we_hit_peak_america> (last accessed September 19, 2016).

Collins, Richard, 'REVIEW: In Captain America: The Winter Soldier, The Enemy is Us,' *Time*, April 2, 2014, <http://time.com/46760/captain-america-the-winter-soldier-movie-review/> (last accessed September 19, 2016).

Congressional Budget Office, *Bipartisan Budget Act of 2013* (Washington DC: Congressional Budget Office, 2013).

Congressional Budget Office, *Estimated Impact of Automatic Budget Enforcement Procedures Specified in the Budget Control Act* (Washington DC: Congressional Budget Office, 2011).

Congressional Research Service, *Pivot to the Pacific? The Obama Administration's 'Rebalancing' Toward Asia* (Washington DC: Congressional Research Service, 2012).

Cooper, Helene, 'Obama Takes Hard Line with Libya after Shift by Clinton,' *New York Times*, March 18, 2011, <http://www.nytimes.com/2011/03/19/world/africa/19policy.html?pagewanted=all> (last accessed September 19, 2016).

Cooper, Helene, 'On the World Stage, Obama Issues an Overture,' *New York Times*, April 2, 2009, <http://www.nytimes.com/2009/04/03/world/europe/03assess.html?_r=0> (last accessed September 19, 2016).

Cooper, Helene, 'Putting Stamp on Afghan War, Obama Will Send 17,000 Troops,' *New York Times*, February 17, 2009, <http://www.nytimes.com/2009/02/18/washington/18web-troops.html> (last accessed September 19, 2016).

Cooper, Michael, 'McCain Sharpens His Foreign Policy Attacks on Obama,' *New York Times*, June 3, 2008, <http://www.nytimes.com/2008/06/03/us/politics/03mccain.html?_r=0> (last accessed September 19, 2016).

Coulter, Ann, *Adios, America: The Left's Plan to Turn Our Country into a Third World Hellhole* (New York: Regnery, 2015).

Council on Foreign Relations, 'Mission Statement,' <http://www.cfr.org/about/mission.html> (last accessed February 25, 2017).

Craig, Campbell, Benjamin H. Friedman, Brendan Rittenhouse Green, Justin Logan, Stephen G. Brooks, G. John Ikenberry, and William C. Wohlforth, 'Debating American Engagement: The Future of U.S. Grand Strategy,' *International Security* 38, no. 2 (2013), pp. 181–199.

Crandall, Russell, 'The Post-American Hemisphere,' *Foreign Affairs* 90, no. 3 (2011), pp. 83–95.

Croft, Stuart, *Culture, Crisis and America's War on Terror* (Cambridge: Cambridge University Press, 2006).

Crowley, Michael, 'This May Be the Real Obama Doctrine,' *TIME*, May 28, 2014, <http://time.com/120645/obama-west-point-doctrine-foreign-poli cy/> (last accessed September 19, 2016).

Crowley, Tony, *The Politics of Discourse* (London: Macmillan, 1989).

Dalby, Simon, 'Imperialism, Domination, Culture: The Continued Relevance of Critical Geopolitics,' *Geopolitics* 13, no. 3 (2008), pp. 413–436.

Dalby, Simon, 'Recontextualising Violence, Power and Nature: The Next Twenty Years of Critical Geopolitics?'*Political Geography* 29, no. 5 (2010), pp. 280–288.

Dalby, Simon, 'Warrior Geopolitics: Gladiator, Black Hawk Down and The Kingdom Of Heaven,' *Political Geography* 27, no. 4 (2008), pp. 439–455.

Dale, Catherine, *The 2014 Quadrennial Defense Review (QDR) and Defense Strategy: Issues for Congress* (Washington DC: Congressional Research Service, 2014).

Dale, Catherine and Pat Towell, *In Brief: Assessing the January 2012 Defense Strategic Guidance (DSG)* (Washington DC: Congressional Research Service, 2013).

De Groot, Gerard, 'Andrew Bacevich's "Washington Rules" and John Dower's "Cultures of War,"' *The Washington Post*, September 12, 2010, <http://www.washingtonpost.com/wp-dyn/content/article/2010/09/10/AR 2010091003604.html> (last accessed March 4, 2013).

Debrix, François, *Tabloid Terror: War, Culture and Geopolitics* (Abingdon and New York: Routledge, 2008).

Dempsey, Martin E., 'From the Chairman,' *Joint Forces Quarterly* 66 (3rd Quarter 2012), pp. 2–3.

Denmark, Abraham M., 'Managing the Global Commons,' *The Washington Quarterly* 33, no. 3 (2010), pp. 165–182.

Der Derian, James, *Virtuous War: Mapping the Military-Industrial-Media-Entertainment Network*, 2nd edn (Boulder: Westview Press, 2001).

Der Derian, James and Michael Shapiro (eds.), *International/Intertextual Relations* (New York: Lexington Books, 1989).

Dijkink, Gertjan, *National Identity and Geopolitical Visions: Maps of Pride and Pain* (London: Routledge, 1996).

DiMaggio, Anthony, *The Rise of the Tea Party: Political Discontent and Corporate Media in the Age of Obama* (New York: Monthly Review Press, 2011).

Dittmer, Jason, 'American Exceptionalism, Visual Effects, and the Post-9/11 Cinematic Superhero Boom,' *Environment and Planning D: Society and Space* 29, no. 1 (2011), pp. 114–130.

Dittmer, Jason, 'Captain America's Empire: Reflections on Identity, Popular Culture, and Post-9/11 Geopolitics,' *Annals of the Association of American Geographers* 95, no. 3 (2005), pp. 626–643.

Dittmer, Jason, *Popular Culture, Geopolitics and Identity* (Lanham: Rowman & Littlefield Publishers, 2010).

Dittmer, Jason and Klaus K. Dodds, 'Popular Geopolitics Past and Future: Fandom, Identities and Audiences,' *Geopolitics* 13, no. 3 (2008), pp. 437–457.

Dixon, Wheeler W., *Lost in the Fifties: Recovering Phantom Hollywood* (Carbondale: Southern Illinois University Press, 2005).

Dodds, Klaus, 'Gender, Geopolitics, and Contemporary Representations of National Security,' *Journal of Popular Film and Television* 38, no. 1 (2010), pp. 21–33.

Dodds, Klaus, 'Hollywood and the Popular Geopolitics of the War on Terror,' *Third World Quarterly* 29, no. 8 (2008), pp. 1624–1625.

Doherty, Patrick, 'A New U.S. Grand Strategy,' *Foreign Policy*, January 9, 2013, <http://www.foreignpolicy.com/articles/2013/01/09/a_new_U.S._grand_strategy> (last accessed August 6, 2014).

Donilon, Tom, 'America is Back in the Pacific and Will Uphold the Rules,' *Financial Times*, November 27, 2011, < http://www.ft.com/cms/s/0/4f3febac-1761-11e1-b00e-00144feabdc0.html#axzz2vlVeZcC4> (last accessed March 11, 2014).

Douthat, Ross, 'Obama the Theologian,' *New York Times*, February 7, 2015, <https://www.nytimes.com/2015/02/08/opinion/sunday/ross-douthat-obama-the-theologian.html> (last accessed February 25, 2017).

Dowd, Maureen, 'Is Barry Whiffing' *New York Times*, April 29, 2014, <http://www.nytimes.com/2014/04/30/opinion/dowd-is-barry-whiffing.html> (last accessed June 2, 2014).

Downs, Erica and Suzanne Maloney, 'Getting China to Sanction Iran,' *Foreign Affairs* 90, no. 2 (2011), pp. 15–21.

Draezen, Yochi J., 'Obama Dips into Think Tank for Talent,' *Wall Street Journal*, November 17, 2008, < http://online.wsj.com/news/articles/SB122688537606232319> (last accessed February 6, 2014).

Drake, Bruce, 'Obama Charts a New Foreign Policy Course for a Public That Wants the Focus to be at Home,' Pew Research Center, May 28, 2014, <http://www.pewresearch.org/fact-tank/2014/05/28/obama-charts-a-new-foreign-policy-course-for-a-public-that-wants-the-focus-to-be-at-home/> (last accessed June 3, 2014).

Drezner, Daniel W., 'Does Obama Have a Grand Strategy?' *Foreign Affairs* 90, no. 4 (2011), pp. 57–67.

Drezner, Daniel W., 'Five Things I Think I Think About U.S. Foreign Policy After Obama's West Point Speech,' *Washington Post*, June 2, 2014, <http://www.washingtonpost.com/posteverything/wp/2014/06/02/five-things-i-think-i-think-about-american-foreign-policy-after-obamas-west-point-speech/> (last accessed June 3, 2014).

Drezner, Daniel W., 'Military Primacy Doesn't Pay (Nearly As Much As You Think),' *International Security* 38, no. 1 (2013), pp. 52–79.

D'Souza, Dinesh, *Obama's America: Unmaking the American Dream* (Washington DC: Regnery, 2012).

Dueck, Colin, 'Realism, Culture and Grand Strategy: Explaining America's Peculiar Path to World Power,' *Security Studies* 14, no. 2 (2005), pp. 195–231.

Dueck, Colin, *Reluctant Crusaders: Power, Culture and Change in American Grand Strategy* (Princeton: Princeton University Press, 2006).

Dueck, Colin, *The Obama Doctrine* (Oxford: Oxford University Press, 2015).

Duss, Matthew, 'The Isolationists Are Coming!' *The American Prospect*, May 2, 2013, <http://prospect.org/article/isolationists-are-coming> (last accessed January 21, 2014).

Eaglen, Mackenzie, 'The Sequester Is Here To Stay – Now the Military Needs To Get To Work,' *Fox News*, May 8, 2013, <http://www.foxnews.com/opin ion/2013/05/08/sequester-is-here-to-stay-now-military-needs-to-get-to-work/> (last accessed February 6, 2014).

Economist, 'The Decline of Deterrence,' May 1, 2014, <http://www.economist. com/news/united-states/21601538-america-no-longer-alarming-its-foes-or-reassuring-its-friends-decline> (last accessed February 23, 2017).

Economy, Elizabeth C., 'The Game Changer,' *Foreign Affairs* 89, no. 6 (2010), pp. 142–152.

Edelstein, David and Ronald Krebs, 'Delusions of Grand Strategy: The Problem with Washington's Planning Obsession,' *Foreign Affairs* 94, no. 6 (2015), pp. 109–118.

Edkins, Jenny, 'Ethics and Practices of Engagement: Intellectuals as Experts,' *International Relations* 19, no. 1 (2005), pp. 64–69.

Edkins, Jenny, *Post-structuralism and International Relations: Bringing the Political Back In* (Boulder: Lynne Rienner Publishers, 1999).

Edwards III., George C. and William G. Howell (eds.), *The Oxford Handbook of the American Presidency* (Oxford: Oxford University Press, 2009).

Edwards-Levy, Ariel, 'Americans Think Putin Has Been More Effective than Obama on Syria,' *Huffington Post*, September 27, 2013, <http://www.huff ingtonpost.com/2013/09/27/putin-obama-syria_n_4002351.html> (last acc- essed April 28, 2014).

Engelhardt, Tom, *The End of Victory Culture. Cold War America and Disillusioning of a Generation* (New York: Basic Books, 1995).

Entous, Adam and Phil Stewart, 'Exclusive: The Warrior-Scholar Versus the Taliban,' *Reuters*, June 25, 2010, <http://www.reuters.com/article/2010/06/ 25/us-petraeus-idU.S.TRE65O0R820100625> (last accessed May 7, 2014).

Erlanger, Steven, 'Iran and Six Powers Agree on Terms for Nuclear Talks,' *New York Times*, February 20, 2014, <http://www.nytimes.com/2014/02/21/ world/middleeast/iran.html> (last accessed May 21, 2014).

Ewing, Philip, 'The Military-Industrial-Entertainment Complex,' *DoD Buzz*, May 23, 2012, <http://www.dodbuzz.com/2012/05/23/the-military-indus trial-congressional-entertainment-complex/> (last accessed July 16, 2013).

Exum, Andrew M., 'CNAS Policy Brief Afghanistan 2011: Three Scenarios,' CNAS, October 20, 2009, <https://www.cnas.org/publications/reports/

cnas-policy-brief-afghanistan-2011-three-scenarios> (last accessed February 25, 2017).

Feaver, Peter, 'American Grand Strategy at the Crossroads: Leading from the Front, Leading from Behind or Not Leading at All,' in Richard Fontaine and Kristin M. Lord (eds.), *America's Path: Grand Strategy for the Next Administration* (Washington DC: Center for a New American Security, 2012), pp. 59–71.

Ferguson, Niall, *Colossus: The Rise and Fall of the American Empire* (Penguin, 2005).

Fisher, Max, 'Our New Isolationism Just Hit a 50-Year High: Why That Matters,' *Washington Post*, December 4, 2013, <https://www.washington post.com/news/worldviews/wp/2013/12/04/american-isolationism-just-hit-a-50-year-high-why-that-matters/?utm_term=.ae479e35d2ab> (last accessed February 25, 2017).

Flournoy, Michèle and Janine Davidson, 'Obama's New Global Posture,' *Foreign Affairs* 91, no. 4 (2012), pp. 54–63.

Flynn, Michael, 'The War Hawks,' *The Chicago Tribune*, April 13, 2003, <http://articles.chicagotribune.com/2003-04-13/news/0304130427_1_iraq-william-kristol-benevolent-hegemony> (last accessed January 21, 2013).

Fontaine, Richard and Kirstin M. Lord (eds.), *America's Path: Grand Strategy for the Next Administration* (Washington DC: Center for a New American Security, 2012).

Fontaine, Richard and Kirstin M. Lord, 'Introduction: Debating America's Future,' in Richard Fontaine and Kristin M. Lord (eds.), *America's Path: Grand Strategy for the Next Administration* (Washington DC: Center for a New American Security, 2012), pp. 3–12.

Forbes, Randy, 'America's Pacific Air-Sea Battle Vision,' *The Diplomat*, March 8, 2012, <http://thediplomat.com/2012/03/americas-pacific-air-sea-battle-vision/> (last accessed November 20, 2013).

Foreign Policy Initiative, American Enterprise Institute, and The Heritage Foundation, *Defending Defense: Defense Spending, the Super Committee and the Price of Greatness* (Washington DC: Foreign Policy Institute, American Enterprise Institute, and The Heritage Foundation, 2011).

Foucault, Michel, *Discipline and Punish: The Birth of the Prison* (London: Penguin Books, 1977).

Foucault, Michel, *Power: Essential Works of Foucault 1954–1985* (New York: The New Press, 2000).

Foucault, Michel, *Power/Knowledge: Selected Interviews and Other Writings 1972–1977* (New York: Pantheon, 1977).

Foucault, Michel, *Society Must Be Defended: Lectures at the Collège de France 1975–76*, translated by David Macey (London: Penguin, 2004).

Foundas, Scott, 'Film Review: "Captain America: The Winter Soldier"' *Variety*, March 20, 2014, <http://variety.com/2014/film/reviews/film-review-cap

tain-america-the-winter-soldier-1201139253/> (last accessed August 11, 2014).

Franke, David, '"White House Down"—What a Waste,' *The American Conservative*, June 28, 2014, <http://www.theamericanconservative.com/white-house-down-what-a-waste/> (last accessed August 12, 2014).

Freedman, Lawrence, *Strategy: A History* (Oxford and New York: Oxford University Press, 2013).

Friedberg, Aaron L., *A Contest for Supremacy: China, America, and the Struggle for Mastery in Asia* (New York and London: W. W. Norton & Company, 2011).

Friedman, Benjamin H. and Christopher Preble, 'Americans Favor Not Isolationism But Restraint,' *Los Angeles Times*, December 27, 2013, <http://www.cato.org/publications/commentary/americans-favor-not-isolationism-restraint> (last accessed June 3, 2014).

Friedman, Benjamin H. and Christopher Preble, *Budgetary Savings from Military Restraint* (Washington DC: CATO, 2010).

Friedman, George, *The Next 100 Years: A Forecast for the 21st Century* (New York: Doubleday, 2009).

Friedman, George, *The Next Decade: Empire and Republic in a Changing World* (New York: Doubleday, 2011).

Friedman, Thomas L. and Michael Mandelbaum, *That Used To Be Us: How America Fell Behind in the World it Invented and How We Can Come Back* (New York: Farrar, Straus and Giroux, 2011).

Fukuyama, Francis, *The End of History and the Last Man* (New York: Free Press, 1992).

Gaddis, John Lewis, *Strategies of Containment: A Critical Appraisal of American National Security Policy During the Cold War* (New York: Oxford University Press, 2005).

Gallup, *The U.S.-Global Leadership Project* (Washington DC: Gallup, 2013).

Gans, John A. Jr., '"This is 50-50": Behind Obama's Decision to Kill Bin Laden,' *Atlantic*, October 10, 2012, <http://www.theatlantic.com/international/archive/2012/10/this-is-50-50-behind-obamas-decision-to-kill-bin-laden/263449/> (last accessed May 27, 2014).

Garnett, John, 'Strategic Studies and its Assumptions,' in John Baylis, Ken Booth, John Garnett, and Phil Williams (eds.), *Contemporary Strategy: Theories and Policies* (London: Croom Helm, 1975), pp. 3–21.

Gates, Robert M., 'A Balanced Strategy,' *Foreign Affairs* 88, no. 1 (2009), pp. 28–40.

Gates, Robert M., *Duty* (New York: Alfred A. Knopf, 2014).

Gates, Robert M., 'Helping Others to Defend Themselves,' *Foreign Affairs* 89, no. 3 (2010), pp. 2–6.

Gelb, Leslie H., 'In Defense of Leading from Behind,' *Foreign Policy*, May/June

2013, <http://www.foreignpolicy.com/articles/2013/04/29/in_defense_of_ leading_from_behind> (last accessed September 24, 2014).

Gelb, Leslie H., 'Necessity, Choice, and Common Sense,' *Foreign Affairs* 88, no. 3 (2009), 56–72.

George, Larry N., 'Pharmacotic War and the Ethical Dilemmas of Engagement,' *International Relations* 19, no. 1 (2005), pp. 115–125.

Gerson, Michael, 'Obama's Foreign Policy and the Risks of Retreat,' *Washington Post*, March 19, 2014, <http://www.washingtonpost.com/opinions/michael- gerson-obamas-foreign-policy-and-the-risks-of-retreat/2013/03/18/526e9 ad6-8ffa-11e2-bdea-e32ad90da239_story.html> (last accessed June 2, 2014).

Giglio, E., *Here's Looking at You: Hollywood, Film, and Politics*, 3rd edn (New York: Peterland, 2010).

Goddard, Stacie E. and Ronald R. Krebs, 'Rhetoric, Legitimation, and Grand Strategy,' *Security Studies* 24, no. 1 (2015), pp. 5–36.

Golan-Vilella, Robert, 'The Results of Threat Inflation,' *National Interest*, March 1, 2013, <http://nationalinterest.org/blog/the-buzz/the-results-threat-infl ation-8175> (last accessed May 7, 2014).

Goldberg, Jeffrey, 'Obama's Crystal-Clear Promise to Stop Iran From Getting a Nuclear Weapon,' *Atlantic*, October 2, 2012, <http://www.theatlantic.com/ international/archive/2012/10/obamas-crystal-clear-promise-to-stop-iran- from-getting-a-nuclear-weapon/262951/> (last accessed May 21, 2014).

Goldberg, Jeffrey, 'The Obama Doctrine,' *Atlantic*, April 2016, pp. 70–90.

Goldgeier, James, 'The "Russia Reset" was Already Dead; Now it's Time for Isolation,' *Washington Post*, March 2, 2014, <http://www.washingtonpost. com/blogs/monkey-cage/wp/2014/03/02/the-russia-reset-was-already- dead-now-its-time-for-isolation/> (last accessed May 21, 2014).

Goldstein, Avery, 'China's Real and Present Danger,' *Foreign Affairs* 92, no. 5 (2013), pp. 136–144.

Gray, Colin S, *Hard Power and Soft Power: The Utility of Military Force as an Instrument of Policy in the 21st Century* (Carlisle: US Army War College, 2011).

Gray, Colin, 'In Defence of the Heartland: Sir Halford Mackinder and His Critics a Hundred Years On,' *Comparative Strategy* 23, no. 1 (2004), pp. 9–25.

Green, Brendan Rittenhouse, 'Two Concepts of Liberty: U.S. Cold War Grand Strategies and the Liberal Tradition,' *International Security* 37, no. 2 (2012), pp. 9–43.

Green, Michael, *Rethinking U.S. Military Presence in Asia and the Pacific* (Washington DC: Center for Strategic and International Studies, 2012).

Green, Michael, Kathleen Hicks, and Mark Cancian, *Asia-Pacific Rebalance 2025: Capabilities, Presence, and Partnerships* (Washington DC: CSIS, 2016).

Guardian, 'The NSA Files,' <http://www.theguardian.com/world/the-nsa- files> (last accessed September 1, 2016).

Guertner, Gary L., 'European Views of Preemption in U.S. National Security Strategy,' *The U.S. Army Professional Writing Collection* 5 (2007/2008), <http://www.army.mil/professionalWriting/volumes/volume5/august_2007/8_07_2.html> (last accessed September 14, 2016).

Haass, Richard, 'America Can Take a Breather. And It Should,' *New York Times*, June 22, 2013, <http://www.nytimes.com/2013/06/23/opinion/sunday/america-can-take-a-breather-and-it-should.html?pagewanted=all&_r=2&> (last accessed September 24, 2016).

Haass, Richard N., 'The Restoration Doctrine,' *The American Interest*, December 9, 2011, <http://www.the-american-interest.com/articles/2011/12/9/the-restoration-doctrine/> (last accessed September 28, 2016).

Hagel, Chuck, 'Remarks by Secretary Hagel at the IISS Asia Security Summit,' June 1, 2013, <http://www.defense.gov/transcripts/transcript.aspx?transcriptid=5251> (last accessed September 11, 2016).

Hansen, Lene, *Security as Practice: Discourse Analysis and the Bosnian War* (New York: Routledge, 2006).

Hantke, Steffen, 'Bush's America and the Return of Cold War Science Fiction: Alien Invasion in Invasion, Threshold, and Surface,' *Journal of Popular Film and Television* 38, no. 3 (2010), pp. 143–151.

Hasian, Marouf Jr., Sean Lawson, and Megan D. McFarlane, *The Rhetorical Invention of America's National Security State* (Lanham: Lexington Books, 2015).

Hastings, Michael, 'The Runaway General,' *Rolling Stone*, June 22, 2010, <http://www.rollingstone.com/politics/news/the-runaway-general-20100622> (last accessed September 7, 2016).

Hayward, Susan, *Cinema Studies: The Key Concepts* (London: Routledge, 2000).

Heilbrunn, Jacob, 'Barack Obama Misfires at West Point,' *National Interest*, May 29, 2014, <http://nationalinterest.org/feature/obamas-west-point-speech-10552> (last accessed September 19, 2016).

Herman, Arthur, 'America's Disarmed Future,' *National Review Online*, January 6, 2012, <http://www.nationalreview.com/articles/287320/america-s-disarmed-future-arthur-herman> (last accessed September 17, 2016).

Hilfrich, Fabian, *Debating American Exceptionalism Empire and Democracy in the Wake of the Spanish-American War* (New York: Palgrave Macmillan, 2012).

Hill, Charles, *Grand Strategies* (New Haven, London: Yale University Press, 2010).

Hirsh, Michael, 'The Clinton Legacy: How Will History Judge the Soft-power Secretary of State,' *Foreign Affairs* 92, no. 3 (2013), pp. 82–91.

Hodge, Nathan, 'The Nation: Who Drives the Think Tanks?,' *NPR*, March 17, 2010, <http://www.npr.org/templates/story/story.php?storyId=124760902> (last accessed September 22, 2016).

Hornaday, Ann, '"Captain America: The Winter Soldier" Review: Maybe the Most Grown-up Avengers Movie Yet,' *Washington Post*, April 3, 2014,

<http://www.washingtonpost.com/goingoutguide/movies/captain-ameri ca-the-winter-soldier-review-maybe-the-most-grown-up-avengers-mov ie-yet/2014/04/03/89bad3d8-ba60-11e3-9a05-c739f29ccb08_story.html> (last accessed September 11, 2016).

Horowitz, Jason, 'Events in Iraq Open Door for Interventionist Revival, Historian Says,' *New York Times*, June 15, 2014, <http://www.nytimes.com/ 2014/06/16/us/politics/historians-critique-of-obama-foreign-policy-is-brou ght-alive-by-events-in-iraq.html?_r=0> (last accessed September 29, 2016).

Human Rights Watch, 'Targeted Killings and Drones,' <http://www.hrw. org/topic/counterterrorism/targeted-killings-and-drones> (last accessed September 10, 2016).

Huntington, Samuel, *Who Are We? Challenges to America's National Identity* (New York: Simon and Schuster, 2004).

Hyndman, Jennifer, 'Mind the Gap: Bridging Feminist and Political Geography Through Geopolitics,' *Political Geography* 23, no. 3 (2004), pp. 307–322.

Ignatieff, Michael, 'American Empire; The Burden,' *New York Times Magazine*, January 5, 2003.

Ikenberry, John, G., *After Victory: Institutions, Strategic Restraint, and the Rebuilding of Order After Major Wars* (Princeton: Princeton University Press, 2009).

Ikenberry, John G., 'The Future of the Liberal World Order,' *Foreign Affairs* 90, no. 3 (2011), pp. 56–68.

Ikenberry, John G., *Liberal Leviathan: The Origins, Crisis and Transformation of the American World Order* (Princeton: Princeton University Press, 2011).

Ikenberry, Karl W., 'The Limits of Counter-Insurgency in Afghanistan: The Other Side of the COIN,' *Foreign Affairs* 92, no. 5 (2013), pp. 59–74.

IMF, *Regional Economic Outlook: Asia and Pacific. Stabilizing and Outperforming Other Regions* (Washington DC: IMF, 2015).

Indyk, Martin S., Kenneth G. Lieberthal, and Michael E. O'Hanlon, *Bending History: Barack Obama's Foreign Policy* (Washington DC: Brookings, 2012).

Indyk, Martin S., Kenneth G. Lieberthal, and Michael E. O'Hanlon, 'Scoring Obama's Foreign Policy,' *Foreign Affairs* 91, no. 3 (2012), pp. 29–43.

Ingraham, Laura, *The Obama Diaries* (Chicago: Threshold Editions, 2010).

Itzkoff, Dave, 'You Saw What in "Avatar"? Pass Those Glasses!' *New York Times*, January 20, 2010, <http://www.nytimes.com/2010/01/20/movies/ 20avatar.html> (last accessed September 15, 2016).

Jackson, Richard, 'Culture, Identity and Hegemony: Continuity and (the Lack of) Change in US Counterterrorism Policy from Bush to Obama,' *International Politics* 48, no. 2–3 (2011), pp. 390–411.

Jaffe, Greg, 'U.S. Model For a Future War Fans Tensions with China and Inside Pentagon,' *Washington Post*, August 1, 2012, <http://www.washingtonpost.

com/world/national-security/us-model-for-a-future-war-fans-tensions-with-china-and-inside-pentagon/2012/08/01/gJQAC6F8PX_story.html> (last accessed September 17, 2016).

Jepperson, Ronald L., Alexander Wendt, and Peter J. Katzenstein, 'Norms, Identity, and Culture in National Security,' in Peter J. Katzenstein (ed.), *The Culture of National Security: Norms and Identity in World Politics* (New York: Columbia University Press, 1996), pp. 33–75.

Joffe, Josef, 'The Default Power,' *Foreign Affairs* 88, no. 4 (2009), pp. 21–35.

Johnson, Chalmers, *Dismantling the Empire: America's Last Best Hope* (New York: Metropolitan Books, 2010).

Johnston, Alastair Iain, *Cultural Realism: Strategic Culture and Grand Strategy in Chinese History* (Princeton: Princeton University Press, 1995).

Joint Chiefs of Staff, *The National Military Strategy of the United States* (Washington DC: US Department of Defense, 2011).

Jones, Bruce, Thomas Wright, and Jane Esberg, *Reviving American Leadership: The Next President Should Continue on the Path Obama Has Set* (Washington DC: Brookings, 2012).

Jones, Julia and Eve Bower, 'American Deaths in Terrorism vs. Gun Violence in One Graph,' *CNN*, December 30, 2015, <http://edition.cnn.com/2015/10/02/us/oregon-shooting-terrorism-gun-violence/> (last accessed September 21, 2016).

Jones, Robert, 'The Eclipse of White Christian America,' *Atlantic*, July 12, 2016, <http://www.theatlantic.com/politics/archive/2016/07/the-eclipse-of-white-christian-america/490724/> (last accessed September 1, 2016).

'Judicial Watch Obtains Department of Defense and CIA Records Detailing Meetings with Bin Laden Raid Filmmakers,' Judicial Watch, May 22, 2012, <http://www.judicialwatch.org/press-room/press-releases/13421/> (last accessed September 10, 2016).

Judis, John B., 'Speak Loudly and Carry a Small Stick,' *New Republic*, March 12, 2014, <http://www.newrepublic.com/article/116988/barack-obama-foreign-policy-speak-loudly-and-carry-small-stick> (last accessed September 13, 2016).

Kagan, Robert, 'Not Fade Away: Against the Myth of American Decline,' *New Republic*, January 11, 2012, <http://www.newrepublic.com/article/politics/magazine/99521/america-world-power-declinism> (last accessed September 14, 2016).

Kagan, Robert, *Of Paradise and Power: America and Europe in the New World Order* (New York: Alfred A. Knopf, 2003).

Kagan, Robert, 'President Obama's Foreign Policy Paradox,' *Washington Post*, March 27, 2016, <http://www.washingtonpost.com/opinions/president-obamas-foreign-policy-paradox/2014/03/26/c5284c2e-b4f8-11e3-8cb6-284052554d74_story.html> (last accessed September 28, 2016).

Kagan, Robert, 'Superpowers Don't Get to Retire,' *New Republic*, May 26,

2014, <http://www.newrepublic.com/article/117859/allure-normalcy-what-america-still-owes-world> (last accessed September 12, 2016).

Kagan, Robert, 'The Benevolent Empire,' *Foreign Affairs* 111 (1998), pp. 24–35.

Kagan, Robert, *The World America Made* (New York: Alfred A. Knopf, 2012).

Kagan, Robert and William Kristol, 'Statement of Principles,' Project for the New American Century, June 3, 1997, <http://web.archive.org/web/20070810113753/www.newamericancentury.org/statementofprinciples.htm> (last accessed September 21, 2016).

Kaplan, Robert D., 'Center Stage for the Twenty-First Century,' *Foreign Affairs* 88, no. 2 (2009), pp. 16–32.

Kaplan, Robert D., *The Revenge of Geography: What the Map Tells Us About Coming Conflicts and the Battle Against Fate* (New York: Random House, 2012).

Kaplan, Robert D., 'Why John J. Mearsheimer is Right (About Some Things),' *Atlantic*, January/February 2012, <http://www.theatlantic.com/magazine/archive/2012/01/why-john-j-mearsheimer-is-right-about-some-things/308839> (last accessed September 24, 2016).

Katzenstein, Peter J. (ed.), *The Culture of National Security: Norms and Identity in World Politics* (New York: Columbia University Press, 1996).

Katzenstein, Peter J., Robert O. Keohane, and Stephen D. Krasner, 'International Organization and the Study of World Politics,' *International Organization* 52, no. 2 (1998), pp. 645–685.

Kaufman, Robert G., *Dangerous Doctrine: How Obama's Grand Strategy Weakened America* (Lexington: University Press of Kentucky, 2016).

Kaufman, Stuart J., 'US National Security Strategy from Bush to Obama,' in Bahram M. Rajaee (ed.), *National Security under the Obama Administration* (New York: Palgrave Macmillan US, 2012), pp. 11–28.

Kearns, Gerry, *Geopolitics and Empire: The Legacy of Halford Mackinder* (Oxford: Oxford University Press, 2009).

Kearns, Gerry, 'Naturalising Empire: Echoes of Mackinder for the Next American Century?' *Geopolitics* 11, no. 1 (2006), pp. 74–98.

Keegan, Rebecca, '"Act of Valor" Must Balance Publicity, Secrecy with Navy SEALs,' *Los Angeles Times*, February 12, 2012, <http://articles.latimes.com/2012/feb/12/entertainment/la-ca-act-of-valor-20120212> (last accessed September 21, 2016).

Kellner, Douglas, *Cinema Wars: Hollywood Film and Politics in the Bush-Cheney Era* (Oxford: Wiley-Blackwell, 2010).

Kellner, Douglas, *Media Culture: Cultural Studies, Identity and Politics Between the Modern and the Post-Modern* (New York: Routledge, 1995).

Kennan, George F., 'The Sources of Soviet Conduct,' *Foreign Affairs* 26, no. 2 (1947), pp. 566–582.

Kennedy, Caroline, 'The Manichean Temptation: Moralising Rhetoric and the

Invocation of Evil in U.S. Foreign Policy,' *International Politics* 50, no. 5 (2013), pp. 623–638.

Kennedy, Paul, *The Rise and Fall of the Great Powers: Economic Change and Military Power from 1500 to 2000* (New York: Random House, 1987).

Keohane, Robert, *After Hegemony: Cooperation and Discord in the World Political Economy* (Princeton: Princeton University Press, 1984).

Kerry, John, 'Opening Remarks Before the Senate Appropriations Subcommittee on Foreign Operations,' March 13, 2016, <http://www.state.gov/secretary/remarks/2014/03/223414.htm> (last accessed September 16, 2016).

Khanna, Parag, *The Second World: Empires and Influence in the New Global Order: How Emerging Powers Are Redefining Global Competition in the Twenty-first Century* (New York: Random House, 2008).

Kissinger, Henry A., 'The Future of U.S.-China Relations,' *Foreign Affairs* 91, no. 2 (2012), pp. 44–53.

Kohut, Andrew, 'Americans: Disengaged, Feeling Less Respected, But Still See U.S. as World's Military Superpower,' Pew Research Center, April 1, 2014, <http://www.pewresearch.org/fact-tank/2014/04/01/americans-disengaged-feeling-less-respected-but-still-see-u-s-as-worlds-military-superpower/> (last accessed September 17, 2016).

Korb, Lawrence J., 'The Right Cuts,' *National Interest*, January 25, 2012, <http://nationalinterest.org/commentary/obamas-overblown-defense-reductions-6379> (last accessed September 17, 2016).

Korb, Lawrence, Sean Duggan, and Laura Conley, *Integrating Security* (Washington DC: CAP, 2009).

Korb, Lawrence J., Max Hoffman, and Katherine Blakeley, 'A User's Guide to the Fiscal Year 2015 Defense Budget,' CAP, April 24, 2014, <https://www.americanprogress.org/issues/security/reports/2014/04/24/88516/a-users-guide-to-the-fiscal-year-2015-defense-budget/> (last accessed February 25, 2017).

Korb, Lawrence J., Max Hoffman, and Kate Blakeley, 'Hagel's Defense Cuts: A Good Idea,' *National Interest*, April 30, 2014, <http://nationalinterest.org/feature/hagels-defense-cuts-good-idea-10322> (last accessed September 17, 2016).

Korb, Lawrence J., Alex Rothman, and Max Hoffman, *$100 Billion in Politically Feasible Defense Cuts for a Budget Deal* (Washington DC: CAP, 2012).

Kornprobst, Markus, 'Building Agreements Upon Agreements: The European Union and Grand Strategy,' *European Journal of International Relations* 21, no. 2 (2015), pp. 267–292.

Krauthammer, Charles, 'How Fractured is the GOP?,' *Washington Post*, August 1, 2013, <http://www.washingtonpost.com/opinions/charles-krauthammer-how-fractured-is-the-gop/2013/08/01/6fd6f816-fada-11e2-9bde-7ddaa186b751_story.html> (last accessed September 21, 2016).

Krauthammer, Charles, 'Krauthammer: Obama Doctrine Forged in Retreat,'

Boston Herald, June 1, 2014, <http://bostonherald.com/news_opinion/opi
nion/op_ed/2014/05/krauthammer_obama_doctrine_forged_in_retreat>
(last accessed September 12, 2014).

Krauthammer, Charles, 'The Bush Doctrine,' *Time*, March 5, 2001, p. 42.

Krauthammer, Charles, 'The Obama Doctrine: Leading from Behind,'
Washington Post, April 28, 2011, <http://www.washingtonpost.com/opi
nions/the-obama-doctrine-leading-from-behind/2011/04/28/AFBCy18E_st
ory.html> (last accessed September 23, 2016).

Krauthammer, Charles, 'The Unipolar Moment,' *Foreign Affairs* 70, no. 1
(1990), pp. 23–33.

Krepinevich Jr., Andrew F., 'Strategy in a Time of Austerity,' *Foreign Affairs* 91,
no. 6 (2012), pp. 58–69.

Krepinevich Jr., Andrew F., 'Statement Before the Senate Armed Services
Committee on Defense Strategy,' October 29, 2015, <http://www.
armed-services.senate.gov/download/15-82_-10-29-15> (last accessed
September 30, 2016).

Krepinevich Jr., Andrew F., 'The Pentagon's Wasting Assets,' *Foreign Affairs*
88, no. 4 (2009), pp. 18–33.

Krepinevich Jr., Andrew F. (ed.), *Why AirSea Battle?* (Washington DC: CSBA,
2010).

Kristof, Nicholas, 'Overreacting to Terrorism?,' *New York Times*, March 24,
2016, <http://www.nytimes.com/2016/03/24/opinion/terrorists-bathtubs-
and-snakes.html?_r=0> (last accessed September 21, 2016).

Kristol, William and Robert Kagan, 'Toward a Reaganite Foreign Policy,'
Foreign Affairs 75, no. 4 (1996), pp.18–32.

Kuhnhenn, Jim, 'Obama Faces "New Chapter" of American Foreign Policy,'
Huffington Post, March 17, 2014, <http://www.huffingtonpost.com/2014/03/
17/obama-foreign-policy_n_4981654.html> (last accessed September 10,
2016).

Kupchan, Charles A., 'Enemies Into Friends,' *Foreign Affairs* 89, no. 2 (2010),
pp. 120–135.

Kupchan, Charles A., 'Grand Strategy: The Four Pillars of the Future,'
Democracy Journal, no. 23 (Winter 2012), <http://www.democracyjournal.
org/23/grand-strategy-the-four-pillars-of-the-future.php?page=all> (last
accessed September 14, 2016).

Kupchan, Charles A., *No One's World: The West, the Rising Rest, and the Coming
Global Turn* (New York: Oxford University Press, 2012).

Kurth Cronin, Audrey, 'National Security Education: A User's Manual,' *War
On the Rocks*, June 17, 2014 <http://warontherocks.com/2014/06/nation
al-security-education-a-users-manual/> (last accessed September 21,
2016).

Kyl, Jon and Jim Talent, 'A Strong and Focused National Security Strategy,'
American Enterprise Institute, October 31, 2013, <http://www.aei.org/

papers/foreign-and-defense-policy/defense/a-strong-and-focused-nation al-security-strategy/> (last accessed September 16, 2014).

Lacy, Mark J., 'War, Cinema, and Moral Anxiety,' *Alternatives* 28, no. 5 (2003), pp. 611–636.

Landler, Mark, *Alter Egos: Hillary Clinton, Barack Obama, and the Twilight Struggle over American Power* (New York: Random House, 2016).

Landler, Mark, 'Ending Asia Trip, Obama Defends His Foreign Policy,' *New York Times*, April 28, 2014, <http://www.nytimes.com/2014/04/29/ world/obama-defends-foreign-policy-against-critics.html> (last accessed September 27, 2016).

Landler, Mark, 'Obama Says Iran Strike is an Option, but Warns Israel,' *New York Times*, March 2, 2012, <http://www.nytimes.com/2012/03/03/world/ middleeast/obama-says-military-option-on-iran-not-a-bluff.html?pagewa nted=all> (last accessed September 21, 2014).

Larison, Daniel, 'Noninterventionism: A Primer,' *American Conservative*, June 11, 2014, <http://www.theamericanconservative.com/articles/noninterven tionism-a-primer/> (last accessed September 16, 2016).

Larison, Daniel, 'The Cliches of "Leadership" and "Resolve,"' *American Conservative*, March 3, 2014, <http://www.theamericanconservative.com/ larison/the-cliches-of-leadership-and-resolve/> (last accessed September 23, 2016).

Layne, Christopher, 'The (Almost) Triumph of Offshore Balancing,' *National Interest*, January 27, 2012, <http://nationalinterest.org/commentary/ almost-triumph-offshore-balancing-6405> (last accessed September 26, 2016).

Layne, Christopher, 'The End of Pax Americana: How Western Decline Became Inevitable,' *Atlantic*, April 26, 2012, <http://www.theatlantic.com/ international/archive/2012/04/the-end-of-pax-americana-how-western- decline-became-inevitable/256388/> (last accessed September 30, 2016).

Layne, Christopher, *The Peace of Illusions: American Grand Strategy from 1940 to the Present* (Ithaca: Cornell University Press, 2006).

Leffler, Melvyn P., '9/11 in Retrospect,' *Foreign Affairs* 90, no. 5 (2011), pp. 33–43.

Leonard, Mark, 'Why Convergence Breeds Conflict,' *Foreign Affairs* 92, no. 5 (2013), pp. 125–135.

Lewis, Paul, 'Most Americans Think U.S. Should "Mind Its Own Business" Abroad, Survey Finds,' *Guardian*, December 3, 2013, <http://www.the guardian.com/world/2013/dec/03/american-public-mind-its-own-busi ness-survey> (last accessed September 26, 2016).

Lieber, Robert J., *Retreat and its Consequences: American Foreign Policy and the Problem of World Order* (Cambridge: Cambridge University Press, 2016).

Lieberman, Joseph I. and Jon Kyl, 'The Danger of Repeating the Cycle of American Isolationism,' *Washington Post*, April 26, 2013, <http://www.wash ingtonpost.com/opinions/the-danger-of-repeating-the-cycle-of-american-is

olationism/2013/04/25/16da45f8-a90c-11e2-a8e2-5b98cb59187f_story.html> (last accessed September 21, 2016).

Lipset, Seymour Martin, *American Exceptionalism: A Double-edged Sword* (New York: W. W. Norton & Company, 1996).

Lipson, Charles, 'America's Meltdown Abroad,' *Chicago Tribune*, May 20, 2014, <http://articles.chicagotribune.com/2014-05-20/opinion/ct-america-stand ing-overseas-europe-lipson-oped-05-20140520_1_john-kerry-achieveme nt-balance-sheet> (last accessed September 11, 2016).

Lizza, Ryan, 'Leading from Behind,' *New Yorker*, April 27, 2011, <http://www.newyorker.com/online/blogs/newsdesk/2011/04/leading-from-behi nd-obama-clinton.html> (last accessed September 27, 2016).

Lizza, Ryan, 'The Consequentialist. How the Arab Spring Remade Obama's Foreign Policy,' *New Yorker*, May 2, 2011, <http://www.newyorker.com/reporting/2011/05/02/110502fa_fact_lizza?currentPage=all> (last accessed September 23, 2016).

Löfflmann, Georg, 'Leading from Behind – American Exceptionalism and President Obama's post-American Vision of Hegemony,' *Geopolitics* 20, no. 2 (2015), pp. 308–332.

Löfflmann, Georg, 'The Pivot Between Containment, Engagement and Restraint – President Obama's Conflicted Grand Strategy in Asia,' *Asian Security* 12, no. 2 (2016), pp. 92–110.

Logan, Justin, *China, America, and the Pivot to Asia* (Washington DC: CATO, 2013).

Logan, Justin, 'Rand Paul is No Isolationist,' *Politico*, August 7, 2013, <http://www.politico.com/story/2013/08/rand-paul-is-no-isolationist-95286.html> (last accessed September 21, 2016).

Londoño, Ernesto, 'The Last Casualties: As a Long War Ends, Risks Still Prove Real,' *Washington Post*, March 4, 2014, <http://www.washingtonpost.com/world/national-security/the-last-casualties-as-a-long-war-ends-risks-still-prove-real/2014/03/04/55905998-8a90-11e3-a5bd-844629433ba3_story.html> (last accessed September 25, 2016).

Lowenthal, Abraham F., 'Obama and the Americas,' *Foreign Affairs* 89, no. 4 (2010), pp. 110–124.

Lozada, Carlos, 'Setting Priorities for the Afghan War,' *Washington Post*, June 7, 2009, <http://www.washingtonpost.com/wpdyn/content/article/2009/06/05/AR2009060501967.html> (last accessed September 15, 2016).

Luce, Edward, *Time to Start Thinking: America and the Specter of Decline* (London: Little, Brown, 2012).

Luke, Timothy W., 'Hyper-Power or Hype-Power? The USA After Kandahar, Karbala, and Katrina,' in Francois Debrix and Mark Lacy (eds.), *The Geopolitics of American Insecurity* (London: Routledge, 2008), pp. 1–17.

MacAskill, Ewen, 'Barack Obama Ends the War in Iraq. "Now It's Time to Turn the Page."' *Guardian*, September 1, 2010, <http://www.theguardian.

com/world/2010/sep/01/obama-formally-ends-iraq-war> (last accessed September 22, 2016).

McCrisken, Trevor, *American Exceptionalism and the Legacy of Vietnam* (Hampshire, New York: Palgrave Macmillan, 2003).

McCrisken, Trevor and Mark Phythian, 'The Offensive Turn,' in Inderjeet Parmar, Linda B. Miller, and Mark Ledwidge (eds.), *Obama and the World: New Directions in US Foreign Policy* (New York and London: Routledge, 2014).

MacDonald, Paul K. and Joseph M. Parent, 'Graceful Decline? The Surprising Success of Great Power Retrenchment,' *International Security* 35, no. 4 (2011), pp. 7–44.

McGann, James G., *2012 Global Go To Think Tanks Report and Policy Advice* (Philadelphia: University of Pennsylvania, 2012).

McGann, James G., *Think Tanks and Policy Advice in the U.S.* (Philadelphia: Foreign Policy Research Institute, 2005).

McGrath, Ben, 'The Movement,' *The New Yorker*, February 1, 2010, <http://www.newyorker.com/reporting/2010/02/01/100201fa_fact_mcgrath?currentPage=all> (last accessed September 16, 2016).Maddow, Rachel, *Drift: The Unmooring of American Military Power* (New York: Crown Publishers, 2012).

Madsen, Deborah, *American Exceptionalism* (Edinburgh: Edinburgh University Press, 1998).

Mahnken, Thomas G., *Asia in the Balance* (Washington DC: American Enterprise Institute, 2012).

Mamadouh, Virginie and Gertjan Dijkink, 'Geopolitics, International Relations and Political Geography: The Politics of Geopolitical Discourse,' *Geopolitics* 11, no. 3 (2006), pp. 349–366.

Mandelbaum, Michael, 'Review Essay. Overpowered?' *Foreign Affairs* 89, no. 3 (2010), pp. 114–119.

Mandelbaum, Michael, *The Frugal Superpower* (New York: PublicAffairs, 2011).

Mann, James, *The Obamians: The Struggle Inside the White House to Redefine American Power* (New York: Penguin, 2012).

Mann, James and Jim Mann, *Rise of the Vulcans: The History of Bush's War Cabinet* (London: Penguin, 2004).

Marshall, Tyrone C., 'DoD Budget Request Adapts to Fiscal Realities, Hagel Says,' *American Forces Press Service*, March 6, 2014, <http://www.defense.gov/news/newsarticle.aspx?id=121784> (last accessed September 13, 2016).

Martel, William C., 'America's Grand Strategy Disaster,' *National Interest*, June 9, 2014, <http://nationalinterest.org/feature/americas-grand-strategy-disaster-10627> (last accessed September 24, 2016).

Martel, William C., *Grand Strategy in Theory and Practice* (Cambridge: Cambridge University Press, 2015).

Martel, William C., 'Why America Needs a Grand Strategy,' *The Diplomat*, July 18, 2012, <http://thediplomat.com/2012/06/why-america-needs-a-grand-strategy/> (last accessed September 28, 2016).

Matlock, Jack F. Jr. *Superpower Illusions: How Myths and False Ideologies Led America Astray – And How to Return to Reality* (New Haven & London: Yale University Press, 2010).

Mazarr, Michael J, 'The Risks of Ignoring Strategic Insolvency,' *The Washington Quarterly* 35, no. 4 (2012), pp. 7–22.

Mazza, Michael, 'Asia's Four Big Questions for Obama's Second Term,' *The Diplomat*, November 7, 2012, <http://thediplomat.com/2012/11/asias-four-big-questions-for-obamas-second-term/> (last accessed September 25, 2016).

Mead, Walter Russell, *Special Providence: American Foreign Policy and How it Shaped the World* (New York and London: Routledge, 2002).

Mead, Walter Russell, 'The Tea Party in American Foreign Policy,' *Foreign Affairs* 90, no. 2 (2011), pp. 28–44.

Meaney, Thomas and Stephen Wertheim, 'Grand Flattery: The Yale Grand Strategy Seminar,' *The Nation*, May 28, 2012, <http://www.thenation.com/article/167807/grand-flattery-yale-grand-strategy-seminar#> (last accessed September 22, 2016).

Mearsheimer, John J., 'Imperial by Design,' *National Interest*, December 16, 2010, <http://nationalinterest.org/print/article/imperial-by-design-4576?page=1> (last accessed September 24, 2016).

Mearsheimer, John J., *The Tragedy of Great Power Politics* (New York: W. W. Norton & Company, 2001).

Mearsheimer, John J. and Stephen Walt, 'The Case for Offshore Balancing,' *Foreign Affairs*, 95 no. 4 (2016), pp. 70–83.

Metz, Stephen, 'A Receding Presence,' *World Politics Review*, October 22, 2013, <http://www.worldpoliticsreview.com/articles/13312/a-receding-presence-the-military-implications-of-american-retrenchment> (last accessed February 26, 2017).

Milliken, Jennifer, 'The Study of Discourse in International Relations: A Critique of Research and Methods,' *European Journal of International Relations* 5, no. 2 (1999), pp. 225–254.

Mills, Donna, 'Obama: Tide of War Receding at "Crossroads of History,"' *American Forces Press Service*, September 21, 2011, <http://www.defense.gov/news/newsarticle.aspx?id=65402> (last accessed September 17, 2016).

Milne, David, 'Pragmatism or What? The Future of U.S. Foreign Policy,' *International Affairs* 88, no. 5 (2012), pp. 935–951.

Mintz, Steven and Randy W. Roberts (eds.), *Hollywood's America: United States History Through its Films,* 2nd edn (New York: Brandywine Press, 1993).

Mitzen, Jennifer, 'Illusion or Intention? Talking Grand Strategy into Existence,' *Security Studies* 24, no. 1 (2015), pp. 61–94.

Morris, Dick and Eileen McGann, *Here Come The Black Helicopters! UN Global Governance and the Loss of Freedom* (New York: Broadside Books, 2012).

Morris, Dick and Eileen McGann, *Screwed!* (New York: Broadside Books, 2012).

Morrissey, John, 'Architects of Empire: The Military–Strategic Studies Complex and the Scripting of U.S. National Security,' *Antipode* 43, no. 2 (2011), pp. 435–470.

Mr. Y (Wayne Porter and Mark Mykleby), 'A National Strategic Narrative,' Woodrow Wilson Center, 2011, <http://www.wilsoncenter.org/sites/default/files/A National Strategic Narrative.pdf> (last accessed September 20, 2016).

Müller, Martin, 'Doing Discourse Analysis in Critical Geopolitics,' *L'Espace Politique* 12, no. 3 (2010), pp. 1–18.

Mutlu, Can E. and Mark B. Salter, 'The Discursive Turn,' in Mark B. Salter and Can E. Mutlu (eds.), *Research Methods in Critical Security Studies: An Introduction* (New York: Routledge, 2013), pp. 113–119.

Narizny, Kevin, *The Political Economy of Grand Strategy* (Ithaca and London: Cornell University Press, 2007).

Nathan, Andrew J. and Andrew Scobell, 'How China Sees America,' *Foreign Affairs* 91, no. 5 (2012), pp. 32–47.

National Intelligence Council, *Global Trends 2025: A Transformed World* (Washington DC: National Intelligence Council, 2008).

National Intelligence Council, *Global Trends 2030: Alternative Worlds*, NIC 2012-001, (Washington DC: National Intelligence Council, 2012).

Neumann, Iver B. and Henrikki Heikka, 'Grand Strategy, Strategic Culture, Practice: The Social Roots of Nordic Defence,' *Cooperation and Conflict* 40, no. 5 (2005), pp. 5–23.

New York Times, 'Transcript: Donald Trump on NATO, Turkey's Coup Attempt and the World,' July 21, 2016, <https://www.nytimes.com/2016/07/22/us/politics/donald-trump-foreign-policy-interview.html?_r=0> (last accessed February 25, 2017).

New York Times, 'Transcript of President Obama's Commencement Address at West Point,' May 28, 2014, <https://www.nytimes.com/2014/05/29/us/politics/transcript-of-president-obamas-commencement-address-at-west-point.html> (last accessed February 24, 2017).

New York Times Editorial Board, 'President Obama and the World,' *New York Times*, May 3, 2014, <http://www.nytimes.com/2014/05/04/opinion/sunday/president-obama-and-the-world.html> (last accessed August 4, 2014).

New York Times Editorial Board, 'President Obama Misses a Chance on Foreign Affairs,' *New York Times*, May 28, 2014, <http://www.nytimes.com/2014/05/29/opinion/president-obama-misses-a-chance-on-foreign-affairs.html?_r=0> (last accessed June 2, 2014).

New York Times Editorial Board, 'The End of the Perpetual War,' *New York Times*, May 23, 2013, <http://www.nytimes.com/2013/05/24/opinion/oba

ma-vows-to-end-of-the-perpetual-war.html?pagewanted=all&_r=0> (last accessed August 18, 2014).

Nexon, Daniel, 'The "Failure" of the "Reset:" Obama's Great Mistake? Or Putin's?' *Washington Post*, March 4, 2014, <http://www.washingtonpost.com/blogs/monkey-cage/wp/2014/03/04/the-failure-of-the-reset-obamas-great-mistake-or-putinss/> (last accessed September 21, 2016).

Niebuhr, Reinhold, *The Irony of American History* (Chicago: Chicago University Press, 1952).

Norris, John, 'The Y Article,' *Foreign Policy*, April 13, 2011, <http://www.foreignpolicy.com/articles/2011/04/13/the_y_article> (last accessed September 24, 2016).

Nye Jr., Joseph S., *Soft Power: The Means to Success in World Politics* (New York: Public Affairs, 2004).

Nye Jr., Joseph S., 'The Future of American Power,' *Foreign Affairs* 89, no. 6 (2010), pp. 2–12.

Nye Jr., Joseph S., *The Paradox of American Power: Why the World's Only Superpower Can't Go It Alone* (New York: Oxford University Press, 2002).

Nye Jr., Joseph S., 'The War on Soft Power,' *Foreign Policy*, April 12, 2011, <http://www.foreignpolicy.com/articles/2011/04/12/the_war_on_soft_power> (last accessed September 14, 2016).

Obama, Barack, 'Renewing American Leadership,' *Foreign Affairs* 86, no. 4 (2007), pp. 2–16.

Obama, Barack, *The Audacity of Hope: Thoughts on Reclaiming the American Dream* (New York: Crown Publishers, 2006).

Obama, Barack, 'Transcript: Obama's Speech Against The Iraq War,' October 2, 2002, <http://www.npr.org/templates/story/story.php?storyId=99591469> (last accessed September 10, 2016).

Obama, Barack, 'Transcript: President Obama's Speech Outlining Strategy to Defeat Islamic State,' *Washington Post*, September 10, 2014, <https://www.washingtonpost.com/politics/full-text-of-president-obamas-speech-outlining-strategy-to-defeat-islamic-state/2014/09/10/af69dec8-3943-11e4-9c9f-ebb47272e40e_story.html?utm_term=.d6655f29cba8> (last accessed February 25, 2017).

O'Hanlon, Michael, *A Moderate Plan for Additional Defense Cuts* (Washington DC: Brookings, 2013).

O'Hanlon, Michael, 'How to Solve Obama's Grand Strategy Dilemma,' May 23, 2014, <http://www.brookings.edu/research/opinions/2014/05/23-obama-grand-strategy-dilemma-ohanlon> (last accessed September 16, 2016).

O'Hanlon, Michael, 'The Obama Defense,' *Foreign Affairs*, May 28, 2014, <http://www.foreignaffairs.com/articles/141473/michael-ohanlon/the-obama-defense?nocache=1> (last accessed September 22, 2016).

O'Hanlon, Michael and David Petraeus, 'America's Awesome Military,' *Foreign Affairs* 95, no. 5 (2016), pp. 10–17.

O'Meara, Dan, Alex Macleod, Frédérick Gagnon, and David Grondin, *Movies, Myth and the National Security State* (Boulder: Lynne Rienner, 2016).

O'Neill, Jim, 'Building Better Global Economic BRICs,' Goldman Sachs, November 30, 2001, <http://www.goldmansachs.com/our-thinking/archive/archive-pdfs/build-better-brics.pdf> (last accessed August 29, 2016).

O'Neill, William L., 'The "Good War": National Security and American Culture,' in Andrew Bacevich (ed.), *The Long War: A New History of U.S. National Security Policy Since World War II* (New York: Columbia University Press, 2007).

O'Reilly, Bill, *Pinheads and Patriots: Where You Stand in the Age of Obama* (New York: HarperCollins, 2010.)

Ó Tuathail, Gearóid, *Critical Geopolitics: The Politics of Writing Global Space* (Minneapolis: University of Minnesota Press, 1996).

Ó Tuathail, Gearóid, 'Postmodern Geopolitics? The Modern Geopolitical Imagination and Beyond,' in Gearóid Ó Tuathail and Simon Dalby (eds.), *Rethinking Geopolitics* (New York: Routledge, 1998), pp. 16–38.

Ó Tuathail, Gearóid, 'The Frustrations of Geopolitics and the Pleasures of War: Behind Enemy Lines and American Geopolitical Culture,' *Geopolitics* 10, no. 2 (2005), pp. 356–377.

Ó Tuathail, Gearóid, 'Understanding Critical Geopolitics: Geopolitics and Risk Society,' *The Journal of Strategic Studies* 22, no. 2–3 (1999), pp. 107–124.

Ó Tuathail, Gearóid and John Agnew, 'Geopolitics and Discourse,' *Political Geography* 11, no. 2 (1992), pp. 190–204.

Ó Tuathail, Gearóid and Simon Dalby, 'Introduction: Rethinking Geopolitics: Towards a Critical Geopolitics,' in Gearóid Ó Tuathail and Simon Dalby (eds.), *Rethinking Geopolitics* (New York: Routledge, 1998), pp. 1–15.

Ó Tuathail, Gearóid and Simon Dalby (eds.), *Rethinking Geopolitics* (New York: Routledge, 1998).

Packard, George R., 'The United States-Japan Security Treaty at 50,' *Foreign Affairs* 89, no. 2 (2010), pp. 92–103.

Panetta, Leon, 'Speech Delivered at the Shangri-La Security Dialogue,' June 2, 2012, <http://www.defense.gov/speeches/speech.aspx?speechid=1681> (last accessed September 27, 2016).

Panetta, Leon, 'Statement on Defense Strategic Guidance,' January 5, 2012, <http://www.defense.gov/speeches/speech.aspx?speechid=1643> (last accessed September 17, 2016).

Parent, Joseph M. and Paul K. MacDonald, 'The Wisdom of Retrenchment,' *Foreign Affairs* 90, no. 6 (2011), pp. 32–47.

Parmar, Inderjeet, 'Foreign Policy Fusion: Liberal Interventionists, Conservative Nationalists and Neoconservatives—The New Alliance Dominating the US Foreign Policy Establishment,' *International Politics* 46, no. 2–3 (2009), pp. 177–209.

Parsons, Christi and Kathleen Hennessy, 'Obama Will Explain "Interventionist" Foreign Policy at West Point,' *Los Angeles Times*, May 25, 2014, <http://www.latimes.com/world/la-fg-obama-foreign-policy-20140525-story.html> (last accessed September 29, 2016).

Payne, Rodger A., 'Cooperative Security: Grand Strategy Meets Critical Theory?' *Millennium* 40, no. 3 (2012), pp. 605–624.

Pellerin, Cheryl, 'DoD Comptroller: Budget Deal Offers Relief, Uncertainty,' DoD News, December 2, 2015, <https://www.defense.gov/News/Article/Article/632078/dod-comptroller-budget-deal-offers-relief-uncertainty> (last accessed February 25, 2017).

Peoples, Columba and Nick Vaughan-Williams, *Critical Security Studies: An Introduction* (Oxon, New York: Routledge, 2010).

Perez-Rivas, Manuel, 'Bush Vows to Rid the World of "Evil-doers,"' *CNN*, September 16, 2001, <http://edition.cnn.com/2001/U.S./09/16/gen.bush.terrorism/> (last accessed September 12, 2016).

Pew Research Center, 'America's Global Image Remains More Positive than China's,' July 18, 2013, <http://www.pewglobal.org/2013/07/18/americas-global-image-remains-more-positive-than-chinas/> (last accessed September 22, 2016).

Pew Research Center, 'Beyond Red vs. Blue: The Political Typology,' May 4, 2011, <http://www.people-press.org/2011/05/04/section-5-views-of-government-constitution-american-exceptionalism/> (last accessed September 1, 2016).

Pew Research Center, 'Confidence in Obama Lifts U.S. Image Around the World,' Pew Research Global Attitudes Project, July 23, 2009, <http://www.pewglobal.org/2009/07/23/confidence-in-obama-lifts-us-image-around-the-world/> (last accessed September 19, 2016).

Pew Research Center, 'Generational Divide Over American Exceptionalism,' November 18, 2011, <http://www.pewresearch.org/daily-number/generational-divide-over-american-exceptionalism/> (last accessed February 26, 2017).

Pew Research Center, 'Public Sees U.S. Power Declining as Support for Global Engagement Slips,' December 3, 2013, <http://www.people-press.org/2013/12/03/public-sees-u-s-power-declining-as-support-for-global-engagement-slips/> (last accessed September 26, 2016).

Pfaff, William, 'Manufacturing Insecurity,' *Foreign Affairs* 89, no. 6 (2010), pp. 133–140.

Pinker, Steven, *The Better Angels of our Nature: Why Violence Has Declined* (London: Penguin, 2012).

Podesta, John, 'U.S. Rebalance to Asia: Japan as the Key Partner,' Speech at the Sasakawa Peace Foundation, April 13, 2012, <http://www.americanprogress.org/issues/security/news/2012/04/13/11491/u-s-rebalance-to-asia-japan-as-the-key-partner/> (last accessed September 23, 2016).

Polelle, Mark, *Raising Cartographic Consciousness – The Social and Foreign Policy Vision of Geopolitics in the Twentieth Century* (Lanham: Lexington, 1999).

Pollard, Tom, 'The Hollywood War Machine,' *New Political Science* 24, no.1 (2002), pp. 121–139.

Posen, Barry R., 'Command of the Commons: The Military Foundation of U.S. Hegemony,' *International Security* 28, no. 1 (2003), pp. 5–46.

Posen, Barry R., 'Pull Back: The Case of a Less Activist Foreign Policy,' *Foreign Affairs* 92, no. 1 (2013), pp. 116–128.

Posen, Barry R., *Restraint. A New Foundation for U.S. Grand Strategy* (Ithaca: Cornell University Press, 2014).

Posen, Barry R., *The Sources of Military Doctrine: France, Britain and Germany Between the World Wars* (New York: Cornell University Press, 1984).

Posen, Barry R. and Andrew L. Ross, 'Competing Visions for U.S. Grand Strategy,' *International Security* 21, no. 3 (1996/1997), pp. 5–53.

Preble, Christopher A., *The Power Problem: How American Military Dominance Makes Us Less Safe, Less Prosperous, and Less Free* (Ithaca: Cornell University Press, 2009).

Preble, Christopher A., 'The Revolving Door, Think Tanks and the MIC,' *National Interest*, December 29, 2010, <http://nationalinterest.org/blog/the-skeptics/the-revolving-door-think-tanks-the-mic-4646> (accessed September 11, 2016).

Preble, Christopher A., 'Testimony: U.S. National Security Strategy after Primacy: Resilience, Self-Reliance, and Restraint,' Senate Armed Services Committee, October 29, 2015, < http://www.armed-services.senate.gov/download/preble_10-29-15> (last accessed September 30, 2016).

Priest, Dana and William, Arkin, 'A Hidden World growing Beyond Control,' *Washington Post*, July 19, 2010, <http://projects.washingtonpost.com/top-secret-america/articles/a-hidden-world-growing-beyond-control/print/> (last accessed September 21, 2016).

Project for the New American Century, 'Statement of Principles,' June 3, 1997, <http://www.rrojasdatabank.info/pfpc/PNAC---statement%20of%20principles.pdf> (last accessed February 17, 2017).

Purple, Matt, 'Ted Cruz's Fourth-Way Foreign Policy,' *National Interest*, December 5, 2015, <http://nationalinterest.org/feature/ted-cruzs-fourth-way-foreign-policy-14520> (last accessed September 5, 2016).

Rachmann, Gideon, 'American Nightmare,' *Financial Times*, March 16, 2012, <http://www.ft.com/cms/s/2/941a0132-6d37-11e1-ab1a-00144feab49a.html#axzz39PtVqDti> (last accessed September 10, 2016).

Rachmann, Gideon, *Zero-Sum World: American Power in an Age of Anxiety* (London: Atlantic Books, 2010).

Rafferty, Kevin, 'Where is the Global Leadership?,' *Japan Times*, November 12, 2013, <http://www.japantimes.co.jp/opinion/2013/11/12/commentary/

world-commentary/where-is-the-global-leadership/#.U9-WrhacIoE> (last accessed September 4, 2016).

Remnick, David, 'Going the Distance,' *The New Yorker*, January 27, 2014, <http://www.newyorker.com/magazine/2014/01/27/going-the-distance-2?currentPage=all>
(last accessed September 4, 2016).

Restad, Hilde Eliassen, *American Exceptionalism: An Idea that Made a Nation and Remade the World* (Oxon: Routledge, 2014).

Rich, Andrew, *Think Tanks, Public Policy, and the Politics of Expertise* (Cambridge: Cambridge University Press, 2004).

Richardson, Paul, '"Blue National Soil" and the Unwelcome Return of "Classical" Geopolitics,' *Global Change, Peace & Security* 27, no. 2 (2015), pp. 229–236.

Robb, David L., *Operation Hollywood: How the Pentagon Shapes and Censors the Movies* (New York: Prometheus Books, 2004).

Rogin, Josh, 'Obama Embraces Romney Advisor's Theory on "The Myth of American Decline,"' *Foreign Policy*, January 25, 2012, <http://thecable.fore ignpolicy.com/posts/2012/01/26/obama_embraces_romney_advisor_s_th eory_on_the_myth_of_american_decline> (last accessed September 4, 2016).

Romney, Mitt, *No Apology: The Case for American Greatness* (New York: St. Martin's Griffin, 2010).

Rose, Gideon, 'What Obama Gets Right,' *Foreign Affairs* 94, no. 4 (2015), pp. 2–12.

Rose, Steve, 'The U.S. Military Storm Hollywood,' *Guardian*, July 6, 2009, <http://www.theguardian.com/film/2009/jul/06/us-military-hollywood> (last accessed September 12, 2016).

Rosecrance, Richard and Arthur A. Stein, 'Beyond Realism: The Study of Grand Strategy,' in Richard Rosecrance and Arthur A. Stein (eds.), *The Domestic Bases of Grand Strategy* (Ithaca: Cornell University Press: 1993), pp. 3–21.

Rosecrance, Richard and Arthur A. Stein (eds.), *The Domestic Bases of Grand Strategy* (Ithaca: Cornell University Press, 1993).

Rotkopf, David, 'Obama's "Don't Do Stupid Shit" Foreign Policy,' *Foreign Policy*, June 4, 2014, <http://www.foreignpolicy.com/articles/2014/06/04/ obama_dont_do_stupid_shit_foreign_policy_bowe_bergdahl> (last accessed September 22, 2016).

Rourke, Ervin J., 'Military Education for the New Age,' in Paul J. Bolt, Damon V. Coletta and Collins G. Shackelford Jr. (eds.), *American Defense Policy* (Baltimore and London: Johns Hopkins University Press, 2005), pp. 322–326.

Rubin, Jennifer, 'Obama is the War-Weary One,' *Washington Post*, September 9, 2014, <http://www.washingtonpost.com/blogs/right-turn/wp/2014/09/ 09/obama-is-the-war-weary-one/> (last accessed September 17, 2016).

Rucker, Philip and Robert Costa, 'Trump Questions Need for NATO, Outlines Noninterventionist Foreign Policy,' *Washington* Post, March 21, 2016, <https://www.washingtonpost.com/news/post-politics/wp/2016/03/21/donald-trump-reveals-foreign-policy-team-in-meeting-with-the-washington-post/?utm_term=.31289eaca4c0> (last accessed February 25, 2017).

Ruggie, John Gerard, 'The Past as Prologue? Interests, Identity, and American Foreign Policy,' *International Security* 21, no. 4 (1997), pp. 89–125.

Ruggie, John Gerard, *Winning the Peace: America and World Order in the New Era* (New York: Columbia University Press, 1996).

Said, Edward H., *Orientalism*. Reprinted with a new preface. (London: Penguin, 2003, original published in 1978).

Salter, Mark B. and Can E. Mutlu (eds.), *Research Methods in Critical Security Studies: An Introduction* (New York: Routledge, 2013).

Sanger, David, *Confront and Conceal: Obama's Secret Wars and the Surprising Use of American Power* (Broadway: New York, 2013, original published in 2012).

Sanger, David, 'In Full Flight Regalia, the President Enjoys a "Top Gun" Moment,' *New York Times*, May 2, 2003, <http://www.nytimes.com/2003/05/02/international/worldspecial/02PLAN.html> (last accessed September 23, 2016).

Sanger, David, 'Pursuing Ambitious Global Goals, But Strategy is More,' *New York Times*, January 20, 2013, <http://www.nytimes.com/2013/01/21/us/politics/obamas-foreign-policy-goals-appear-more-modest.html> (last accessed September 12, 2016).

Sapolsky, Harvey M., Eugene Gholz, and Caitlin Talmadge, *U.S. Defense Politics: The Origins of Security Policy* (New York and London: Routledge, 2009).

Sasgupta, Sunil and Stephen P. Cohen, 'Arms Sales for India,' *Foreign Affairs* 90, no. 2 (2011), pp. 22–26.

Sauer, Abe, 'Retreat, Sell! "Battle: LA" and Product Placing the Marines,' *Brandchannel*, March 14, 2011, <http://www.brandchannel.com/home/post/2011/03/14/retreat-sell!-battle-la-and-marine-corps-product-placement.aspx> (last accessed September 16, 2016).

Saunders, Paul J., 'The Five Most Abused Foreign-Policy Cliches,' *National Interest*, March 1, 2014, <http://nationalinterest.org/commentary/the-five-most-abused-foreign-policy-cliches-9978?page=2> (last accessed September 3, 2016).

Savage, Michael, *Trickle Down Tyranny* (New York: William Morrow, 2012).

Scheinmann, Gabriel M. and Raphael S. Cohen, 'The Myth of "Securing the Commons,"' *The Washington Quarterly* 35, no. 1 (2012), pp. 115–128.

Schmitt, Gary and Tom Donnelly, 'No Superpower Here,' Center for Defense Studies, January 9, 2012, <http://www.defensestudies.org/cds/no-superpower-here/> (last accessed September 7, 2016).

Schogol, Jeff, 'Transformers Beat G.I. Joe in Battle for DOD Support for

Summer Blockbusters,' *Stars and Stripes*, May 27, 2009, <http://www.stripes. com/news/transformers-beat-g-i-joe-in-battle-for-dod-support-for-sum mer-blockbusters-1.92061> (last accessed September 14, 2016).

Scott, A. O., 'One Small Step for Man, One Giant Leap for Autobots,' *New York Times*, June 28, 2011, <http://movies.nytimes.com/2011/06/29/movies/ transformers-dark-of-the-moon-theyre-at-it-again-movie-review.html?re f=movies&_r=0> (last accessed September 22, 2016).

Scott, A. O. and Manohla Dargis, 'Super-Dreams of an Alternate World Order,' *New York Times*, June 27, 2012, <http://www.nytimes.com/2012/07/01/ movies/the-amazing-spider-man-and-the-modern-comic-book-movie. html?pagewanted=all&_r=0 See also> (last accessed September 15, 2016).

Scott, Mike, 'Aaron Eckhart Went Through Military Training to Make "Battle: Los Angeles" Seem Real,' *The Times-Picayune*, March 14, 2011, <http:// www.nola.com/movies/index.ssf/2011/03/aaron_eckhart_went_through_ mil.html> (last accessed September 16, 2016).

Shanker, Tom, 'Warning Against Wars Like Iraq and Afghanistan,' *New York Times*, February 25, 2011, <http://www.nytimes.com/2011/02/26/world/ 26gates.html?_r=0> (last accessed September 27, 2016).

Shapiro, Michael J., *Cinematic Geopolitics* (London and New York: Routledge, 2009).

Shapiro, Michael J., *Methods and Nations. Cultural Governance and the Indigenous Subject* (London and New York: Routledge, 2004).

Sharkey, Betsy, 'Movie Review G.I. Joe: The Rise of Cobra,' *Los Angeles Times*, August 8, 2009, <http://articles.latimes.com/2009/aug/08/entertainment/ et-gi-joe8> (last accessed September 8, 2016).

Sharp, Joanne, *Condensing the Cold War: Reader's Digest and American Identity* (Minneapolis: University of Minnesota Press, 2000).

Sharp, Joanne, 'Geopolitics at the Margins? Reconsidering Genealogies of Critical Geopolitics,' *Political Geography* 37 (2013), pp. 20–29.

Sharp, Joanne P., 'Reel Geographies of the New World Order: Patriotism, Masculinity, and Geopolitics in Post-Cold War American Movies,' in Simon Dalby and Gearóid Ó Tuathail (eds.), *Rethinking Geopolitics* (New York: Routledge, 1998), pp. 152–170.

Shear, Michael D., 'Obama Insists U.S. Will Not Get Drawn Into Ground War in Iraq,' *New York Times*, September 17, 2014, <http://www.nytimes.com/ 2014/09/18/world/middleeast/obama-speech-central-command-isis-milita ry-resolve.html?_r=0> (last accessed September 17, 2016).

Shelton, Henry H. 'Chairman of the Joint Chiefs of Staff,' *Joint Vision* 2020, no. 8 (2000).

Shone, Tom, 'James Cameron Hates America: The Conservative Attack on Avatar,' *Slate*, January 14, 2010, <http://www.slate.com/articles/arts/cult urebox/2010/01/james_cameron_hates_america.html> (last accessed September 23, 2016).

Sieren, Frank, 'Opinion: The World's Superpower No More,' *Deutsche Welle*, July 15, 2014, <http://www.dw.de/opinion-the-worlds-superpower-no-more/a-17788131> (last accessed September 24, 2016).

Singer, Peter W., 'Bad Idea for the Pentagon's Idea Shop,' *Brookings*, October 29, 2013, <http://www.brookings.edu/research/opinions/2013/10/29-bad-idea-for-pentagons-office-of-net-assessment-singer> (last accessed September 29, 2016).

Singh, Abhijit, 'Rebalancing the Maritime Pivot to Asia,' *The Diplomat*, September 17, 2013, <http://thediplomat.com/2013/09/rebalancing-the-maritime-pivot-to-asia/> (last accessed September 20, 2016).

Singh, Robert, *Barack Obama's Post-American Foreign Policy: The Limits of Engagement* (London: Bloomsbury, 2012).

Sirota, David, '25 Years Later, How "Top Gun" Made America Love War,' *Washington Post*, August 26, 2011, <http://articles.washingtonpost.com/2011-08-26/opinions/35271385_1_pentagon-brass-military-budget-top-gun> (last accessed September 17, 2016).

Skypek, Thomas M., 'In Defense of Net Assessment,' *National Interest*, November 16, 2013, <http://nationalinterest.org/commentary/defense-net-assessment-9411> (last accessed September 25, 2016).

Slaughter, Anne-Marie, 'A Grand Strategy of Network Centrality,' in Richard Fontaine and Kristin M. Lord (eds.), *America's Path: Grand Strategy for the Next Administration* (Washington DC: Center for a New American Security, 2012), pp. 45–56.

Slaughter, Anne-Marie, 'America's Edge,' *Foreign Affairs* 88, no. 1 (2009), pp. 94–113.

Slaughter, Anne-Marie, 'Does Obama Have a Grand Strategy for His Second Term? If Not, He Could Try One of These,' *Washington Post*, January 18, 2013, <http://www.washingtonpost.com/opinions/does-obama-have-a-grand-strategy-for-his-second-term-if-not-he-could-try-one-of-these/2013/01/18/ec78cede-5f27-11e2-a389-ee565c81c565_story.html> (last accessed September 28, 2016).

Slaughter, Anne-Marie, 'Power Shifts: "The Revenge of Geography," by Robert D. Kaplan,' *New York Times*, October 5, 2012, <http://www.nytimes.com/2012/10/07/books/review/the-revenge-of-geography-by-robert-d-kaplan.html> (last accessed February 24, 2017).

Smith, Gayle E., *In Search of Sustainable Security* (Washington DC: Center for American Progress, 2008).

Smith, Steve, 'The Discipline of International Relations: Still an American Social Science?' *British Journal of Politics and International Relations* 2, no. 3 (2000), pp. 374–402.

Smith, Steve, 'The United States and the Discipline of International Relations: "Hegemonic Country, Hegemonic Discipline,"' *International Studies Review* 4, no. 2 (2002), pp. 67–85.

Spetalnick, Matt, 'Obama's Syria "Red Line" Has Echoes in His Warning to Ukraine,' *Reuters*, February 20, 2014, <http://www.reuters.com/article/2014/02/20/us-ukraine-crisis-obama-idU.S.BREA1J2C920140220> (last accessed September 23, 2016).

Steinberg, James and Michael O'Hanlon, 'Keep Hope Alive,' *Foreign Affairs* 93, no. 4 (2014), pp. 107–117.

Steinmetz, Katy, 'Top 10 Buzzwords: 10. *Leading from Behind*,' *TIME*, December 7, 2011, <http://content.time.com/time/specials/packages/article/0,28804,2101344_2100571_2100582,00.html> (last accessed September 23, 2016).

Steyn, Mark, *After America: Get Ready for Armageddon* (Washington DC: Regnery, 2011).

Stolberg, Sheryl Gay, 'Obama Defends Strategy in Afghanistan,' *New York Times*, August 17, 2009, <http://www.nytimes.com/2009/08/18/us/politics/18vets.html> (last accessed September 10, 2016).

Stone, Diane, *Capturing the Political Imagination: Think Tanks and the Policy Process* (New York: Psychology Press, 1996).

Stone, Oliver and Peter Kuznick, *The Untold History of the United States* (New York: Simon and Schuster, 2013).

Stritzel, Holger, 'Securitization, Power, Intertextuality: Discourse Theory and the Translations of Organized Crime,' *Security Dialogue* 43, no. 6 (2012), pp. 549–567.

Subramanian, Arvind, 'Globalization in Retreat,' *Foreign Affairs* 88, no. 2 (2009), pp. 2–7.

Subramanian, Arvind, 'The Inevitable Superpower,' *Foreign Affairs* 90, no. 5 (2011), pp. 66–78.

Suid, Lawrence H., *Guts and Glory: The Making of the Military Image in Film*. Revised and expanded edition. (Lexington: The University Press of Kentucky, 2002).

Szalai, Jennifer, 'Inside the List,' *New York Times*, August 19, 2016, <http://www.nytimes.com/2016/08/28/books/review/inside-the-list.html> (last accessed September 29, 2016).

Talbott, Strobe, *The Russia Hand: A Memoir of Presidential Diplomacy* (New York: Random House, 2002).

Talkers Magazine, 'The Top Talk Radio Audiences,' <http://www.talkers.com/top-talk-radio-audiences/> (last accessed September 7, 2016).

Taraby, Jamie, 'Hollywood and the Pentagon: A Relationship of Mutual Exploitation,' *Al Jazeera America*, July 29, 2014, <http://america.aljazeera.com/articles/2014/7/29/hollywood-and-thepentagonarelationshipofmutualexploitation.html> (last accessed September 23, 2016).

Thompson, Mark, 'Michèle Flournoy Departs,' *TIME*, December 14, 2011, <http://nation.time.com/2011/12/14/michele-flournoy-departs/> (last accessed September 3, 2016).

Thompson, Mark, 'The Two-MRC Strategy: Major Regional Contingencies, or Mythical Routine Canards?,' *TIME*, January 4, 2012, <http://nation.time.com/2012/01/04/the-two-mrc-strategy-major-regional-contingencies-or-mythical-routine-canards/> (last accessed September 27, 2016).

Thompson, Nicholas, 'Review Essay. Ideas Man,' *Foreign Affairs* 91, no. 1 (2012), pp. 148–152.

Thompson Reuters, 'Thomson Reuters Research Analytics Unveils 2013 Release of its Journal Citation Reports,' <http://thomsonreuters.com/press-releases/062013/2013-journal-citation-reports> (last accessed September 17, 2016).

Thornberry, Mac and Andrew F. Krepinevich Jr., 'Preserving Primacy,' *Foreign Affairs* 95, no. 5 (2016), pp. 26–35.

Three-Brennan, Megan, 'Poll Shows Isolationist Streak in Americans,' *New York Times*, April 30, 2013, <http://www.nytimes.com/2013/05/01/world/american-public-opposes-action-in-syria-and-north-korea.html?_r=1&> (last accessed September 20, 2016).

Trotta, Daniel, 'Iraq War Costs U.S. More Than $2 Trillion: Study,' *Reuters*, March 14, 2013, <http://www.reuters.com/article/2013/03/14/us-iraq-war-anniversary-idU.S.BRE92D0PG20130314> (last accessed September 17, 2016).

Trump, Donald J., *Crippled America: How to Make America Great Again* (New York: Threshold Editions, 2015).

Twombly, Jim, *The Progression of the American Presidency: Individuals, Empire, and Change* (New York: Palgrave Macmillan, 2013).

Ucko, David H., *The New Counterinsurgency Era: Transforming the U.S. Military for Modern Wars* (Washington DC: Georgetown University Press, 2009).

US Air Force, 'Transformers: Dark of the Moon Filmed at Hurlburt; Airmen Included as Extras,' <http://www.af.mil/news/story.asp?id=123262258> (last accessed September 23, 2016).

US Army/US Marine Corps, *Counter-Insurgency Field Manual* (New York: Cosimo, 2006).

US Department of Defense, *Asia-Pacific Maritime Security Strategy* (Washington DC: US DoD, 2015).

US Department of Defense, 'Department of Defense (DoD) Releases Fiscal Year 2017 President's Budget Proposal,' <http://www.defense.gov/News/News-Releases/News-Release-View/Article/652687/department-of-defense-dod-releases-fiscal-year-2017-presidents-budget-proposal> (last accessed September 21, 2016).

US Department of Defense, Office of the Undersecretary of Defense, *National Defense Budget Estimates FY 2016* (Washington DC: US DoD, 2015).

US Department of Defense, *Overview – FY 2013 Defense Budget* (Washington DC: US DoD, 2012).

US Department of Defense, *Quadrennial Defense Review Report* (Washington DC: US DoD, 2006).

US Department of Defense, *Quadrennial Defense Review Report* (Washington DC: US DoD, 2010).

US Department of Defense, *Quadrennial Defense Review Report* (Washington DC: US DoD, 2014).

US Department of Defense, *Sustaining U.S. Global Leadership: Priorities for 21st Century Defense* (Washington DC: US DoD, 2012).

US Government Spending, 'Government Spending Chart,' <http://www.usgovernmentspending.com/spending_chart_2004_2018U.S.r_09s1li 111mcn_30f> (last accessed September 17, 2016).

US National War College, *Course 1, Syllabus – Block A: Philosophies of Statecraft* (Year: 1999–2000), <http://www.resdal.org/Archivo/syl1-a.htm> (last accessed September 2, 2016).

US Senate Committee on Armed Services, *Department of Defense Authorization of Appropriations for Fiscal Year 2015 and the Future Years Defense Program*, March 5, 2014, <http://www.armed-services.senate.gov/download/hearing_03-05-14-a> (last accessed 2 September 29, 2016).

Valantin, Jean-Michel, *Hollywood, the Pentagon and Washington: The Movies and National Security from World War II to the Present Day* (London: Anthem Press, 2005).

van Apeldoorn Bastiaan and Naná de Graaff, 'Corporate Elite Networks and US Post-Cold War Grand Strategy from Clinton to Obama,' *European Journal of International Relations*, 20, no. 1 (2015), pp. 29–55.

van Tol, Jan, Mark Gunzinger, Andrew Krepinevich, and Jim Thomas, *AirSea Battle: A Point-of-Departure Operational Concept* (Washington DC: Center for Strategic and Budgetary Assessments, 2010).

Vergun, David, 'Soldiers' take on Godzilla, *US Army*, May 19, 2014, <https://www.army.mil/article/126174> (last accessed September 22, 2016).

Walker, R. B. J., 'History and Structure in the Theory of International Relations,' in James Der Derian (ed.), *International Theory: Critical Investigations* (New York: New York University Press, 1995), pp. 308–339.

Walker, R. B. J., *Inside/Outside: International Relations as Political Theory* (Cambridge: Cambridge University Press, 1993).

Wallerstein, Immanuel, *Geopolitics and Geoculture: Essays on the Changing World-System* (Cambridge: Cambridge University Press, 1991).

Walt, Stephen M., 'A Bandwagon for Offshore Balancing?,' *Foreign Policy*, December 1, 2011, <http://walt.foreignpolicy.com/posts/2011/12/01/a_bandwagon_for_offshore_balancing> (last accessed September 28, 2016).

Walt, Stephen M., 'Military-Intellectual complex?,' *Foreign Policy*, April 27, 2012, <http://foreignpolicy.com/2012/04/27/military-intellectual-complex/> (last accessed September 21, 2016).

Walt, Stephen M., 'Offshore Balancing: An Idea Whose Time Has Come,' *Foreign Policy*, September 2, 2011, <http://www.foreignpolicy.com/posts/

2011/11/02/offshore_balancing_an_idea_whose_time_has_come> (last accessed September 4, 2016).

Walt, Stephen M., 'Sloppy Journalism at the *New York Times*,' *Foreign Policy*, May 1, 2013, <http://www.foreignpolicy.com/posts/2013/05/01/sloppy_journalism_at_the_new_york_times> (last accessed September 13, 2016).

Walt, Stephen M., 'Ten Lessons on Empire,' *Foreign Policy*, July 13, 2009, <http://walt.foreignpolicy.com/posts/2009/07/13/ten_lessons_on_empire> (last accessed September 20, 2016).

Walt, Stephen M, 'The Renaissance of Security Studies,' *International Studies Quarterly* 35, no. 2 (1991), pp. 211–239.

Waltz, Kenneth, *Theory of International Politics* (Reading, MA: Addison-Wesley, 1979).

Washington Post, 'Transcript: Senate Intelligence Hearing on National Security Threats,' January 29, 2014, <http://www.washingtonpost.com/world/national-security/transcript-senate-intelligence-hearing-on-national-security-threats/2014/01/29/b5913184-8912-11e3-833c-33098f9e5267_story.html> (last accessed September 5, 2016).

Washington Post Editorial Board, 'President Obama Continues His Retreat from Afghanistan,' *Washington Post*, May 28, 2014, <http://www.washingtonpost.com/opinions/president-obama-continues-his-retreat-from-afghanistan/2014/05/27/ae01686e-e5c2-11e3-8f90-73e071f3d637_story.html> (last accessed June 2, 2014).

Washington Post Editorial Board, 'President Obama's Foreign Policy is Based on Fantasy,' *Washington Post*, March 3, 2014, <http://www.washingtonpost.com/opinions/president-obamas-foreign-policy-is-based-on-fantasy/2014/03/02/c7854436-a238-11e3-a5fa-55f0c77bf39c_story.html> (last accessed May 5, 2014).

Waxman, Matthew, C., 'Obama's Guantanamo Legacy,' CFR, June 12, 2013, <http://www.cfr.org/terrorism-and-the-law/obamas-guantanamo-legacy/p30926> (last accessed February 26, 2017).

Weber, Cynthia, *Imagining America at War: Morality, Politics, and Film* (New York: Routledge, 2007).

Weber, Cynthia, *International Relations Theory: A Critical Introduction* (London: Routledge, 2010).

Weisgerber, Marcus and John T. Bennett, 'Pentagon Determining Fate of Revered Net Assessment Office,' *Defense News*, October 15, 2013, <http://www.defensenews.com/article/20131015/DEFREG02/310150031/Pentagon-Determining-Fate-Revered-Net-Assessment-Office> (last accessed September 4, 2016).

Weldes, Jutta (ed.), *To Seek Out New Worlds: Exploring Links Between Science Fiction and World Politics* (New York: Palgrave Macmillan, 2003).

Weldes, Jutta, Mark Laffey, Hugh Gusterson, and Raymond Duvall (eds.),

Cultures of Insecurity: States, Communities, and the Production of Danger (Minneapolis: University of Minnesota Press, 1999).

White House, 'Inaugural Address by President Barack Obama,' January 21, 2013, <http://www.whitehouse.gov/the-press-office/2013/01/21/inaugural -address-president-barack-obama> (last accessed September 22, 2016).

White House, *National Security Strategy* (Washington DC: White House, 2010).

White House, *National Security Strategy* (Washington DC: White House, 2015).

White House, 'President Barack Obama's State of the Union address,' January 28, 2014, <http://www.whitehouse.gov/the-press-office/2014/01/28/presi dent-barack-obamas-state-union-address> (last accessed September 22, 2016).

White House, 'President Bush Delivers State of the Union address,' January 28, 2008, <http://georgewbush-whitehouse.archives.gov/news/releases/2008/ 01/20080128-13.html> (last accessed September 5, 2016).

White House, 'President Obama's 2016 State of the Union address,' January 13, 2016, <https://medium.com/the-white-house/president-obama-s- 2016-state-of-the-union-address-7c06300f9726#.60e0tp2v6> (last accessed September 29, 2016).

White House, 'Remarks by President Obama and Vice President Xi of the People's Republic of China Before Bilateral Meeting,' February 14, 2012, <http://www.whitehouse.gov/the-press-office/2012/02/14/remarks-presid ent-obama-and-vice-president-xi-peoples-republic-china-bil> (last acces- sed September 13, 2016).

White House, 'Remarks by President Obama to the Australian Parliament,' November 17, 2011, <http://www.whitehouse.gov/the-press-office/2011/ 11/17/remarks-president-obama-australian-parliament> (last accessed September 11, 2016).

White House, 'Remarks by the President at the Acceptance of the Nobel Peace Prize,' December 10, 2009, <https://www.whitehouse.gov/the-press-offi ce/remarks-president-acceptance-nobel-peace-prize> (last accessed Sep- tember 30, 2016).

White House, 'Remarks by the President at the National Defense University,' May 23, 2013, <http://www.whitehouse.gov/the-press-office/2013/05/23/ remarks-president-national-defense-university> (last accessed September 23, 2016).

White House, 'Remarks by the President at the United States Military Academy Commencement Ceremony,' May 28, 2014, <https://www.whitehouse. gov/the-press-office/2014/05/28/remarks-president-united-states-military- academy-commencement-ceremony> (last accessed September 22, 2016).

White House, 'Remarks by the President in Address to the Nation on Syria,' September 10, 2013, <http://www.whitehouse.gov/the-press-office/2013/ 09/10/remarks-president-address-nation-syria> (last accessed September 28, 2016).

White House, 'Remarks by the President in Address to the Nation on the Way Forward in Afghanistan and Pakistan,' December 1, 2009, <http://www.whitehouse.gov/the-press-office/remarks-president-address-nation-way-forward-afghanistan-and-pakistan> (last accessed September 10, 2016).

White House, 'Remarks by the President in State of the Union address,' January 27, 2010, <http://www.whitehouse.gov/the-press-office/remarks-president-state-union-address> (last accessed September 5, 2016).

White House, 'Remarks by the President in State of the Union address,' January 24, 2012, <http://www.whitehouse.gov/the-press-office/2012/01/24/remarks-president-state-union-address> (last accessed September 12, 2016).

White House, 'Remarks by the President on a New Beginning,' June 4, 2009, <http://www.whitehouse.gov/the_press_office/Remarks-by-the-President-at-Cairo-University-6-04-09> (last accessed September 10, 2016).

White House, 'Remarks by the President on the Way Forward in Afghanistan,' June 22, 2011, <https://obamawhitehouse.archives.gov/blog/2011/06/22/president-obama-way-forward-afghanistan> (last accessed February 24, 2017).

White House, 'Remarks by Tom Donilon, National Security Advisor to the President: "The United States and the Asia-Pacific in 2013,"' March 11, 2013, <https://obamawhitehouse.archives.gov/the-press-office/2013/03/11/remarks-tom-donilon-national-security-advisor-president-united-states-an> (last accessed February 25, 2017).

White House, 'Remarks of President Barack Obama – As Prepared for Delivery Address to Joint Session of Congress,' February 24, 2009, <http://www.whitehouse.gov/the_press_office/Remarks-of-President-Barack-Obama-Address-to-Joint-Session-of-Congress> (last accessed September 25, 2016).

White House, 'Statement by the President on ISIL,' *Washington Post*, September 10, 2014, <https://www.whitehouse.gov/the-press-office/2014/09/10/statement-president-isil-1> (last accessed September 17, 2016).

White House, *The National Security Strategy of the United States of America* (Washington DC: White House, 2002).

Whitlock, Craig, 'Drone Strikes Killing More Civilians Than U.S. Admits, Human Rights Groups Say,' *Washington Post*, October 22, 2013, <http://www.washingtonpost.com/world/national-security/drone-strikes-killing-more-civilians-than-us-admits-human-rights-groups-say/2013/10/21/a99cbe78-3a81-11e3-b7ba-503fb5822c3e_story.html> (last accessed September 10, 2016).

Wilson, Scott, 'Obama, Romney Differ on U.S. Exceptionalism,' *Washington Post*, September 26, 2012, <http://articles.washingtonpost.com/2012-09-26/politics/35497342_1_obama-and-romney-exceptionalism-clinton-global-initiative> (last accessed September 28, 2016).

Wilson, Scott, 'On Syria, Obama's Past Words Collide with National Security Implications,' *Washington Post*, February 2, 2014, <http://www.washington post.com/politics/on-syria-obamas-past-words-collide-with-national-secu rity-implications/2014/02/20/2f61ad7a-9969-11e3-b931-0204122c514b_sto ry.html> (last accessed September 23, 2016).

Wilson, Scott and Al Kamen, '"Global War on Terror" is Given a New Name,' *Washington Post*, March 25, 2009, <http://www.washingtonpost.com/ wpdyn/content/article/2009/03/24/AR2009032402818.html> (last accessed September 14, 2016).

Wohlforth, William C, 'The Stability of a Unipolar World,' *International Security* 24, no. 1 (1999), pp. 5–41.

Wood, Dakota L., 'Testimony before the Senate Armed Services Committee,' October 29, 2015, <http://www.armed-services.senate.gov/imo/media/doc/ 15-82%20-%2010-29-15.pdf> (last accessed September 30, 2016).

Woodward, Bob, *Obama's Wars* (London: Simon & Schuster, 2010).

Work, Robert O. and Shawn Brimley, *20YY: Preparing for War in the Robotic Age* (Washington DC: Center for a New American Security, 2014).

Yale University, 'The Brady-Johnson Program in Grand Strategy,' <http:// grandstrategy.yale.edu/> (last accessed February 25, 2017).

Zakaria, Fareed, 'Obama's Leadership is Right For Today,' *Washington Post*, May 29, 2014, <http://www.washingtonpost.com/opinions/fareed-zakaria-oba mas-disciplined-leadership-is-right-for-today/2014/05/29/7b4eb460-e76d-11e3-afc6-a1dd9407abcf_story.html> (last accessed September 10, 2016).

Zakaria, Fareed, 'Stop Searching For an Obama Doctrine,' *Washington Post*, July 6, 2011, <http://www.washingtonpost.com/opinions/stop-search ing-for-an-obama-doctrine/2011/07/06/gIQAQMmI1H_story.html> (last accessed September 15, 2016).

Zakaria, Fareed, *The Post-American World* (New York: W. W. Norton & Company, 2008).

Zakaria, Fareed, *The Post-American World: Release 2.0* (New York: W. W. Norton & Company, 2011).

Zakheim, Dov, 'A Budget Strategy That Courts Disaster,' *Foreign Policy*, January 5, 2012, <http://shadow.foreignpolicy.com/posts/2012/01/05/a_budget_str ategy_that_courts_disaster> (last accessed September 17, 2016).

Zengerle, Patricia and Matt Spetalnick, 'Obama Wants to End "War on Terror" But Congress Balks,' *Reuters*, May 24, 2013, <http://www.reuters.com/arti cle/2013/05/24/us-usa-obama-speech-idU.S.BRE94M04Y20130524> (last accessed September 23, 2016).

Zenko, Micah, 'Most. Dangerous. World. Ever,' *Foreign Policy*, February 26, 2013, <http://www.foreignpolicy.com/articles/2013/02/26/most_danger ous_world_ever> (last accessed September 17, 2016).

Zenko, Micah and Michael A. Cohen, 'Clear and Present Safety,' *Foreign Affairs* 90, no. 2 (2011), pp. 79–93.

INDEX

═══════

EU representative:
Easy Access System Europe
Mustamäe tee 50, 10621 Tallinn, Estonia
Gpsr.requests@easproject.com

www.ingramcontent.com/pod-product-compliance
Lightning Source LLC
Chambersburg PA
CBHW070611270326
41926CB00013B/2503